TWO SIDES OF GLORY

TWO SIDES OF GLORY

THE 1986 BOSTON RED SOX IN THEIR OWN WORDS

ERIK SHERMAN | FOREWORD BY JOE CASTIGLIONE

University of Nebraska Press | LINCOLN

Library of Congress Cataloging-in-Publication Data
Names: Sherman, Erik, author.
Title: Two sides of glory: the 1986 Boston Red Sox in their own
words / Erik Sherman; foreword by Joe Castiglione.
Description: Lincoln, Nebraska: University of Nebraska Press,
[2021]
Identifiers: LCCN 2020018145
ISBN 9781496219329 (hardback)
ISBN 9781496225337 (epub)
ISBN 9781496225344 (mobi)
ISBN 9781496225351 (pdf)
Subjects: LCSH: Boston Red Sox (Baseball team)—History.
Classification: LCC GV875.B62 S54 2021 |
DDC 796.357/640974461—dc23
LC record available at https://lccn.loc.gov/2020018145

Set in Scala OT by Laura Buis.

Dedicated to
Habiba, Alex, and Sabrina
and the memory of
my friend the great Bill Buckner;
long-time Red Sox public relations director Dick Bresciani;
and a young Red Sox fan, Arthur Remy, who left us too soon

Sometimes the greatest achievements in life aren't what you accomplish; it's what you've overcome.

—BRUCE HURST

CONTENTS

ILLUSTRATIONS

FOREWORD

JOE CASTIGLIONE

When you've been broadcasting Red Sox baseball on the radio for thirty-eight years like I have, trying to rank the best or my favorite team over that time is as difficult as choosing among one's children. But I will say that the 1986 Red Sox, with Hall of Famers and should-be Hall of Famers, were right up there talent-wise with the magnificent 2018 World Series champions. And, at least up to Game Six of the '86 World Series, they had the same kind of magic as the 2013 championship team. But when it comes to a cast of characters with the grit, courage, and dignity of the '86 Red Sox, few could compare.

Now—about that magic.

It all started on a cool April evening at Fenway before a sparse crowd when Roger Clemens stunned the baseball world with his complete dominance over the Seattle Mariners by striking out a Major League–record twenty batters. What was so amazing about that Tuesday night game was that Clemens was not pitching on his regular turn. He was supposed to pitch on that Sunday in Kansas City, but the game was rained out. Monday was an off day, so he had two extra days' rest. Plus he was just coming off shoulder surgery from the year before, so he was a question mark to even pitch that game in at least a couple of different ways. But I had the sense early on that something amazing was happening.

Around the third inning of that game I said to my broadcasting partner, Ken Coleman, that Clemens's performance looked different—that it could be a special night. After all, the Mariners weren't even hitting foul balls; they were swinging and missing or taking strikes. Still, the Red Sox were losing in the seventh, 1–0. But Dwight "Dewey" Evans quickly changed all of that, hitting a three-run homer into the center-field bleachers off of Mike Moore—the difference in the game.

Quite honestly I thought Clemens would end up with twenty-one strikeouts after he struck out Phil Bradley, but Ken Phelps, the last batter of the game, grounded out to short. I remember Roger coming on the postgame show, and the first thing he did was look for his wife, Debbie—they were newlyweds at the time. Then he came on the air with Ken and me, and he couldn't have been more excited. Of all the things that had happened that year, Clemens's record-setting night was the biggest highlight of them all, and it set the tone for the rest of the season. But there were so many other things that happened that showed this team had some magic working for it.

Perhaps the craziest of them all took place in an extra-inning game in July against the Angels, when California led by three runs going into the bottom of the twelfth. With two outs sure-handed third baseman Rick Burleson dropped a pop-up that would have ended the game, allowing Donnie Baylor to reach first base. Baylor would eventually come around to score on a Rich Gedman single to tie the game. Then, later in that same inning, Dwight Evans would incredibly score the winning run on a *balk*.

Other examples that come to mind were when Marc Sullivan was hit in the butt with the bases loaded to win a game and when Mike Stenhouse walked to end another—his lone RBI of the season.

But the one that gets the most attention, of course, occurred that October. I've never gotten such chills at a ball game as I did when Dave Henderson hit that home run in the American League Championship Series (ALCS) against the Angels. I'll just never forget the visual of the state troopers on horseback and the police dogs surrounding the field as sixty-four thousand screaming fans were about to go crazy. But Henderson hit the home run to give us the lead; then, after almost losing it in the bottom of the ninth, after the Angels had tied it and loaded the bases, we pulled it out in extra innings. Incredibly it was Steve Crawford, who was 0-2 during the regular season, who came in and got the win. "Shag" would also get credit for the victory in Game Two of the World Series in that marquee match-up between Clemens and Dwight "Doc" Gooden.

Despite the Sox's losing in seven games, the World Series was memorable too, with plenty of its own magic. First of all, we were shocked at the start to be up two games to none because the Mets were heavy favorites, having won 108 games that season. So taking a two-game lead, especially on the road, was pretty amazing.

After Bruce Hurst won Game Five to give us a 3–2 edge, I thought we would end it in Game Six at Shea Stadium with Roger pitching. Even in extra innings, with Clemens out of the game, I was still confident. After Henderson hit the ball off the *Newsday* sign—a home run call I purposely waited to confirm because I didn't want to blow it—and later, when Marty Barrett singled home Wade Boggs with an insurance run, I thought the title was ours. In fact I was so confident that between innings I turned to Coleman, who had been there twenty years, and asked, "Do you want me to do the bottom of the tenth, or would you rather I go to the clubhouse for the postgame interviews?" He said, "It's strictly up to you." But I thought, "Well, he's been there for so long that he should probably call the first Red Sox championship ever on radio and the first in sixty-eight years." With that in mind I told him he could do the bottom of the inning. Besides, I really wanted to be down there in that joyous clubhouse with the guys.

I made my way downstairs to the Red Sox clubhouse and watched as champagne was brought in, cellophane protective gear was put up to cover the lockers, and Mrs. Yawkey and Lou Gorman were escorted in. As we were standing around, waiting for the final out, a security guard had a little radio with the game on. At one point longtime Mets broadcaster Bob Murphy could be heard saying, "It gets away! Gets away! Here comes Mitchell! Here comes Mitchell!" when Kevin Mitchell scored on Bob Stanley's wild pitch to tie the game.

Shea Stadium was just so archaic—the elevators were terrible—so I had to run back upstairs to the booth. While on the ramp, I couldn't see what was happening on the field, but when I heard the crowd roar once more, after Mookie Wilson hit the ball that went by Buckner for the winning run, I knew it was over. In fact I wouldn't actually see the play until around two o'clock in the morning on *Sports Center*. On the subject of the Buckner play, I have to clear up a misnomer. Dave Stapleton, Buckner's defensive replacement in so many games during the regular and postseason, *should* have been at first base by that point. Some things have been said and written in the years since about how Stapleton had been nicknamed "Shaky" by some in the organization, and that was why he wasn't out there. That is total BS, and I never heard anyone on the team ever say that—and I don't know anyone who ever heard it either.

But back to Buckner. When you think about grit and dignity, you have to think of this warrior. It's so unfair that he got branded and pinned with the goat horns when we had already blown the lead in Game Six. There was no guarantee that we would have won the game if he had made that play. In addition, there was still Game Seven to be played, a game in which we couldn't hold on to a 3–0 lead. The fact is that we wouldn't have gotten to the World Series without Buckner. He had had a tremendous year despite fighting through pain every day of the season. When we were on the road, he always wanted a room closest to the ice machine to treat the swelling of his throbbing heels. Everybody saw the limp in his step, so it was totally unfair and mean-spirited on the part of some Red Sox fans to put any blame on him for the World Series loss. We're talking about a guy who gave everything he had in a near–Hall of Fame career.

Obviously there was some pain after the '86 World Series ended, but the positives outweighed the negatives by a large margin. And I think that after all these years what that Red Sox team accomplished is appreciated more than ever. I certainly believe the fact that the organization has won four World Series in the last fifteen years—exorcising "the Curse of the Bambino" once and for all—has helped. The onus of, "Oh, woe is me, woe is you" and the ball that went through Buckner's legs or Bucky Dent's home run—those kinds of things aren't dwelled on by the fans like they used to be.

So now instead of the fans in Red Sox Nation pointing at '86 as the one they blew, they see the great talent and the characters on that ball club more than ever before. There are guys in the Hall of Fame like Jim Rice and Wade Boggs and others, like Roger, that should be. The fans—even the ones that weren't old enough to see them play—know their numbers and the stats they put up. In the years since, fences have been mended, like when Buckner came back for Opening Day in 2008, walked across left field, and threw out the first pitch as part of the championship flag-raising ceremony. Sadly some are no longer with us. Along with Buckner, we lost Baylor and Henderson too young; the legendary Tom Seaver, who meant so much to that young pitching staff as a mentor; and their manager, John McNamara.

Thirty-five years later the '86 Red Sox team still feels like a family to me. Whenever one of the players comes to a Red Sox game, he always comes up to see me in the booth—and we put him on the air. Maybe it's because I'm the only one up there from that era, but it still means a lot to me when they visit.

I remain especially close with Roger, who is a very loyal guy and a friend since '84. If you are a friend of the Rocket, you are a friend for life. And he certainly was an all-time great. If it were up to me, Roger would have been voted into the Baseball Hall of Fame a long time ago. I think he will get there, but it's a travesty that he is not there yet, considering that he was never proven guilty of any wrongdoing. It was a thrill to be inducted into the Red Sox Hall of Fame with Roger and two of my other favorites, Nomar Garciaparra and Pedro Martinez. I remember when the four of us threw out the first pitches together that day. Roger said, "Let's throw on three." When we got to two, I threw my pitch so that it would arrive at home plate the same time as theirs!

Rich Gedman is another from that team that remains a very close friend whom I see often at Fantasy Camp, as well as Marty Barrett and Oil Can Boyd. What I love about Can is that he can talk pitching with anybody—and how he would approach hitters like Aaron Judge. His love of the game is just so refreshing. Some people think he's a little off the wall, but when you get him one-on-one, he's really a solid, sensitive guy.

Then there are other guys like Al Nipper, a pal for so long that our friendship extends back to the days when he taught my daughter how to roller skate. And Joe Sambito, whom I run into whenever I'm in Anaheim.

I've also always been a confidant and admirer of Bob Stanley and his wife Joan. Bob did so much service for the Jimmy Fund as a player, and then, shortly after his career concluded, he ended up using Jimmy Fund services after his son Kyle was diagnosed with cancer. It's those kinds of experiences—and reality checks—that bring friends even closer together.

And there's Dewey, a very philosophical man with a strong faith. I have always been aware of all the surgeries and hospitalizations of his two sons. I think it was remarkable that he could concentrate on the game of baseball when he had all these health issues with the children at home. He was always a great right fielder—with a canon for an arm—but then he blossomed into a fearsome hitter after his first few years in the Majors. He had more home runs than any other American League hitter in the '80s—and he specialized in Saturday afternoon walk-off home runs. Suffice it to say that I believe Dewey deserves Hall of Fame consideration.

It's wonderful to see them all come back to Fenway from time to time at various events and celebrations. The Red Sox have truly done a terrific job of honoring their past, and it enables me to see the guys fairly often.

There is no question that the '86 Red Sox wanted to win it all, not just for themselves but for their fans and the city of Boston. In a sense, because they were so supremely talented and adored by Red Sox fans yet came up just short in dramatic fashion, they are tragic heroes. Enjoy this look back to a golden age in Red Sox history—and why the '86 Red Sox are still revered today.

PREFACE

When I decided to write a book on the '86 Red Sox, I fully expected casual fans to ask, with various degrees of bewilderment, "Why?" Surely, some would say in various forms, "Wasn't that the team that broke New England's heart by blowing the '86 World Series in epic proportion?" But for the truly knowledgeable baseball historians and Red Sox fans with whom I shared the idea, the reaction was uniformly enthusiastic. Most immediately understood that a highly personal, in-depth look into a team that, within a two-week period in October '86, experienced the highest of highs and lowest of lows like no other team in the history of the game—and how the experience affected the rest of their lives—would be fascinating. And through one-on-one interviews with the key and most intriguing players, I wouldn't just tell the tale of the '86 Red Sox but would try to capture the team's very soul.

With the benefit of years of reflection and perspective from the men that made up the '86 Red Sox, my goal, through deep and sometimes emotional interviews, was to write the definitive book on this iconic yet Shakespearean drama–like team. To my great satisfaction, at nearly every turn there was the thrill of discovering history never told.

Make no mistake: in spite of their World Series misery, the '86 Red Sox were a beloved, magical team. All these years later they are instantly recalled by just nicknames like "Oil Can,"

"Rocket," "Spike," "Buck," and "Dewey." They were—and have remained—baseball royalty in "The Hub."

I admit that I tried once before to write a book about this team back in 1993. It was to be co-written with their sparkplug second baseman, Marty Barrett. But as it had been only seven years since the crushing World Series defeat to the Mets, the publishing industry deemed it "too soon" to appeal to the target audience of Red Sox fans.

Now, four Red Sox World Series championships later, the time had at long last arrived. The opportunity had arisen to give this historic team its due. It was also time to dispel some of the myths, inaccuracies, and misnomers that have been written and spoken about the team and accepted as truth. It was time to set free long-held feelings and thoughts that have been bottled up in the hearts and minds of some of the players for more than three decades. And it was time to resolve long-held mysteries that the players were now more comfortable revealing.

What left the greatest impression on me from meeting with the players was their raw emotion and transparency. I could see the passion in their eyes and hear it in their voices. It would be a book far less about the rehashing of that season but rather more about the riveting lives each of them have endured because of it.

The venues where the interviews took place tell much about the former players' lives today. The hope is that readers will feel like they're sitting in the living rooms, dugouts, ballpark stands, and restaurants where they took place, eavesdropping in on the conversations while feeling the ocean breezes, smelling the fresh-cut grass, tasting the hotdogs, or walking through the vineyards of the Napa Valley.

I chose sixteen players to profile for this project, fourteen of them face to face. The meetings would take place in cities large and small, as diverse as the players themselves: Las Vegas, Nevada, and Kinston, North Carolina; Boston, Massachusetts, and Phoenix, Arizona; Pawtucket, Rhode Island, and Hermosa

Beach, California; Queens, New York, and Tampa, Florida; Calistoga, California; Fort Myers, Florida; and Austin, Texas.

Those profiled were the indomitable Roger Clemens, the outspoken Oil Can Boyd, the dignified Bill Buckner, the dry-witted Bob Stanley, the eloquent Wade Boggs, the intense Jim Rice, the compassionate Rich Gedman, the upbeat Marty Barrett, the humble Bruce Hurst, the gritty Spike Owen, the spiritual Dwight Evans, the gregarious Steve Lyons, the uber-intelligent Tom Seaver, the persevering Calvin Schiraldi, the virtuous Don Baylor, and the affable Dave Henderson. All were known for their heroics on the field. But when that '86 pennant-winning season ended, so did much of their aura of invincibility. One faced battles with addiction, and another remains in Hall of Fame purgatory; some dealt with serious illnesses or unfathomable family tragedies, while others struggled mightily to shake off the stigma of the '86 World Series defeat. Saddest of all, four players and their manager have passed away, including Buckner, whose final major interview is in these pages and includes his admission that despite his positive public persona, he never got over the pain he and his family endured from the fallout of his infamous error.

The interviews, which are at the heart of these literary portraits, lasted anywhere from one to as many as seven hours, with three of them conducted over two separate days. There was much joy and laughter during those encounters—but a few tears as well. What was so poignant was the closeness the team still has to this day—like a brotherhood. This was evident in how most of the players lighted up when talking about their teammates. They'll always have a pennant-winning season and struggling in the trenches together as their bond—with the camaraderie and friendships that goes along with it.

So beloved were the '86 Sox in Boston that even with the ultimate defeat, the city held a rally for them at Government Center that rivaled the celebrations of the championship clubs that would come later. And why not? A .500 team the year before, with plenty of question marks, the '86 Sox weren't expected to finish much higher than fifth place before a twenty-strikeout performance on a chilly April night by the young Clemens changed everything. It lifted the players' expectations of themselves and the team. It made every Clemens start "must-see TV." It made them all believers.

In the years since leaving the Red Sox, some of the players profiled in this book have had their numbers retired, and most have been inducted into the team's Hall of Fame. To celebrate the thirtieth anniversary of the '86 season, the players were brought back to Fenway Park and honored in a grand celebration for everything they had accomplished that season. They were feted like lords of Lansdowne Street. They were, for all intents and purposes, a once-in-a-generation team.

The '86 Sox currently have three Hall of Famers—and three others who arguably belong there. They were a highly exciting and likable group, and had they gotten just one more strike in Game Six of the World Series, they would have been a team for the ages. Given all of the Red Sox organization's success in recent years, it's easy to forget that the '86 team was its only pennant winner over a twenty-eight season period (1976–2003). Thus it was the *only* club that a generation of Red Sox fans saw make it to the World Series.

Ultimately this is a story about a team that transcended baseball. It's about a club that enjoyed exhilarating victory and suffered heart-wrenching defeat—and then overcame that failure by moving on in various ways. It's about being human and understanding what's really important in this world. It's about how a city that lived and died with a club that came one pitch away from ending the sixty-eight-year Curse of the Bambino has reconciled the agonizing end to the '86 World Series and now embraces this collection of all-time greats more than ever before.

TWO SIDES OF GLORY

1.

Safe at Home

....

You can be grateful to God for what He's given you, or you can worry about things and complain. For the most part I've taken the positive way.

—BILL BUCKNER

I first met Bill Buckner on a wintry February evening in 2013 inside a dimly lit "green room" in the back of the 1930s-era Gramercy Theater in New York City. I had been invited there by Mookie Wilson, with whom I was working on his autobiography at the time. Buckner was still a ruggedly handsome man, with his signature full mustache and everlasting tan, sitting on a sofa and relaxing while sipping a can of beer. He was friendly enough, though a reserved man of few and measured words. We casually talked about Mookie's book project, the current state of baseball broadcasting, and how a close bond of mutual admiration had formed over the years between the two main characters involved in the so-called Buckner play, which infamously ended Game Six of the '86 World Series.

For me the thirty minutes that the three of us spent together—as Bill and Mookie waited for the crowd to settle into the intimate 499-seat playhouse for an event dubbed *An Evening with Mookie Wilson and Bill Buckner*—was a bit surreal. I was amazed at how well the two of them got along—considering that nearly thirty years before it was Mookie's ground ball that made him a "hero" and Buckner—who had the ball go through his legs—a "scapegoat," in the most unfair sense of the word.

Imagine this if you will. You're Bill Buckner. You have a career that touched four decades, beginning in the sixties and ending in the nineties. You hit over .300 seven times in your career. You won a batting title. You amassed more lifetime hits than Ted Williams and Joe DiMaggio. You never struck out more than twice per game in 2,517 games. You were a superb defensive first baseman with a better lifetime fielding percentage than Lou Gehrig and set a record for most assists in a season at the position. You played the game the way it's supposed to be played—with a reckless abandon and intensity—all while being plagued by ankle and knee injuries since the beginning of your career. But in what could be described as a Greek tragedy, your outstanding, borderline–Hall of Fame career is overshadowed by a single error that was only one of several Red Sox gaffes that contributed to Boston's losing one particular game. You sometimes feel as if you didn't just receive a disproportionate amount of blame for the loss but rather *all of the blame*. You have run-ins with fans, and even your children have to deal with inappropriate comments about it. And you can never get away from the error, as it's been replayed again and again on national television—usually every October during the postseason. Simply put, it would be enough to break any person.

And yet here was Bill Buckner, all these years after that night at Shea Stadium, enjoying a light conversation with me and the always engaging Wilson, the man who hit the ball that caused all the chaos in Buckner's life. His and Mookie's friendship and spiritual bond had blossomed over the last two decades as they teamed up at countless autograph shows to sign copies of the famous photo now frozen in time: Wilson running up the first-base line at the exact moment his batted ball got past Buckner. They had become the modern-day Ralph Branca and Bobby Thomson, another pair of adversaries-turned-friends and business partners in the years following Thomson's "Shot Heard 'Round the World" at the Polo Grounds in 1951.

To my surprise the next day Mookie informed me that Buckner was interested in perhaps doing a book, either one in tandem with him or possibly his own autobiography. The latter idea would be considered more seriously, bounced back and forth for three years with several book proposals written and reviewed but ultimately filed away. Buckner was torn. In the end the project, which would have delved deeply into his sometimes painful past and for which he would have had to endure a book tour and answer the same old questions again and again about the '86 World Series, would have been too much for him.

While I understood his position, the book, like the man, would have been inspiring and in many ways a roadmap in overcoming obstacles in life. But, alas, it wasn't to be. We would remain friendly—a breakfast here, a coffee there—as Buck would come to the New York area regularly for card show signings, often with Mookie. He never failed to impress me with his inner-strength and fortitude.

Bill Buckner's Final Major Interview

Bill Buckner and I would meet nearly five years after our first encounter one November afternoon for lunch at a Holiday Inn across the street from, ironically enough, Citi Field—home to the Mets. Life had presented him with another obstacle to overcome: a serious, though now under control, health issue. Having lost some weight, he appeared a bit frailer compared to how physically fit he had always been, and his speech was a little slower than usual. Having great empathy and tremendous respect for the man and pleased to hear he had gotten past the worst of his ailment, I was sincerely concerned at the pace of his recovery.

I handed a book across the table to Buck, *Diamond Redemptions*, which he had lent to me the last time we had met. According to Bill, the author of the book, C. Terry Williams, had given him the copy. One of the chapters in the book—about Buckner's plight—was aptly called "The Salvation of Billy Buck." The piece offered alternative endings to Game Six of the 1986

World Series, some of which I found plausible and others a bit ridiculous but all of them interesting to read.

"The one I found most reasonable," I relay to Buckner, "was how different your life would have been had that inside wild pitch that tied the game actually come in just another inch or so and hit Mookie. If that had happened, it would have changed the entire complexion of the game, and there never would have been a 'Buckner play.' The book takes an interesting approach on how the smallest of things could have changed the history of baseball."

"You could say that for most of that [Game Six]," Buck notes.

"Of course so much has been written about that game and the error," I say. "When the Boston media started asking you about it all the following spring, were you ever like, 'Hey, I don't deserve this'? How did you handle it then?"

"It depended," Buckner says. "Sometimes you'd have someone that would ask a stupid question, and I'd get offended. It's just the fact that I understand that people who know the game at all know what happened. They don't blame me totally. I'm part of a team. What bothered me and what I couldn't understand was how, right after the World Series, they *tortured* me. I think I handled that all right, but there are wounds from it that have left a lot of scar tissue that didn't totally go away. Do I think I lost the World Series? Obviously no. But it wasn't good. The only good that came out of it was that I had a lot of people who were inspired by it. I got so many nice letters. People were writing from the heart. They actually were helped by what had happened to me and how I dealt with it. That kind of got me through it, but without my faith it would've been a lot harder. God doesn't put you in situations that you can't handle. It may seem like they are [impossible], but they do work out in the long run, even though you can't see it at the time."

I ponder Buck's message for a moment before asking if, in a quiet moment, he ever wondered why God chose him to deal with all he went through.

"I didn't question Him or why He did it," Buckner tells me. "Maybe I wouldn't have wanted to know, but it definitely at times seemed unfair. And that's a lot harder than maybe if I'd made an error that cost the game. Then I'd say, 'Okay, if I'd caught the ball, we would've won.' I would rather that have happened than the way it worked out—with those [nonfactual] criticisms."

I've always felt that not enough attention was given to one factor: Buckner could barely walk during that entire World Series, yet he played through his Achilles heel injuries, which he had battled throughout the season, so as to keep his bat in the lineup.

"Your injuries were so bad you had to wear special high-top spikes," I begin. "I remember your telling me that even though [Red Sox manager John] McNamara would bring Stapleton into games to replace you in the late innings, in Game Six you still felt you were the better option in the field. Did you talk to Mac about finishing the sixth game?"

"I was standing next to Marty [Barrett] in the dugout when McNamara asked me, 'You wanna finish the game?' I said, 'Yeah, sure.' I suppose he could have taken me out like he did in Game Two, but that game was a blowout, so of course he would take me out of that one. But here's the thing: during the first couple of games I could barely move. But then the Achilles tendon got better as the Series went on. It got better to the point where the problems I had with it didn't keep me from getting to [Mookie's] ball. If I hadn't been able to get there, then you could say it was a bad move. The whole problem was that Marty had the pickoff sign on, so he was over closer to second, and I had to move over away from first. You know Mookie could fly, so any ground ball was gonna be close. There was a big deal made about Stanley not being able to get [to first]—he took some heat for it—but I don't even think about that. The fans were booing Stanley when I got to the team [in '84], and I still don't know why. Anyway I was out there. If McNamara had told me, 'I'm putting in Stapleton,' I would have been fine with it."

And one can only guess what alternative ending that could have presented.

Often lost in all the attention paid to Buckner's error was what an extraordinarily productive hitter he had been for the club during his first two full seasons with the Red Sox in '85 and '86, driving in over a hundred runs each year. Without his bat it's hard to conceive that Boston would have made it to the '86 World Series at all. And he gives much of the credit for the resurgence of his offensive numbers to Red Sox hitting coach Walter Hriniak.

"In past discussions you've told me what a difference Walt Hriniak made after you joined the Sox," I recall. "Do you feel like he was one of the unsung heroes of that pennant-winning coaching staff?"

"Yeah, I do, and he took a lot of unfair criticism that mostly stemmed from Ted Williams," Buckner says. "Sometimes great hitters don't study the game as much as guys who aren't [so great]. And Ted wasn't a very good manager either. But he was probably the best hitter that ever played, and I respected that. It bothered me that Ted felt like he had to knock Walter down. Walter was the hardest-working baseball guy ever and cared about you more than anybody else that ever coached. Walter was a Charlie Lau [legendary batting coach] guy and didn't waver from what he believed in. [The most notable of Lau's absolutes of hitting was a weight shift from a firm rigid back side to a firm rigid front side.] Walter and I became friends, and we both lived in the Boston area during the wintertime before the '85 season. I was doing all right but always thought I could hit better [and be] more like a George Brett type of hitter. So one day we were in my basement in Andover, and I said, 'Walter, I wanna be more like Brett—same swing and everything.' He said, 'I'm all for it.' It was tough for me because I was already a legitimate hitter. I mean, I didn't have to change."

"Yeah, you were a former batting champion," I point out.

"But I wanted to be better," Buckner continues. "So Walter said to me, 'You've gotta promise me that no matter what, from here on out, you're gonna stick with what I'm telling you; otherwise forget about it. I told him I was good with that. So we went to spring training, and for some reason I just kept getting jammed—couldn't get the bat through the zone. With six days left of spring training the brass, the manager, and the coaches were having a meeting. Walter told me someone said, 'What about Buckner? He can't get the ball out of the infield.' Walter stood up for me and said, 'Don't worry about Buckner; he's fine.' But after another tough game in Sarasota, where I got jammed and broke about three bats, I said to Hriniak, 'Walter, meet me in the cage.' So we went down there, and he gave me soft tosses to hit and said to me, 'Try releasing your top hand off the bat after you make contact.' I did that, and it was just like somebody had cut the ropes off. Now I could get a good finish to my swing. I played the next day and hit a home run, got four hits, and ended up having what I thought was my best year. I ended up playing another six years, which never would have happened without Walter. I wish I had had him as my hitting coach when I was twenty years old. I think I could have hit like Brett because I had great hand-eye coordination and didn't strike out."

Also overshadowed by the "Buckner play" was Buck's role in the historic Game Five comeback of the ALCS that year, when he led off the fateful top of the ninth inning with a single off of Angels starter Mike Witt, who had been cruising up until that point.

"Would you say that being a part of that Red Sox team that came back against the Angels was the highlight of your career?" I ask.

"Oh yeah. Team-wise I can't figure anything better," Buck says, his voice rising enthusiastically. "The only thing that would have been better would've been winning one more [World Series] game. Anaheim that day was the loudest stadium I'd ever been in. I can still just close my eyes and picture Reggie Jackson over in their dugout high-fiving Gene Mauch. And I remember the mounted policemen on the field to keep the fans in the stands. It was amazing, and it was nice to be a part of it. And I got the hit that started the rally—that's a positive thing. But everything was unbelievable."

Buckner decided to skip the 2004 World Series championship ring ceremony at Fenway on opening day in 2005 to avoid all the attention it would conjure up. And he didn't return for the twentieth reunion celebration of the '86 pennant winner in 2006, as he was three thousand miles away on a college visit with his son in Washington state. How ironic it was then that of all the '86 Red Sox who were introduced that night, it was Buckner in absentia who received the loudest and longest ovation of any of his teammates. It was that crowd reaction, along with some prodding by then longtime Red Sox public relations director Dick Bresciani, that no doubt contributed to Buck's ultimately deciding to return to Fenway the spring following the Red Sox next championship in 2007.

On that day as Buckner slowly walked toward the pitcher's mound—with tears in his eyes—to throw out the ceremonial first pitch, the crowd erupted in thunderous applause.

"Dwight Evans told me how touched he was to catch the first pitch you threw out prior to the Red Sox home opener in 2008," I tell Bill. "It was the first time you had returned to Fenway in many years, and he said you were overcome with emotion over the standing ovation you received as you two hugged. What did that moment mean to you?"

Buckner, a little choked up, doesn't hesitate. "It was actually an honor, and I was very impressed with the 'new' Red Sox," Buck says. "When they finally won the World Series after I was gone [in 2004], reporters kept asking me, 'Do you feel better now? Do you feel relieved?'"

Buck shakes his head in disbelief. "I mean, how can I answer that?" he asks rhetorically. "If I'd been on that team that won, yeah, I would've felt better, but it wasn't my team. You know I was a good Red Sock, a good player, and I'm happy they won. I had been rooting for them, and I would have loved to have been on that team."

"You were watching that game with your son, right?"

"Yeah, I was," Buck says. "If I had to pick a dream, it would've been for *him* to have been on that World Series team."

"Back to your return to Fenway. You once told me that you saw a sign that read, 'We forgive you.' As great a return as it was for you, what was your reaction to something so ridiculous, and shouldn't it have been the other way around—something like, 'Hey Buck—forgive us!'?"

"*That*," Buck says, with a pause for effect, "made me angry. To feel that that's what some Boston people thought—that really bothered me. But then afterward I was in a room at Fenway with some famous Boston sports figures like Bobby Orr, and the way they treated me was special. They know how sports work. If you play for a relatively long period of time, either you or some of your teammates are going to have some tough times. So I think those guys could appreciate what happened to me. And most of my teammates were good about it too."

Buck pauses for a moment before adding to that last sentence. "Well, maybe Dave Stapleton's the *only* one that wasn't," he grins, referring to his backup.

I steer the conversation away from '86 to an endearing story that Wilson had once told me.

"Soon after Mookie was traded by the Mets to the Toronto Blue Jays, he spotted you in the outfield warming up before a game against the Kansas City Royals," I begin. "He had forgotten you were now a Royal, and since he hadn't spoken with you in the three years since the '86 World Series, he was a little apprehensive about approaching you, knowing full well everything you had been through. But you eased his anxiety over the potentially uncomfortable situation when you asked him if he could hit you some ground balls. Your humor at that moment was so endearing. What prompted you to do that?"

"Mookie's just a good friend, a class guy," Buckner says. "I obviously knew that he knew what had happened to me and my family, so to kind of make an icebreaker, to make a joke, it was pretty funny. At first he didn't know whether to laugh or not."

"One of the positives that came out of that encounter was a friendship and partnership with Mookie," I say. "On the business end the two of you signed enough autographs together to put your kids through college, right?"

"Yeah, we did," Buckner confirms. "And more than that, I think. My wife wasn't real happy about me signing that photo with Mookie because of how that moment would go on to affect our whole family. But you know what? At first I agreed with her, saying, 'No way; I'm not going to do this.' But then I thought, 'I need to get something back from this torture, man! Somebody needs to repay me a lot of money for me being tortured!' So that's how it got started, and then it just took off. And you know Mookie—he's such a good guy, so likable. We got to become really good friends."

"Like Mookie, who is a pastor at his church and sings in the choir, you're also a man of faith," I say. "Can you talk a little bit about how your life experiences—certainly not limited to baseball—have enabled you to help others, particularly young people confronting challenges in their lives?"

"Well, that's what we're supposed to do—to give back," Buck says with sincerity. "As hard as it was, I had something to give back. I've done a lot of talks and appearances where people want to hear what I thought about what happened to me. So I step out and do it, even though it's hard to talk about."

Buck takes a moment before continuing what are difficult topics for him to discuss, even today. "There are things I've experienced, Erik," he says solemnly. "My father died [by suicide] when I was young. That was a tough one. My wife thinks, and I kind of agree with her, that his death and all the things that happened during my childhood that weren't healthy—you know, there was some abuse—they left scars. Baseball has its scars too. So you can go two ways. I grew up living in an area that was kind of shaky—a little bit on the wrong side of the tracks. I saw a lot of kids that went the wrong way. Fortunately I chose the right way, where things I cared about were school and sports. I became obsessed [to the point that] if I didn't get the best score on a test or if I didn't do the most push-ups, it really bothered me. There were things that affected how I ended up. You can be grateful to God for what He's given you, or you can worry about things and complain. For the most part I've taken the positive way."

"Has talking about your experiences been therapeutic for you?" I ask. "I know you do a lot of shows, and the fallout from the '86 World Series gets brought up a lot."

Buckner smiles as a thought comes to mind. "You know, it's surprising," he begins. "Last week was the first postseason since [the error] happened that it wasn't shown on TV. They always show the Mets celebrating, but they've also always shown me missing the ball. They didn't do that this year. So I *appreciate* them at Fox, ESPN, and Turner! Finally they have enough class to take that off of there. Believe me, I've watched most all of the playoffs over the years and have always been a little gun shy of seeing it shown. It took some of the pleasure away from watching the games."

"What about your wife, Jody?" I ask. "I've talked to her on the phone, and I know she has been a great source of support for you all these years. Can you talk about her and some of the things she's done to help you and the family?"

"Well, she didn't release me," Buck says with a sly smile. "She's a good lady—very strong, tough. It's probably been tougher on the family than it was on me, I would think, because you know how it is when something happens to one of your kids. And then she saw how tough it was on me and how unfair it was. So that bothered her a lot."

In reference to his kids, the one incident that probably hurt the most was when his then four-year-old son was actually told by an adult at his preschool, "Your daddy had to quit baseball because he missed the ball." For himself a few incidents stood out, including one in 1993. As a roving batting instructor for the Blue Jays, Buckner was asked by a youngster to sign a baseball card outside the Red Sox Triple-A facility in Pawtucket. That's when an eighteen-year-old man shouted out, "Don't give him a ball; he'd drop it anyway." Buckner went to his truck, put his bag inside, and then returned to the heckler, lifted him off the ground by the collar of his shirt, and pretty much scared the hell out of him.

But what also bothered the Buckners were the erroneous reports delivered by some in the Boston media on why he moved the family out of Boston.

"After you retired from baseball," I say, "you left Boston and moved to Boise, Idaho, where you already owned a two-thousand-acre ranch."

"That's right," Buckner says, appearing to know where I am going with my statement. "I had a lot of property and a cattle ranch. It was *always* my plan to move there. It had nothing to do with getting away from Red Sox fans or any trouble we were still having. I actually stayed in Boston quite a while after I finished playing because the economy was so bad that I couldn't sell my house. But writers kept putting into their articles that we were forced to move because of the fans. It was so stupid."

"What was the appeal of Idaho?" I ask. "After all, you grew up in California."

"I had a step-uncle out there," he explains, "and as a hunter, I loved it. It was great hunting. So I would come up at the end of a season to go hunting with my brother, who played pro ball, and we decided to get a ranch in Murphy, Idaho. We used to watch *Bonanza* when we were kids, so I thought that would be pretty cool. So we had that ranch for twenty-five years."

A waiter comes by and does a double take, clearly recognizing the former baseball star, before asking him if he is still working on his half-eaten pasta.

"No, I'm good," Buckner tells him, as the waiter takes his plate away. "I need to start putting some weight back on," Buck confides to me.

It's been said that laughter is the best medicine. For Buckner in recent years some of his healing from Game Six came in the form of a couple of hilarious, cleverly done television appearances. I ask Bill about his guest role on the popular HBO series *Curb Your Enthusiasm*, in which Bill makes a great diving catch to save a baby dropped from a burning building so as to, at last, absolve him from the error in '86.

"That all started because Larry David [creator of the show] was friends with the Red Sox owners," Buck begins. "So Larry called them to see if I would do the show, and I said, 'No way.' But then he called again and kind of presented it a little differently. He said [my wife and I] could look at the script if we wanted. I wouldn't even think about doing something like that without running it by Jody, as she's got a better feel for stuff like that. Anyway we talked to Larry on the phone, and Jody said, 'Let's do it.' So it ended up being fun, and people keep telling me it's their favorite episode. They still show it a lot."

"Oh, it was *outstanding*," I say.

"Yeah, it was fun," Buck says with a grin. "It was kind of, in a way, a release from all the shit. Some good laughs."

"And then there was the television commercial you did for the MLB Network with Mookie in 2016—thirty years after the '86 Series—titled *Catching Up*," I say. "That was so well done, and it looked like you two really enjoyed doing it."

"Yeah, I don't laugh enough, so they were just giving me the opportunity to have a laugh," Buckner says.

"All these years later you and your '86 Red Sox teammates are treated like legends when returning to Fenway," I point out. "Do you think the reason is nostalgia, or could it be that the Boston fans have come to admire how hard you guys played the game?"

"I think the fans were frustrated for so many years, and it's almost like a relief now," Buck says. "We were their team, they enjoyed us, and it was an obsession for the fans. I didn't understand that. New England is such a large area. And if you live in New England, you're pretty much a Red Sox fan. It's important for people in that part of the country."

"The fans are pretty intense in this town too," I say of New York. "It's a Northeast thing."

"So when we played the Mets, we were two historic teams," Buck notes. "All the stars lined up."

"The networks loved it," I say. "Game Seven was the highest rated World Series game of all time."

"And Game Six?" Buckner asks.

"That was the second most watched of all-time."

"I guess I picked a bad time to have a bad day, didn't I?" Buck says self-deprecatingly and with a grin. "But at least I got through the last game."

For Buckner to speak now with humor over a tortuous experience that would have made lesser men crumble speaks volumes for this modern-day baseball warrior. He's an example for us all.

At just before 2 p.m. on Monday, May 27, 2019, my cell phone began lighting up like a Christmas tree. The news coming across the texts was as tragic as it was shocking. Buck had lost his battle with Lewy body dementia at age sixty-nine. My first impulse was to call Mookie—to gently find out if he had heard about his dear friend. He had not—and was similarly jarred by the news. After all, Wilson told me, he had just done a signing with him a couple of months before, and everything had seemed fine. Ironically, perhaps, Buck had told Mookie just prior to that event that he wanted to do one more signing with him for old time's sake. Maybe Buck knew his time was short.

A private memorial service would be held on June 22—the month and day of Buck's two uniform numbers: six and twenty-two. In a statement Buckner's family said, "Bill fought with courage and grit as he did all things in life. Our hearts are broken, but we are at peace knowing he is in the arms of his Lord and Savior Jesus Christ."

Bill Buckner is, at last, safe at home.

2.

High Heat

....

Baseball's what I did; it's not who I am. I was a fierce competitor with
a big, loving heart. I really enjoyed helping others, but everyone knew
on game day I was going to bring my best.

—ROGER CLEMENS

The undisputed greatest pitcher of his generation
and arguably the best of all time burst into the
Red Sox dugout at Fenway Park one early overcast
August afternoon. "How ya'll doin'?!" bellowed out a grinning
Roger Clemens in his Texas drawl to a couple dozen fans who
had made pledges to the Roger Clemens Foundation and the
Jimmy Fund for the privilege to hit against him in the batting
cage. A day after his fifty-fifth birthday, the pitcher who had
struck fear into the hearts of opposing hitters through intimidation and an ungodly fastball was raring to go, dressed in a
Red Sox T-shirt and pumped up as if it were a Game Seven of
the World Series. To say the living legend—he of the unprec-
edented *seven* Cy Young Awards and 354 career wins—was a
larger-than-life figure would be no exaggeration.

But the Roger Clemens of today is far different from the one
I interviewed for the first time on April 17, 1986, a day game at
Fenway against the defending champion Kansas City Royals.
Clemens was the starting pitcher, and—under the category of
"something you would never see today"—I interviewed him
in the Red Sox dugout two hours *before* game time. Clemens

had yet to become the Rocket, a nickname bestowed on him by teammate Bruce Hurst after he struck out a Major League record twenty Seattle Mariners just twelve days later. Instead Clemens seemed somewhat shy and reserved, spoke softly, and gave little eye contact. But while his trademark bravado, which Roger would soon adopt with the media, wasn't there yet, there were clearly already glimpses of greatness out on the mound. The result on that particular day was a complete game, 6–2 win over the Royals.

As Roger finished throwing batting practice to the fans and enjoying every moment of it—playfully razzing or encouraging each hitter before every single pitch—I sentimentally arranged for our talk to take place in the *exact* area of the Red Sox bench where we first chatted over thirty years before. Clemens, accompanied on the trip by his stylish and effervescent wife Debbie (who would take a few swings against her husband as well) and a couple of friends from back home in Houston, was in great spirits. He was gregarious with a youthful enthusiasm not unlike that of a big kid. It was easy to get a sense that he was at peace with his world, the life he had built for his family, and his joy at returning to the city that had watched him quickly blossom into a superstar. If you think he harbors any resentment toward the Red Sox for not resigning him following the '96 season and hearing general manager Dan Duquette say at the time that Clemens was "in the twilight of his career," think again.

"This place feels like home," Clemens tells me as he surveys the old-fashioned ballpark from the dugout. "I spent thirteen wonderful years here and really worked my tail off. You have so much pride to have an opportunity to come to a club that's so rich in tradition. When I came out of the University of Texas, the Astros and Rangers had like the third and fifth picks in the country, so they had scouts looking at me quite a bit. I figured I was going to end up staying close to home. But then Boston, which is so deep in history, drafted me. I had gotten to know the Bush family at home and then, up here, got to meet the Kennedys. What's interesting is that Debbie was a young girl in my mother-in-law's arms on the route where the JFK assassination took place in Dallas. They saw JFK drive by about a mile from where he got shot. I'm a big JFK fan, and Deb still stays in touch with his daughter Caroline; they talk and text. So obviously I was excited, but I was trying to figure out Boston and get up to speed on everything. Actually my mother helped me out quite a bit with the history. She wrote me a poem about the area around Fenway Park—her own kind of poem to get me up to speed on where I was going to play and start my career. That was really cool."

Another way Clemens became familiar with the city was through jogging every day. One of his daily routines when in town was to run five miles along the Charles River. Feeling nostalgic, Clemens planned to go for a run before a scheduled flight to Scotland for a golf vacation the next day.

"I'll go retrace some of my runs around the river," he says. "Back in the day we'd get done with batting practice maybe an hour before the game started. I used that time to get my distance running in. And it's so easy here in Boston because there are so many runners that have a nice little pace going and you can always jump in behind. It's just such a running town; everybody runs here."

"Wouldn't people recognize you?" I ask with a chuckle.

"Oh yeah! They take a quick glance—and then *another* glance—and go, 'Are you . . . ?' And I'd say something like, 'Yeah. You've got a nice pace. You mind if I run with you?' It was just hilarious. There weren't a lot of cell phones back then, but I could only image their conversations—like, 'Hey, I was running with the Rocket,' with the other person on the phone going, 'Yeah, right!' So it was an easy run, and you met so many people and fans. After a while they began to catch on to when I would do my running—pretty fun stuff."

But for all the fame and fortune that Clemens would go on to receive over a career that would span twenty-four seasons, it almost wasn't to be. In the midst of a promising sophomore season in 1985, he was shut down due to a small flap tear that kept getting caught in his rotator cuff joint.

"I would get to the sixty to seventy pitch mark, and that thing would swell and click," Clemens explains. "It felt like someone was hitting me with an ice pick in the back of my shoulder. Any surgery for a pitcher is devastating, and I was in actual tears in the hallway in Anaheim when I realized I was going to be shut down. But Dr. James Andrews fixed me up and told me during my first rehab session, 'There are going to be days when you feel like you can throw ninety. *Don't!* And there are going to be days when you're going to think I didn't fix you. But it's going to be okay.' So I was really religious about the throwing program and wearing the three- to five-pound cuff weights he prescribed. In fact that's why I'm still able to throw at a high rate of speed at my age because I wear my cuff weights a lot."

What the surgery and therapy also did for Clemens was help position him to pitch one of the greatest seasons ever in 1986 and lead a Red Sox club, which many had picked for fifth place, all the way to the World Series. For Roger his coming-out party would begin with a record-setting performance on a chilly late-April night at Fenway Park against the Mariners. Aside from the twenty strikeouts, five of the Mariners who didn't strike out had two strikes on them, and Clemens didn't walk a single batter. But as Roger would explain, the most dominating pitching performance of his career—and perhaps in baseball history—came perilously close to never happening.

"I got stuck on Storrow Drive and almost *missed* that game!" Clemens says incredulously, then glances over to Debbie, who had just wandered over to hear one of her favorite stories. "We lived out in Malden in a one-bedroom condo with my mother-in-law's quilts on the windows—a good twenty-five minutes outside of town. It was a 7:35 p.m. starting time back then, and I liked to arrive at about five—enough time to go to the bull-pen, warm up, and be ready to pitch. So coming down Storrow, we were about two miles away from Fenway, but I could see the Citgo sign, so I thought, 'No problem.' But after forty-five minutes we'd gone maybe ten car lengths. I'm in boots, jeans, and a golf shirt, but I turn to Deb and say, 'I'm going to run for it. I'm going to run to the ballpark.' I get out of the car, open up the trunk, and grab my running shoes. In the traffic people are honking at me, but I'm panicking that I'm going to miss my start. Then I hear a police siren. I turn around, and it's a motorcycle cop with his siren blasting—*Whir! Whir! Whir!*—to get my attention. Then he goes, 'What's the problem?' I tell him, and he goes, 'Follow me.' The next thing I know he parts the sea of cars and escorts us to the ballpark. I walk through the clubhouse door at about 7:05. My entire team is looking at me, and I feel like the biggest heel. My pitching coach, Bill Fischer, goes, 'Come into McNamara's office.' So I walk in, and Mac says, 'We're going to scratch you. We got a guy getting ready to warm up. A long reliever.' I say, 'No, you're not. You're not going to do this to me. I'll get ready. I can *do* this! Let's go, Fish!' Poor Fish. I made him run at his age (he was fifty-five), and we sprinted the whole way to the bullpen."

"So how did you feel warming up?" I ask.

"I was a mess! I didn't come close to throwing a strike, and now I had a temple headache. I knew Fish was calling to get the long man going. I think the only time I got to catch my breath was when they played the anthem. So I tried to get my wits about me, backtrack to the day before—an off day—when I played golf with a couple of my friends from college. Spike Owen, who was then the leadoff hitter for the Mariners, was one of my teammates at Texas [University], and my friends wanted me to knock him down just for fun—just to bug him. So with all this craziness happening, I'm on the mound thinking, 'Geez, I can't believe this. I just got to the ball park, the crowd is cheering, and the fella batting number one for the Mariners is Spike. Oh gosh; I told those guys I was going to buzz him.' So I throw one just kind of up and in; he hits the dirt and just stares back at me. So with that out of the way, I'm thinking, 'Okay, here we go.' I push off extremely hard on the very next pitch, as hard as I can, whistle it in there, and it goes right at his ear hole! I knock him down, he spins out and gets up, and I can't even tell you the cuss words he was hollering at me. I was like, 'Gosh, I'm going to be all over the place tonight. I'm not gonna have it.' Well, in what seemed like a blink of an eye, I strike out twenty. I don't walk a guy. Everybody was going crazy."

The impact of what Clemens had accomplished wasn't lost on his teammates.

"The night Roger struck out twenty," Hurst tells me in a separate interview, "I remember driving home with my wife and saying, 'Our life just changed because of this guy.' All of a sudden I had credibility where I had had none before. All of us pitchers on the staff had credibility now because we were Roger's teammates. It was amazing!"

Roger then reminisces with me about a tender moment he had with his pitching coach following the game. "I get up to my locker and Fish comes over, sits next to me, and says two things. 'After your arm injury, that's unbelievable what you did,' he starts out. 'But you know what? I'm most proud that you threw that hard and didn't walk anybody.'" Bill Fischer, who was himself once a pitcher, still holds the Major League record to this day of 84⅓ consecutive innings without a walk. Roger concludes: "As Fish got up to leave, he goes, 'By the way, you get here *whenever* you want!'"

From that point on Clemens's world would never be the same. He graced the cover of *Sports Illustrated*; his cap, glove, and spikes were shipped to the National Baseball Hall of Fame in Cooperstown. A local Boston radio station even creatively changed the lyrics to Falco's hit song at the time "Rock Me Amadeus!" to "Rock Me Roger Clemens!" He was the most sought-after interview not just in baseball, but in all of popular culture, with appearances on every major national broadcast network, while publications like *Newsweek*, *People*, the *New York Times*, the *Washington Post*, and *USA Today* sent reporters to follow him around the country. It's what happens when you pitch the first twenty-strikeout game in 111 years of Major League base-ball, covering over 150,000 games. But most important to him, Roger now gave the Red Sox a sense of invincibility every time he took the mound.

"After a period of pedestrian baseball," I say, "you were chang-ing the culture around the Red Sox."

"There's no question about that," Roger agrees. "I showed the club that I was healthy and ready for that long run, that good pennant and playoff run that we had in '86. As for the spot-light, as I mentioned, we only had a one bedroom condo, so we had to pull the mattress out into the family room because that was the only room where we had a phone jack, and the phone was ringing nonstop. I got calls from everybody from the White House and Secret Service guys we knew to friends and family. Some of the guys I had played ball with before called the morning after the twenty-strikeout game because they had read the box score in their papers and thought there was a mis-print, that their paper had added the zero after the two by mis-take. And they were like, 'You've got to be kidding me!' And I was like, 'Yeah, man, it was unbelievable.' That game put me on the national stage for sure."

I ask Clemens if he felt a heavy burden to deliver a title as a young, twenty-four-year-old pitcher, especially when consider-ing that fourteen of his twenty-four victories that season came after a Red Sox loss. His answered surprised me.

"I really didn't feel *any* burden. That's because I had some great veteran pitchers with me—like Bruce Hurst, who really came along that year, and Oil Can Boyd. I learned over the twenty-four years that I played that when you have somebody like Hursty, that number two guy that can win seventeen or eighteen games, you've got a chance to go to the dance. That's the most important thing. You can win a Cy Young Award, but if you end up watching the playoffs on TV, it's not a lot of fun. The Cy Youngs that I've won that were attached to a really super year as far as the team goes are really the most import-ant ones to me. As for the rest of the staff, you need a good number three. As for the number four and five guys—I don't want to belittle them—but they can be very average, pitch to a 12-12 record, give me thirty-one to thirty-three starts and two hundred innings. Hey, those guys get five-year deals now; you know what I'm saying? It's crazy! I tell young guys that. I say things like, 'You know what you're messing with? If you just get locked in where you're healthy, be upright, don't get hurt, don't get hurt in the shower, run out there thirty-one times, 4.5 ERA, you're going to be alright.'"

"When you pitched in '86 and beyond in this town, it was *an event*," I say. "The city stopped. Local news outlets teased whenever you were pitching throughout the day. Fenway Park was regularly sold out. If someone was sitting at home, a Roger Clemens start was 'must-see TV.' That's because on any given night you could challenge the strikeout record you set or throw a no-hitter. Were you aware at that time the extent of the hold you had on this city? Or were you just so locked into what you were doing on the field?"

"I was definitely locked in," Clemens replies without pause. "I was very prideful. But I knew what was going on. It was cool for me on a day I pitched to see the different license plates from all the surrounding states coming to Fenway—New Hampshire, Rhode Island, Connecticut. They would see me in my car and honk. And I would receive so many cool letters. Some folks would write that they were counting every five days and buying their tickets so they could see me pitch. Some would complain when the coaching staff would decide to push me back a day. They would be like, 'Hey, we bought tickets thinking you would pitch,' like it was my fault. Of course I didn't have any control over it. But it was all good stuff."

"One of the things that set you apart from other elite hurlers was that you pitched with an edge, an aggression much in the same vein as Bob Gibson," I point out. "I've heard from guys who have played with and against your old Texas and Red Sox teammate Calvin Schiraldi that he had as much pure talent as anybody but lacked that intimidation factor that you possessed.

How psychologically important is it for a pitcher to have that element of intimation—to be unafraid to pitch inside?"

At that very moment I sense a change in Clemens's demeanor. I had hit on a subject that went to the core of what made him such a devastating competitor. I recalled the great Mets manager Davey Johnson once telling me that as outstanding as his New York staff was in the eighties, he wished they all induced more fear in hitters like Clemens did.

"Yeah. *Why* learn to pitch inside?" Clemens asks rhetorically in a serious tone. "I *had* to. I had to make a seventeen-inch plate into a twenty-four-inch plate. That's not throwing at or hitting guys. You're just trying to keep both sides of the plate open. It's *your job* as a pitcher. You want the hitter to feel uncomfortable—like the way Nolan Ryan and Gibson did. When I faced the likes of Dave Kingman, Greg Luzinski, and Carlton Fisk, I knew they could hurt me really bad if I wasn't able to command the inside of the strike zone. When I did Don Drysdale's radio show, he turned off the recorder and we talked personally. I'm just a kid then, and Drysdale looks at me—I'm shaking in my boots because here's '*Big D!*' Don Drysdale!—and he goes, 'Kid, you know what my best pitch of the game was?' I go, 'No sir, I don't.' And he goes, 'It was my *second* damn knock-down pitch. You know why kid?' I go, 'No, sir.' And Big D goes, 'That way the hitter knew the *first* one wasn't a damn mistake!'"

We both chuckle at his anecdote, but the point is driven home. Clemens then finishes his thoughts on my question: "You're right about Calvin, Erik. He had a devastating slider. And I know he desperately wanted to do well against the Mets [in the '86 World Series] because that was the team he came up with. I would not want anybody more on the mound than Calvin because I knew what kind of competitor he was from watching him up close and personal in our Texas days together, when we won the College World Series. But intimidation is winning. And you've *got* to win. Without intimidation you're going to lose out there. When the other team sees my name in the paper that I'm pitching the next day, it *better* get some rest because I'm getting mine!"

Roger's use of the present tense and how he emphatically expresses that last statement leave little question in my mind that the Rocket still had that signature fire in his belly.

Clemens was nothing short of a phenomenon the first three months of the 1986 season, going 14-0 and not losing his first game until July 2. By this point the Red Sox had jumped out to a remarkable 50-25 record, with an eight-game cushion in the AL East. Despite Boston's history of blowing big leads late in the season, the domination of Clemens overcame those ghosts from the past, as he won fourteen games following a Red Sox loss. So critical to Boston's regular season success of winning a division title, Roger not only won the Cy Young Award, but was also the rarest of pitchers to be voted AL Most Valuable Player, a distinction almost always given to the best everyday position player.

Despite a slide following the All-Star break, the Red Sox never lost hold of their first-place standing, which they had reached on May 14. Winning the division crown would set up an epic ALCS against a veteran California Angels team—a series in which the Red Sox were one strike away from elimination in Game Five. Clemens remembers vividly the helpless feeling he had as he felt the Red Sox's season slipping away.

"I've long been close with Reggie Jackson," Roger says of the Angels slugger at that time. "I make sure Reggie knows he was one of the reasons that at the age of twenty-one I wanted to get to the Major Leagues in time to face him before he retired. He was one of my favorites growing up. I remember [in Game Five] seeing Reggie with his arm around [Angels manager] Gene Mauch, like, 'We're done.' And I'm thinking, 'Okay, I'm going to get back to Boston, pack and fly to Texas, then rest for two weeks before starting workouts again.' But then we started coming back, and I turn to Oil Can and say, 'We might win [the pennant] if we can get this thing back to Boston. You got to get me the ball for Game Seven. You're going to win Game Six, Can.' And he says, 'Yup, I got it.' Then *Bam, bam, bam!* Hendu [Dave Henderson] hits that home run [to tie it] and jumps up in the air and sprains his knee. I couldn't believe he ended up playing in the World Series because he messed his knee up big time."

"So you end up winning that game for the ages, and Oil Can does indeed win Game Six here to get you the ball in the seventh and decisive game," I say. "This was your third start of the ALCS. Considering the Sox had all the momentum back on their side, what was your mindset going into that game?"

"You know the Red Sox had never won a Game Seven before that game," Clemens says. "I didn't know that before I had already bartered my four extra World Series tickets in exchange for stereo equipment for my apartment. On my way out of the [stereo] guy's door, he looks at me and says, 'Rocket, what if you don't win tonight? You know the Red Sox have *never* won a Game Seven, right?' So I play it cool and go, 'Well, you just hang in there and watch.' When I got three steps out the door, I was like, 'Oh gosh, I didn't know all this. Now what am I going to do?' The other thing was that Game Seven was the 'get healthy and try and save all the energy I had' game. I got the flu on the flight back from California and had an allergy outbreak. Those were the days when you could smoke on a plane, and we had a number of front office people and friends who were smoking. I'm allergic to menthol. So it got the best of me, and it ended up knocking my immune system down. I went seven innings [leaving with an 8–0 lead], but I knew that I was just trying to empty the tank. The first handful of innings I stayed in control, a bit underthrowing the ball and just playing pitch and catch even though I had really good stuff. After I came out of the game, they had me in with our doctor, who was giving me fluids, monitoring me, taking my heart rate, and taking all kinds of tests. I could hear the guys celebrate in the locker room after the game was over. I was still in the doctor's office. But it all worked out."

Roger's seven shutout innings in his weakened condition showed a blood-and-guts effort that would come to define his career.

The Red Sox would move on to the World Series against a historically good New York Mets team that had won 108 regular-season games and had had its own thrilling playoff series against the Houston Astros. It was a match-up made in network heaven, breaking every ratings record for baseball in the books for NBC. After a nail-biting 1–0 Sox victory in Game One behind Hurst, Clemens would pitch the second game, looking to put Boston up two games in the series.

"Game Two was touted as the pitching duel of the century," I begin. "You were facing Doc Gooden, who was the other outstanding young pitcher in baseball. What do you recall about all the hype going into that game?"

"I don't remember all the particulars, but what was really cool about it was that I got drafted by the Mets in 1981 but did not sign," Clemens says. "I do remember everybody talking about how if I had signed with them, Doc and I would have been on the same staff. Doc just had electric stuff. There is a backstory to Doc and me that is interesting. We both started in the All-Star Game—my first one—earlier that year in Houston, my hometown. We had to do an interview together the day before, so we were chatting behind the scenes. Because the All-Star Game was in a National League city, if I pitched the first three innings, I would have to hit. As we were departing, we wished each other good luck, and then he goes, 'Hey Rog, straight up tomorrow, right?' And I said, 'I don't understand; what are you talking about?' He goes, 'Straight up. If we face each other, just fastballs, right?' I go, 'Yeah, absolutely,' answering him quickly without even thinking about it. Well, I come up to hit, and Doc's out there throwing ninety-six or ninety-seven miles an hour. When a pitcher stands at home plate and sees a ball at that speed on the outside corner, it looks like a block away or in the other dugout. I tell the [home plate] umpire, 'Wow, that thing looked outside.' And he goes, 'Oh Rog, the whole ball's over the plate.' So it gave me a great perspective: I didn't have to be so fine when I was pitching. Anyway, with two strikes, I'm looking for another fastball, and I'm just going to swing at it no matter what. But Doc launches a curveball right at my earflap. Of course when he let it go, I thought it was coming right at me. As it broke down for a strike, it looked like I was riding a roller coaster trying to get back into the box—I almost fell down! I just stared at him and was like, 'Ooooh, okay.' I ran back out to the mound for my third inning, and after quickly going through Dale Murphy and Ozzie Smith, I was so excited because Gooden had to come up, and I was going to throw a curveball right at him. But they pinch-hit for him! I was like, 'Gosh dang it!' So I faced him that second game of the World Series you alluded to, and we beat him, which was extra satisfying."

In that game Gooden had perhaps the worst start of his career, getting pummeled by the Red Sox for six runs through five innings. Clemens, while more effective than his counter-part, wasn't his usual dominant self and was removed in the fifth inning.

"There was no carryover from not feeling well in Game Seven [of the ALCS]," Clemens tells me. "I was fine. I don't know what happened to us in that game. It wasn't like we didn't have good stuff. I guess the teams just got base hits."

So what was billed as a classic pitching match-up ended with the Red Sox amassing eighteen hits in a 9–3 rout of the Mets. The Mets would bounce back to win the next two at Fenway before Hurst would win his second game of the Series in Game Five. The Sox were now one win away from their first World Series championship in sixty-eight years with their ace on the hill to close it out. Our conversation leads to the contro-versial decision by Red Sox manager John McNamara to pull Clemens from Game Six, still one of the biggest mysteries in baseball lore—until now.

"You returned to the mound for the sixth game at Shea, which would have clinched the World Series for the Red Sox had you won," I recount. "This time you're pitching a terrific game—your A game for sure. I've watched this game again and again. In the top of the eighth, leading the game, 3–2, you've got your batting helmet on ready to hit, but you're removed for pinch hitter Mike Greenwell. It would seem to me that since you had your helmet on, you wanted to stay in the game. But Johnny Mac has stated that you insinuated that you wanted out of the game because a blister had developed on your pitching hand, impeding you from finishing the game. So just how bad was that blister, and what was the disconnect between you and John?"

Still clearly perplexed by the move and the contradictions that followed, Clemens addresses the question without hesitation: "I have *no idea* how it got the light that it did," Roger begins. "Not just my family but also Bill Fischer, my pitching coach, said it was *laughable* that [McNamara] tried to say that I asked out of the game—or something like that. That obviously *never* happened. All you have to do is look at the video tape. I was on deck swinging a bat and ready to go when I got called back for a pinch hitter. I had really good stuff. When the blister would open up or bleed, they just had to throw out a few baseballs because I was getting blood on them. But that only happened when I threw sliders. So I put the slider away and told Geddy [Rich Gedman], 'We're going to go with fastballs and only curveballs if need be.' Or, I thought, a little baby changeup that I had. But at the time I had given up only four hits, and they were all off of sliders anyway, so it was probably a good thing not to throw it anymore. But I was doing fine. And the weather's perfect that time of year for a power pitcher like myself. Your legs never get tired. But it was real simple to see. Like you said, all you have to do is go back to the video tape, and it pretty much says it all."

Marty Barrett's account to me in a separate interview would back up Clemens's side of the story: "I was right there in the middle of the conversation," Barrett said. "Roger left it up to Mac. Roger said, 'I got a little blister, but I can go back out there. Whatever you think, Mac.' So there was no asking to go out, and there was no asking to stay in. Mac just made the decision to take him out. Me? I probably would have been like, 'Okay, let's go out there and see how you do. Pitch to one hitter, and we'll just see how you finish up.' But no way did Roger ask out. If that's a story that's been said, it's not true."

The conversation moves on to the Mets' miraculous comeback in the tenth inning of that game—and how it all began with two outs and nobody on base while the Red Sox held a two-run lead. "Certainly, it was a heart-wrenching defeat," I begin. "As a professional athlete and as competitive as you've always been, was a defeat like that something you ever get over?"

"Some MIT guy sent me over something that put the odds on that comeback, with all the two-strike counts and [the Mets] not making any outs, as almost astronomical," Clemens says, shaking his head. "There was just a jam shot here, an off-the-end-of-the-bat hit there. We had what they called the 'Austin Red Sox' out there—Calvin trying like heck to get the last strike; Spike [Owen], who was a flat-out winner, at shortstop. Once I got removed from the game, I went in to ice my arm for fifteen minutes. . . . I went back out to [the dugout] to watch everything going down. On my way through our clubhouse [I saw] they had already started covering the lockers and putting the champagne in there. At one point I actually saw the World Series trophy. They ended up getting Mrs. Yawkey down there early because she was an elderly lady at the time, and they knew it would take time to walk her there. They were actually setting up a little stage for Bob Costas, who was going to do the [postgame] interviews. I was thinking, 'Wow, this is kind of crazy.' I tell people I'm not very superstitious, but I think we all are."

Schiraldi was removed after giving up three singles, and the Mets tied it on a Bob Stanley wild pitch; then Mookie Wilson's slow roller up along first went through Bill Buckner's legs, and the Series was tied at three games apiece to force a Game Seven.

"Everybody talks about Billy Buckner and that ground ball," Clemens begins in his defense of the gritty first baseman. "But Buckner deserved to be on that field. We don't get anywhere or accomplish anything at all if we don't have Billy Buck. And I tell people who aren't in the know that if they had come to the stadium at about 2 p.m. for a 7:35 p.m. start, Bill Buckner would have been there no later than 3 p.m., already icing and numbing his ankles in ice buckets to get himself ready to go through batting practice and his early work. Then he would have to go through it all over again and re-tape his ankles to go out, play the game, and have the career he had. That man *deserved* to be on the field!"

Despite his disappointment in not finishing off the Mets in Game Six, Clemens is convincing in his conviction that the Red Sox had a strong chance of winning the next game: "After it all fell apart, I was fired up because [before the rainout] we had a fresh Oil Can Boyd ready to go. But then we got that rainout, so now we also had a very fresh Bruce Hurst, who had been pitching incredibly well during the World Series. We had to chew on it a little bit more to decide who would pitch, and McNamara named Hurst the starter. I know Oil Can was a little upset and hot under the collar—and rightfully so because he wanted the ball—but Hursty had pitched some outstanding games."

Hurst would pitch very well early—five shutout innings before facing trouble in the next frame—and left after six innings in a 3–3 tie. But another one of the great mysteries of this World Series was why Clemens, the Red Sox's best option, wasn't used in relief.

"I went out there to the bullpen *ready* to pitch for an inning or two," Clemens exclaims. "I'm sitting out there, watching arm after arm come out of the bullpen before me. I was hoping I was going to get a chance to get in, even if they just needed an out or an inning. I was out there stretching and just waiting for the phone to ring. I don't know if they were protecting me or were worried about next year because I was so young. But right then, that's when the floodgates opened."

McNamara would use five pitchers—including Game Four losing starter Al Nipper—in the seventh and eighth innings in an effort that would yield five runs to the Mets in their 8–5 victory. It left Red Sox fans wondering what could have been had Clemens (or even Boyd) been brought into the game. I bring this up to Roger, though he just pauses in reflection and takes the high road in his response.

"It was a tremendous season. I mean it was *off-the-charts* special. And now that time has passed, I think it's really cool that you hear from some of the Red Sox players, the media, the coaches, and everybody on the inside [of the organization] saying that the '86 team got Boston back on the map. It got them back to their winning ways and desire to win. So that's a huge compliment to everybody on our team. When the Red Sox finally won it all in 2004, I was with the Astros, and I told people I was smiling the most after it happened because I wasn't just happy for those guys and our fans there in New England, but I was also thinking how a little piece of that ring belongs to Jim Rice and Dwight Evans and Bruce Hurst and Marty Barrett and Wade Boggs and Richie Gedman and so on and so forth. I'm hoping all those guys had a nice smile on their faces too because we were a part of that stepping stone in building a championship. I know the Yawkeys were gone, and they had new owners and everything—and what they've done is incredible—but there were definitely some stepping stones left from the '86 championship season."

"It seems like the '86 team now gets honored and celebrated more than ever," I observe. "Do you get that sense too?"

"Yeah, absolutely!" Clemens exclaims. "There is just so much excitement about it. It's kind of like what you're doing with me today—reliving it and realizing how special a year it was. It's not something to look down on or feel bad about. It was a *fantastic* year! Unbelievably exciting! We went from one series and kind of ripped the hearts out of [the Angels] and then had it done to ourselves a week later. Of my six World Series '86 was, along with 2001, one of the most emotional ones."

The Rocket is called away to sign autographs and have lunch with the fans who had earlier batted against him. Our interview had run a little long, and rain had now begun to fall gently on the playing field. There was more to cover, and Clemens, clearly in his element talking about the game he loves, vowed to call me back following his trip to Scotland so that we could finish our conversation.

"Erik, I will be free tonight to visit by phone if you are. Want to make sure you get what you need—Rocket," reads Clemens's text message to me. I was impressed by Clemens's follow-up and found charming his use of his nickname in this and all of his texts to me. But such usage is hardly news in baseball. For example, Pete Rose refers to himself in texts as "the Hit King." There is something endearing in the pride the great ones take in what they accomplished during their glory years. But I was most astonished by Roger's follow-through with me considering its timing. Clemens was dealing with the devastation that massive floods had caused in Houston in the wake of Hurricane Harvey. Not only had flood waters entered his home, but a good deal more was also taking a toll on his property near Lake Conroe. And when he wasn't dealing with his own flood-related problems, he was tirelessly helping out others and raising money for relief efforts. It spoke volumes about the man's character.

Speaking from Vancouver, where his son Kacy—drafted in the eighth round of the 2017 draft by the Toronto Blue Jays—was playing first base that night for the short-league Vancouver Canadians, Clemens talks about doing what he could during the ongoing crisis in Houston.

"Erik, I'm doing what I love to do. I'm putting smiles on other people's faces. I'm doing stuff that, at one time when I was a kid, I hoped to be able to do when I became an adult. I'm actually DJing this weekend at an NCAA ladies' event. I'll be spinning some tunes and having some people get out there and dance and sing. I think music is a great outlet for all this stuff we're going through in Houston. If we can get some people's minds off of what's been happening at home, that'd be great. As you can tell, in Texas people extend not just a hand but the whole arm and leg. Right when you think you have a good plan and your schedule is set, something throws a rake in it, and you make adjustments to help somebody else out. I'm fortunate I'm in a position to do that."

But on this day Roger's focus could be on Kacy, one of his four sons, all of whom have a love of baseball and have enjoyed various degrees of success in great part due to Roger's involvement with them since they were old enough to walk. Red Sox legend Johnny Pesky was once asked to rate Clemens as a father, not a pitcher, to which he replied, "That's an easy one. I'd give him a perfect 10."

"I've heard wonderful things about Vancouver," Roger tells me. "I've gotten to meet a lot of cool people, met the guys on Kacy's team, signed a couple dozen baseballs. The pitching coach had me visit with the pitchers. All the kids on the team are pretty excited. I'm just having a great time."

"All right, here's a classic story about you and one of your boys that I absolutely love," I say. "When you were training for the World Baseball Classic in 2006, you pitched in a simulated game with some of the Astros and your oldest son Koby's Minor League team. Now Koby was the real deal—a good hitter who had played in ten professional seasons and got as high as Triple-A in the Astros' organization. In Koby's first at-bat of that scrimmage he hit a home run against you. So in his next at-bat you threw an inside pitch to kind of brush him back, didn't you?"

Clemens gives a hearty laugh. "Yeah, it was pretty fun," he says. "And Koby tells the story as good as anyone. I had to get three or four innings in. We were on a back field, so we were away from all the hoopla. Still there were obviously some media there. I was warming up in the bullpen and knew I would be facing five or six players without knowing if they were going to be big league guys, Triple-A guys, or what. When I got over to the field, I looked over, and Koby was in the dugout with about five other guys. Since I was just trying to get locked in and see how my body was, I wasn't paying a lot of attention to who I would be facing. The way Koby tells the story, he's in the dugout, and while he usually hit third, fourth, or fifth in the lineup, the rest of the guys are like, 'No way we're getting up first! It's your dad! You're going to hit first off him.' So next thing I know, Koby steps into the box first to lead off. I throw him a ninety-two-mile-an-hour fastball down and away, and as he describes it, he 'ambushed me,' hitting one over the left-center-field fence. There are no fielders, so Koby said he wasn't sure if he was supposed to run. So he just jogged around the bases. I just stared at him like, 'You little pisspot! You jumped me on my pitches.' I thought he would at least have let me get a strike in there. So his next time up—five or six batters later—I start out throwing a fastball down and away. Then for the next pitch I come up and in on him! And of course the guys were all like, 'Oh he threw it at you!' I think that got his attention, but I don't think he would have expected anything different. I was working both sides of the zone. But it made for good theater, that's for sure!"

Nothing seems to bring Roger more enjoyment than when he talks about his boys. You can hear it in his voice.

"I'll give you another story about Koby and me," Roger says enthusiastically. "When I came out of retirement to play with Houston, they sent me to Lexington, Kentucky [the A ball Legends]. It took me about ten days working out to get prepared for my first start. As the day got closer and closer, the media got bigger and bigger. I think there were nine or ten thousand people at that first Lexington game I started. Standing room only and a ton of media. I'm having lunch with Koby that day, and he says, 'Dad, I'm so glad this day's here.' And I go, 'Why— because I'm going to start and we're going to actually get to play in a professional game together?' And he goes, 'No, because I want you to get the start over with and get the heck out of town and take the circus with you so we can get back to our normalcy here!' Before the game, when we're in the locker room, I grabbed him and said, 'Son, make sure at some point during my three or four innings, when the infielders throw the ball around the infield, that you jog over to me from third base and actually hand it to me on the mound. Because there's going to be a ton of cameras, we'll have a great keepsake photo. It may never happen again.' So in the fourth inning, after one of my strikeouts, Koby grabs the ball and starts walking over toward me. As he's getting close to the mound, he stares at the hitter who's getting ready in the batter's box. So I turned around and looked at the hitter too. He was kind of a big left-handed hitter, so I think Koby's going to give me a scouting report on him—like, 'Hey, Dad, this guy can hit a fastball down, so stay away from him'—because they've played against this team a few times. As he makes it to the mound, I can hear the cameras all going off in the stadium from fans and photographers. He puts the ball in my glove and says, 'Let me run this by you, Pops. If you punch this guy out, everybody in the building gets a free gallon of window wiper fluid.' Then as he jogs back to his position at third base, I'm just looking at him and go, 'Are you kidding me?' I strike the guy out, we're running off the field, and he goes, 'Geez, Pops, if I'd known you were going to take him down in three pitches, I would have told you that even sooner!' Here I'm thinking I'm going to get a scouting report, and he tells me about this typical Minor League giveaway! So when people ask me about what it was like to play with my son, that's one of the funnier stories."

Clemens would once again get a chance to play professional ball with Koby—in 2012 at the age of fifty—for the independent Sugar Land Skeeters of the Atlantic League. This time Koby was his battery mate—a moment that any father, much less a legendary pitcher, could only dream of.

"The reason I ended up playing for the Skeeters was that I had a really good friend who owned a portion of that team," Clemens explains. "Not that they were struggling financially, but I knew that if I was able to go back and make a start, I would consider doing it. I told him, 'It will take me a good two or three weeks to get ready.' So I was throwing a lot of batting practice and the kids would see the velocity was there. My boy was like, 'Dad, you're throwing somewhere between eighty-seven and ninety miles an hour! This is crazy! And your split finger is still as nasty as ever! You need to think about coming back!' I did two Sugar Land starts and made sure that my son would catch my last pitch thrown in a professional setting—*or any setting.* And so we made it happen. ESPN picked up the game, it helped the bottom line of the team, and I pitched 4⅔ scoreless innings, so everybody won. I ended up throwing eight scoreless innings in those two games, but there was zero consideration about making a comeback. I had already been through that."

After Clemens recorded his final out of the game, he shared an embrace with Koby on the mound and walked off to a standing ovation—the final one of his storied career—from the record crowd at Constellation Field. A better sendoff would have been unfathomable.

Clemens is currently the only eligible member of the three-hundred-win club not to be inducted into the National Baseball Hall of Fame. By any statistical measurement—his 4,672 strikeouts (third of all time), the 354 victories, the seven Cy Young Awards, the twice striking out of twenty batters in a game, and the two World Series trophies (as well as his becoming one of the great ambassadors in promoting the game)—Clemens should have been a first-ballot, *if not unanimous,* Hall of Fame inductee. The clear-cut reason for why he is not in Cooperstown stems from accusations by the *Mitchell Report* of performance-enhancing drug (PED) use late in his career—despite the fact that Clemens challenged the findings in the report on Capitol Hill, ultimately proving that they didn't hold up under due process. Despite his efforts, much of the misinformation about Clemens has been repeated so often that it has been accepted as fact by many. As a result, his otherwise sterling reputation has taken a battering.

Since 2012, when he was found *not guilty* on all six counts of lying to Congress, Roger has said very little about his Hall of Fame prospects and PED accusations. Still these remain the elephant in the room and issues inconceivable to *not* bring up. They simply had to be addressed.

"Roger, with the career you had, you should have been a lock for the Hall of Fame, and your voting totals continue to climb. [At the time of the interview Clemens had collected 54 percent with 75 percent needed for enshrinement.] Yet post-career a lot has been said and written about the allegations against you. I think you're going to get into the Hall of Fame one day—as do obviously a lot of writers with votes. What will it mean to you if you are one day enshrined into Cooperstown?"

At first Clemens touches on where his unmatched work ethic came from and how it helped rejuvenate and extend his career before addressing the Hall of Fame issue.

"As far as my attitude and vision, my vision on the mound—whatever you want to call it—that came strictly from the background of watching my grandma and my mother and how hard they worked. And because of them, I was always very serious about my work; there's no doubt about that. And that translated into my longevity and everything else.

"As far as the Hall of Fame goes, I have zero control over that, so it doesn't change my life one way or the other to be a Hall of Famer. If it happened, I wouldn't even care that people would even introduce me as that because I think it's a disservice to all the many players and teammates I had who would probably never have an opportunity to get there. And they're the reason why I shined—whether they knocked in runs for me or played fantastic defense behind me. I have had, probably, thirty-five-plus catchers. And even if some of them caught only five games for me, they counted. Like you said, it was an event when I went to the mound. And credit needs to go to catchers I worked with like Gedman, Tony Pena, Charlie O'Brien, Johnny Marzano, Darin Fletcher, and Jorge Posada, who was probably the best combination of a hitter and catcher I worked with. The list goes on and on. They really paid attention to detail when I was out there working. So those would be the guys that, in a selfish, Hall of Fame speech way, you get up there and talk about. All right, I know people thank their families and their mothers—and I think that's really cool—but there would not be enough time in a week for me to thank the teammates that I had that made me shine. They're the most important people to me. If I make the Hall, that's great. I have no control over that. What I do have control over, though, is keeping my name in order. If I was single, didn't have a family, and didn't have all my brothers and sisters who have to listen to all that absolute nonsense [about me]—which really hurts them also—I would have told everybody to basically go shit in their hat—like I told people on Joe Buck's show."

Clemens then turns his ire toward Brian McNamee, his former part-time strength and conditioning coach while he was with the Yankees and Blue Jays. McNamee had made claims that he injected Clemens with anabolic steroids and human growth hormone on several occasions.

"We stopped [McNamee] from going around the country trying to tell people he was my personal trainer," Clemens says. "Nobody writes that he made money, sold my name to two different companies, and everything else that went on. It was pretty much a *Jerry Springer Show* out there! I learned a lot; it opened my eyes to a lot. But I tell people that I appreciate the writers who are voting who look at *the facts*. And it was awesome to get in a setting [a courtroom] where only facts mattered and we were on a level playing field. It wasn't people saying [nonsense] or people putting all their marbles into a known liar."

The facts would bear out what Clemens was saying. The government had nothing on him except the word of a witness with a sordid past. At the trial a string of witnesses, including Yankee general manager Brian Cashman, attacked the integrity of McNamee, the formerly disciplined New York City cop-turned-disgruntled trainer. It was noted that McNamee had falsely claimed to having an accredited doctorate in his various side jobs away from his position as Yankee trainer. Then in 2001 McNamee was investigated for rape following an incident that took place at a St. Petersburg, Florida, hotel, where the Yankees were staying. The charges were eventually dropped, though the Yankees relieved McNamee of his duties with the club.

"Everybody behind the scenes at Yankee Stadium and at Toronto [where McNamee was a strength and conditioning coach during the 1998 season] thought it was laughable," Roger comments. "They'd hear some of [McNamee's] stories, and they'd say, 'Well, that didn't happen.' And the same thing with the team doctors. I did all my checkups with them, and I've always made the statement that I'm not breaking down and I'm not shrinking [typical post-steroid-use symptoms]. It's all about how I obviously took care of myself and the way I went about it. I was thorough, so [the PED allegations] were very hurtful. I did get a little emotional a couple of times because I have extended family that was really hurting [from the accusations]. But I appreciate that I've been really blessed with all the fan support and the support through my foundation. So if [election into the Hall of Fame] happens, it will be awesome."

I talked about that prospect, as well as Clemens's conditioning program, with several prominent '86 Red Sox. Their answers tell you all you need to know about Roger as a competitor, a teammate, and a person.

"Nobody could keep up with Clem, except maybe Roy Halladay," Hurst told me. "Clem's workout was legendary. When he walked into a big league clubhouse, he was the most prepared guy I've ever seen for a young pitcher. His work ethic was epic at that time. I couldn't keep up with him, but he motivated me to do better and to do things that I had been taught weren't prudent for pitchers. He was shattering myths. So the Roger I knew was the most naturally hard worker from day one. I love Roger. If he did [PEDS], then no, he shouldn't make the Hall of Fame. It hurts me to say that because I love the guy. I owe so much to him, but I respect the game and it's history and what the people before us did and what we're leaving for those who come after us."

"Roger's the *greatest!*" exclaimed Barrett. "He's like a little kid. I always tell people when they ask something like, 'Is he depressed?' I'll say, 'No! You would laugh your ass off at Roger Clemens.' Go play a round of golf with Roger; you're going to have fun because he always wants to have fun. He is smarter than heck too. But when it was time to work, he worked. Roger's got that Texas drawl, but he's smart about everything and is probably the *fiercest* competitor I've ever seen—a great work ethic. I am absolutely certain he will make the Hall of Fame. . . . He is creeping up [in the voting]."

Spike Owen, who has known Clemens since their college days at Texas, didn't hesitate with his opinion about Roger's Hall of Fame worthiness. "No doubt about it—he should get in! Do I think he will? I don't know how them people vote. I know the premise of it all, but there's so many staunch people against anybody in that era that did good and hadn't even been caught of doing anything—which I don't understand. Some say, 'Well, everybody knows he did it.' How do they know? I'm not playing dumb or naïve about that. Seriously! People are going to discredit a man of something that you have no facts over? I mean he's one of the greatest pitchers that's played the game of baseball—*in history*! So he definitely belongs in the Hall of Fame. And I think at some point they'll vote him in."

Hall of Famer Wade Boggs took it a step further, telling me how the whole voting system needs to at last address the era and its players as a whole. "There's an issue that is revolving around that [Roger], as well as Barry Bonds, were caught up in the steroid era, and there are accusations that they were using steroids. I think it should be put on the baseball writers' agenda that these questions have to be answered. Statistics-wise there's no question they belong. But when we talk about guys getting ready to [be eligible] for the Hall of Fame—guys like Alex Rodriguez who have been caught twice and admitted to using—what do you do with their stats? [Alex's] numbers are such that anybody in their right mind would put him in the Hall of Fame, but he was caught after testing positive for steroids. Some sportswriters will *still* vote for him and other steroid players—and that's their prerogative. And some won't. But it gets back to is coffee a performance-enhancing drug? I played with Roger and I played against him, and there's no question that with his stats—354 wins—he would get in. But he carries that cloud of uncertainty."

Roger's battery mate Rich Gedman, with a degree of emotion in his voice, was the most poignant of all in talking about Clemens. "Roger ended up being a Hall of Fame–type pitcher, but more than anything he was a Hall of Fame guy. If people only knew the way he was with his teammates. He picked them up and carried and nurtured guys. Not the stars but the twenty-fourth and twenty-fifth men on the team that he was watching out for, making sure that they were okay. To me there's something to be said for someone who is a star that actually thinks way beyond or outside of the box, where he's not self-absorbed and notices other things that go on. With Roger it was incredible. I sit sometimes and think, 'Okay, I'm his friend. I was his teammate. People can say what they want. Whether he did or didn't use really doesn't matter to me. I knew what he was like on the field. I knew what he was like as a teammate. And I know what he's like as a friend—and the friend he was to others.' Roger came from a wonderful family. If someone wants to put him down and say, 'I accuse him of this' and 'He did that,' I look at it this way: when the American government goes after you and can't prove you guilty, you're *innocent*! Plain and simple! They spent millions and millions of dollars trying to prove that he did something wrong. [I think] he didn't. And to people who say I'm naïve, I'll tell them, 'No. I've had friends do things that some people think are awful, but they're still my friends despite having made a mistake. In Roger's case you haven't proven him guilty of anything, but you assume he's guilty. I tell people, 'This is America. I thought you were innocent until proven guilty. Not alleged. Not assumed. But you're innocent until proven guilty.' So now we're going to take somebody's career and say, 'He cheated.' Why? Because he was good at it? Because he did something that somebody said you're not supposed to do? Couldn't it be hard work? Could it not be part evolution of what we're talking about now in the game? Could it be that he knew somebody sooner that showed him a different way? Look at Chuck Norris. He's like seventy years old, and he looks like a kid in his body. I'm just throwing that out there. Things change."

I pointed out Nolan Ryan and his longevity, and Gedman stopped me midsentence. "Right!" he exclaimed. "Ahead of his time, right? You watch an older guy—a forty-year-old playing basketball with the kids—and you're thinking, 'What the hell's he doing?' You know what I mean? They even look different nowadays. You've got fifty-, sixty-, seventy-year-olds that look like young people. Fifty is the new forty. Things are changing."

The allegations have made it easy for some voters to overlook the brilliance of Roger Clemens's overall career and play judge and jury, a situation that has hurt him and those important in his life.

But on this day in Vancouver, the joyful Clemens has other things on his mind. It is time to take in his son's ballgame.

3.

Captain of His Own Ship

....

I didn't play the game for accolades; I played the game because I had a gift. But once you put all you got into the game . . . and dominate for a few years, the accolades will come.

—JIM RICE

On a sun-splashed breezy late morning at the Red Sox spring training facility at JetBlue Fenway South ballpark in Fort Myers, Florida, the atmosphere was as laid back as it gets. The adjoining player development complex had pitcher Rick Porcello getting some light work in against a group of young Minor Leaguers on one field, while Rich Gedman was giving instructions on hitting at another diamond with some other prospects. The legendary Luis Tiant rode around in a covered golf cart from one field to another, simply just taking it all in. These are the lazy days of baseball, especially for a powerhouse team like the Red Sox, with few doubts regarding their big league roster and with their players simply using the time to get game ready for the long season ahead.

It should have been a relaxing morning, yet I was a little uneasy. The day's assignment was to meet up with Jim Rice, who, though now in his midsixties, had maintained the demeanor of a hard-to-get-to-know personality—easily one of the more challenging interviews in baseball.

There were always two sides to Rice during his playing days. There was the kind-hearted soul who treated clubhouse kids like his own; the superstar that never denied an autograph; the warm and funny personality who was revered by practically all of his teammates; and, most famously, the savior to a bloodied four-year-old boy struck in the head by a screaming foul ball at Fenway Park in 1982. Rice saved the little boy's life that day by racing into the stands and carrying him in his arms to the dugout to a waiting Red Sox medical staff. He watched as they rushed the youngster to the hospital. Memorably Rice played the rest of the game in a blood-stained uniform.

But Rice's history with writers had always been, by contrast, pretty brutal. In fact some of his clashes with the media were downright legendary. There was the time he tore the shirt off of Steve Fainaru of the *Hartford Courant*; the instance he lifted Larry Whiteside of the *Boston Globe* off the ground by the collar of his shirt; and the occasion when he threatened to throw venerable columnist Tom Boswell of the *Washington Post* or any other reporters assembled by his locker into a trash can if they asked Rice what he deemed "another stupid question." Rice had a general intolerance for the media, believing (sometimes justifiably so) that they couldn't be trusted to accurately report a story or the contents of an interview. In essence he felt he was often depicted unfairly.

So despite having interviewed hundreds of ballplayers over the years—some of them difficult—I admit to having been a little intimidated by this task of interviewing Rice. While I had my questions to ask—some of them contentious enough to hit a nerve—I didn't want to get on his bad side. I needed an icebreaker.

As I approach Rice, who was sitting at a metal picnic table in the shadows of the ballpark finishing up an interview with the affable WEEI.com reporter Rob Bradford, he is instantly recognizable as the imposing figure who devastated opposing pitchers more than three decades ago. Wearing a blue Red Sox windbreaker and 1970s-era Red Sox cap, his short-cropped hair still black with just a touch of gray in his mustache, he remained at his playing weight from his prime—a still solid

220 pounds—a far cry from so many former sluggers at his age who tend to let themselves go.

Bradford, familiar with some of my books, does me a solid. "You're talking with Erik next?" he rhetorically asks Rice. "He's *the man.*"

For a writer seeking some credibility and a warm opening for an interview with Rice, the comment was most welcome. But our talk would have to wait, as Rice was headed into the training room to have his surgically repaired right knee worked on. He requested that we meet in an hour. Attempting to make small talk before he left, I told him that I was familiar with the area of Anderson, South Carolina, where he grew up, explaining that my mother had retired to Salem, roughly just forty miles to the north.

"Salem?" Rice quizzically asks. "I've never heard of Salem!"

"It's close to Clemson," I say. "About twenty minutes from there."

For whatever reason Rice is greatly amused by not knowing this, grinning ear to ear and letting out a big laugh. "I've got to think about that. *Salem*, huh? Gotta look that up." As he leaves the picnic area and enters the bowels of the ballpark, I think, "This is great! An ice-breaking moment. I got Rice to laugh and relax a little bit with me. The interview will now most assuredly go smoothly."

When Rice returns, there is no smile, no laughter. So it is back to square one. He sits down at the picnic table stone faced, then grabs his right knee with a strained expression. I ask if he is in pain.

"Not now," he says. "That's because of where I just came from. These guys got every freaking thing. They got boots now up to your thighs that just squeeze the pressure and soreness out of you, give you more flexibility. Then you have the cold whirlpool, the hot whirlpool; you got everything down there. I try to do it every day. I walk six fields every day too. Guys that get hurt now, there ain't no way to stay on the disabled list for thirty days. They got too much shit down there, too much stuff to get you back in a couple of days. I had my knee done in December. Lost about seventeen pounds. I'm trying to keep the weight off."

"You've done a great job," I say. "I write about players often from your era, and some of them are tipping the scales at three hundred pounds."

"I know," Rice says, looking straight ahead at the field behind me. "When I retired, I was like 245. But I didn't have a big gut and everything. It was all in my legs and everywhere else. Now that I lost everything from my legs, I'm less than usual."

Since he is in his Red Sox attire, I ask if he is helping some of the younger players with their hitting.

"I'm not a hitting instructor here," Rice says tersely. "I have a contract with NESN [New England Sports Network]. And I make a couple of appearances a year here. I know about hitting, but I don't have that job."

Of course Rice knows a little something about hitting. He always has. During his first full season with the Red Sox in 1975 he quickly established himself as a fearsome hitter with unmatched strength and a marvelous swing. So naturally strong was Rice, who never lifted weights, that he made headlines in his rookie year by breaking a bat on a checked swing one night in Detroit. Henry Aaron, the home run king at the time and finishing his career in the American League with the Milwaukee Brewers, observed Rice and claimed that if anyone had the chance to break his record, he thought it would be him.

The Red Sox in 1975 were in the midst of their best season since the pennant-winning "Impossible Dream" year of 1967. And while the twenty-two-year-old Rice was having a terrific campaign, driving in 102 runs with a .309 batting average, he shared the spotlight with another first-full-year star, center fielder Fred Lynn.

"When you came up with Lynn, you were a part of what the media called 'the Gold Dust Twins,'" I begin, before Rice quickly cuts me off.

"Let's clear this up," Rice says. "Lynn came up with *me*! You said I came up with Lynn. Let's get that straight. Everybody says, 'You came up with Fred.' No. No. No."

Rice's point is that while both he and Lynn saw limited action during the '74 campaign, he appeared in twenty-four games to Lynn's fifteen games that season. Rice had also been to the Red Sox Major League camp in '74 while Lynn had not. These minute details are clearly important to Rice.

"You two were such a great combo," I say. "Did you understand the significance of what you were doing—leading the Red Sox to the pennant—or were you just too young?"

"I knew what I was doing," Rice recalls. "That's because I had already been to the Major League camp and had been around Rico [Petrocelli] and Yaz [Carl Yastrzemski] and 'Louie' [Tiant], so I had an idea already about the game of baseball, what it was all about, and about not just getting [to the Majors] but staying there. Plus I had Major League experience [in '74]. So then you have an opportunity to do the things we did my first year—go to a World Series."

"Typically rookies are to be seen and not heard," I say. "But you came up and were a star right away. What was your experience like that first year, and what were some of the challenges you faced on the ball club?"

"I don't think there were any challenges," Rice says. "You have to know the opposing team and the opposing pitchers. But, yes, you're right; you had to show up and be seen, not heard. We had guys when I came up like Rico, Tiant, Yaz, [Bob] Montgomery, [Carlton] Fisk, and a lot of other guys who were older and had kids. I was still just a kid—twenty-one years old. So you came in and you respected those guys. Going back to spring training in Major League camp, you kept your mouth shut, and when they say you're going on a road trip, you go on a road trip. It was what it was; you did what you had to do. You knew [your place]. But that's the thing about it. Then you have an opportunity to do the things we did my first year—go to the World Series."

It was cruel that with just six games to go and with the AL Eastern Division title all but wrapped up, a Vern Ruhle fastball broke Rice's wrist, costing him a chance to play in both the ALCS and the classic World Series match-up against the Cincinnati Reds. When this comes up in our conversation, the disappointment for Rice is still very much apparent.

"I still think about it," he says with a sigh, melancholy about the timing of his injury. "First, you wanted to play in that World Series in '75 because when you think about the Big Red Machine and when you think about the Red Sox, without a doubt you had the two top teams playing and it's your first year in the big leagues. Then in another situation you're fighting [Lynn] for MVP and Rookie of the Year."

The last part of that comment is telling. Aside from the honor if Rice had won one or both of those distinguished American League awards, he sensed that a rivalry existed between himself and Lynn. For one thing, the two players couldn't be any more different. Lynn was California cool, a young white man with matinee idol looks and perfect smile; a smooth, effortless left-handed stroke; and a gracefulness patrolling centerfield perhaps not seen since Joe DiMaggio a generation before. He didn't simply cover the outfield and run around the bases; he glided. By contrast, Rice was an African American from the deep South; had a serious demeanor that was all business; hammered balls with a powerful, compact swing; and, while a good outfielder with a strong arm—given his chiseled, muscular physique—ran like a power halfback. To say that race didn't figure into this rivalry would be naïve. This was 1975 Boston, a city that was predominantly of Irish and Italian descent and in the midst of a new state-sponsored busing program that had inflamed racial tensions by transporting Black children to predominantly white schools. Despite being largely silent publicly on the topic of race throughout his career, Rice was the first home-grown African American star in Red Sox history and was, by extension, innocently caught in the middle of the city's turmoil and the common belief that Boston would never fully accept a Black star.

"I have more respect for Jim Rice than any guy I have *ever* known," Bruce Hurst told me. "A magnificent man and a Hall of Famer in every sense of the word. With race relations in Boston what they were—I don't want to pick a scab, but it needs to be said: what Jimmy had to endure coming up was [hard]. There were headwinds being a Black player, especially Rice, because he was quieter than most. Every Black player would get [hate] mail. It was tough. I loved Jimmy. He went through and endured a lot to do what he did."

Lynn would end up winning both the Rookie of the Year and MVP Awards in 1975, though Rice, decades later, would ultimately earn the more prominent piece of hardware: a Hall of Fame plaque.

In reflecting on his earliest days in Boston, however, Rice prefers not to focus on the negative but to look back at the '75 Red Sox in glowing terms. Now more cordial and comfortable with our meeting, he wants us to play a game.

"Hypothetically let's compare the World Series team of 2004 with our team in '75," Rice starts out. "Everybody says, 'Man, that '04 team was a really good team.' So you go with the '04 team, and I'll give you the '75 team, position by position. Who's your catcher?"

"Jason Varitek."

"I've got Fisk. Who's your first baseman?"

I'm embarrassed that Kevin Millar's name doesn't come immediately to mind.

"You don't even remember," Rice says quickly. "And this is like my thing, man, okay? I got Yaz at first, [Denny] Doyle at second, Boyles [Rick Burleson] at short, Rico at third. You got me in left, Freddy in center, and Evans in right. The '04 team can't compare! Everybody says Manny [Ramirez] in left [could compare], but Manny couldn't do what I did at that time, so don't give me that bullshit. Nah, nah, nah! That was *a team*!

And look at the pitchers we had. That's the team right there—
our '75 team!"

Rice's eyes light up. He is having fun with a writer.

Much had changed on the Red Sox by the spring of 1985. Petrocelli and Doyle had long since retired. Gone was Tiant, via
free agency to the Yankees of all teams, and Bill Lee, the most
colorful of them all, was traded to the Expos—both following
the '78 season. Gone was Burleson, the gritty sparkplug of the
club, traded to the Angels in 1980. Gone was Lynn, the golden
child, traded to the Angels in 1981. Gone was Fisk, the heart and
soul of the team, via free agency to the White Sox—also in 1981.
And of course the most celebrated exit had come two seasons
earlier with the retirement of team captain Carl Yastrzemski
following a magnificent twenty-three-year Hall of Fame career.

Aside from Dwight Evans manning right field, the only other
constant over the previous decade had been the remarkable run
of excellence by Rice; it included an MVP award, 307 home runs,
and seven All-Star Game appearances. The team's best player, he
had signed a five-year deal with the club worth more than $10
million that offseason—a staggering sum at that time. And in
a move that would have been unthinkable in Boston earlier in
Rice's career, he was bestowed with the ultimate honor a club
can give: he was named team captain by newly installed manager John McNamara. It was a sign the club—and the city—had
come a long way since the racial turmoil of the midseventies
and even further along since the Sox had been the last team
in baseball to put their first African American player, Pump-
sie Green, on the field, in 1959—a full twelve years after Jackie
Robinson had integrated the game.

In a foreshadowing of Rice's being named captain, it was Yaz
who, in his final game with the Red Sox in 1983, waved farewell to the Fenway faithful from the top step of the Red Sox
dugout, then turned to Rice and said, "Now it's yours."

"When Yaz retired, did you feel like you had to take on more
of a leadership role on the team?" I ask.

"You lead by example," Rice says, leaning back in his chair. "I'd had some pretty good years by then, and I was becoming one of the oldest guys after everybody left. But it was more my upbringing through the organization, the footsteps that I followed with [Ted] Williams, Yaz, and now myself. I enjoy the game of baseball, and I wasn't a follower. Being a follower can get you into trouble. You want to be a leader, and I led by example. You lead by a plan every day."

And lead Rice would. Another year, another All-Star appearance, and another hundred-plus RBIS—the seventh time of his career. But it would be the following season, 1986, when he would get perhaps more clutch hits than any other hitter in the American League. If not for all-time great performances turned in by Clemens and the Yankees' Don Mattingly, Rice, who finished third to them in the MVP balloting, would have earned a second trophy eight years after his first one—a nod to his endurance.

Getting to the World Series in '86 was especially meaningful for Rice considering that he had been sidelined the last time the Red Sox had reached the Fall Classic in '75. And it was his big three-run homer in Game Seven of the ALCS against the Angels at Fenway Park that sealed the deal. But to get to that seventh game the Red Sox had to miraculously snatch victory from the jaws of defeat in Game Five in Anaheim.

"At any point in the ninth inning of that fifth game did you believe it was over and you were going home?" I ask.

"At any given time it could have been over, you know," Rice proclaims. "I think we were the underdogs when we played the Angels, just like we were the underdogs in '75, when we played the Oakland A's [in the ALCS]. So there's nothing wrong with being the underdog. In fact I would rather be an underdog because no one expects you to win. Sometimes it pulls teammates together."

The Red Sox would be major underdogs entering their World Series match-up against the Mets. Of course the tables would be turned, and Boston, just one strike away from winning its first

World Series since 1918, would fall victim to a stunning Mets comeback in Game Six and then lose a 3–0 lead in the finale.

"Did the defeat in the World Series take anything away from the historic comeback of the ALCS?" I ask.

Rice is pragmatic, quick to compartmentalize his feelings—an altogether different reaction than most Red Sox fans had in dealing with the loss. "No. I think any time you're playing sports, there's a winner and there's a loser. You accept it and think, 'We'll get them next year.' That's all you can do. Once you win or lose, it's in the past. You can't do anything about it. You just hope you can regroup and make your team better for the coming year by adding a player here, switching something up, or letting someone go. Maybe some kid wasn't good in the clubhouse, so we don't need him. So that's what you look at. You have to look at the positives and not look back at the negatives. The negative part is that we lost. The positive is, 'Hey, we've got another year.' Fans remember *everything*—from spring training until the end of the season. I don't look back and try to dissect everything. I'm not a fan; I'm a player with one thing I'm trying to do: go out there and win."

As it turned out, 1986 would be Rice's last great season of his storied career. In fact if we consider the mountaintop on which he had resided throughout his first twelve full seasons, his decline would be stunning. Never again would he come close to hitting twenty home runs or batting .300. By 1988 the writing was on the wall for this proud man when new manager Joe Morgan pinch-hit for Rice with shortstop Spike Owen (in a sacrifice bunt situation) during a late July game at Fenway. Enraged and humiliated, Rice slammed his bat into the rack, threw his helmet on the floor, and got into a physical confrontation with Morgan before several players stepped between them. A suspension followed. Following the next season, the Red Sox unceremoniously placed Rice on waivers—a far different ending to his time in Boston than anyone would have fathomed just a couple of years earlier. Rice would blast the front office and Morgan on his way out, calling the move "classless."

The bad taste it left Rice had many wondering if he would ever return to Fenway Park. However, with new management and later a different ownership group, Rice would return to the Red Sox family several years later—first as a roving hitting instructor, then as a batting coach. But then, in an irony of all ironies, Rice was hired in 2003 as a commentator for NESN. He was now a member of the same media with which he had once sparred.

"What is the biggest thing you've learned about the press that you didn't realize as a player?" I ask.

"I don't have to write any stories like you guys write," he answers. "By doing TV, I've got to realize that the players are listening. Their wives are listening. Their families are listening. So you have to be careful what you say. Before I say anything about a player, I will go and talk to him, ask him what happened, and get his side of the story because I don't want to make him look bad or make myself look bad by getting something wrong. I think a lot of times when you're dealing with the media, reporters will get stories from a partner. They'll go, 'I didn't make it there, but this is what I got from someone else.' If you're going to do it right, you've got to go right to the source. That's what I do if I have anything to say about someone."

By all accounts Rice has done an admirable job as a commentator, using his experience as a player to break down games and individual player performances. He's also a great listen for his directness, never afraid to call out a Red Sox player or opponent when he deems it necessary. He is now a long-standing member of the same media that foolishly, in large part out of spite and revenge, didn't vote him into the Baseball Hall of Fame until his final year of eligibility in 2009.

"Jim, I followed your entire career, as did colleagues of mine closely involved in the game," I start out. "Everyone is in agreement that you were the most feared hitter over a ten-year period in the game, that you would be an automatic for enshrinement into the Hall of Fame once you had been out of the game for five years. But it took some time—fifteen years—to get voted in. As all those years went by, what were you thinking about the process?"

"I wasn't thinking anything because it wasn't in my control," Rice says. "It's in the control of the people that were voting. I didn't play for the Hall of Fame. I played because I had a gift and an opportunity to play the game of baseball, and what I accomplished on the field was great. But that one last hurrah was not there [for those years]. As far as going to the Hall of Fame, I guess I just had to wait, and I waited long enough."

"It's funny, but I heard at the time of the Hall of Fame phone call that you were watching the soap *The Young and the Restless*. Is that really true?"

"Yep. I watch it every day. Even when I played. Comes on about 6:30 p.m. here tonight as a matter of fact. It's on right about now too. Comes on at 12:30." Rice checks his watch. "Yep, it's 12:44 now."

"Did it become a ritual for you?"

"It did. Ballplayers have a lot of time. Back when I played, you couldn't go to the ballpark early like you do now. You had lunch and things like that, but you didn't have the TVs; you didn't have the trainers like we have down here now. You didn't have all the data of opposing pitchers. The clubhouse didn't open until around three o'clock because that's when we would take extra batting practice. Now guys come to the ballpark around noon—no later than one o'clock—for a seven o'clock game."

Later that July, just days after Rice was inducted into the Hall of Fame and a full twenty years from his final embattled season in Boston as a player, the Red Sox finally retired Rice's number 14 in a moving pregame ceremony at Fenway Park.

"Jim, I was at Fenway for the final weekend series of David Ortiz's regular season career. I have never seen celebrations for any player like those bestowed on him for each of those three games. They were nothing short of epic. So epic that even just one of those days would have been enough to have adequately celebrated his career. You had just the opposite experience when your days in Boston ended: no fanfare at all. Looking back at your own experience, do you ever wish it had gone better?"

"No, I feel like I could have played a couple more years if I had had surgery, but nothing can compare with what they did for David. It's a different era, different time, and even different fans. When I played, it was more adults. Now you see a lot of kids and everything. We didn't have kids walking around with our jerseys on or things like that. So it's a different time now. And of course [it was unusual] the way we received David from Minnesota—by way of his being released—and then all of a sudden he became a household name. David became even more of a household name with his charities, with the kids, and with everything else, just like Dustin [Pedroia]. Once you do what he did and really mingle with the kids, you don't need anything else."

"Your point about it being a different time is so true," I point out. "With the Yankees, for instance, it seems like every 'very good' player gets his own day; they put a plaque out in Monument Park, and they market it to the fans. It wasn't like that back in 1989."

"You know, it's good, but like I said, I didn't play for that. And it's not my decision [to have a number retired]. Plus the ownership has changed. When I played in '75, it was Tom Yawkey and not John Henry. You know what I did I did for the Yawkeys. I didn't do anything with John Henry. But, again, I don't worry about things like this. As long as I know I got a job, I enjoy what I'm doing, so what the hell."

"With that being the case, what did having your number finally retired mean to you?"

"It meant that I played for one organization and that there's a history of left fielders with the Red Sox. I'm in the same category with Williams and Yaz. But accolades? I didn't play the game for accolades; I played the game because I had a gift. But once you put all you got into the game and accumulate top numbers and dominate for a few years, the accolades will come. And if you can't dominate, you're not going to get them. That's just the way it is."

And with that the most fearsome hitter of his time and a man who played the game on his own terms gets up from his chair to take in a ballgame. As he walks away, I ask, "Oh, did you look up Salem, South Carolina?"

Smiling, the big man answers back, "Okay, I believe you. *I believe you!*"

4.

Chicken, Beer, and Batting Titles

Walt [Hriniak] said to me my second day of my first spring training, "Few dare to be great." I took those words to heart.

—WADE BOGGS

A couple of days after meeting with Rice, I would take the two hour drive up Interstate-75 along Florida's west coast to meet with another Hall of Famer from the '86 Red Sox, Wade Boggs. After driving past the tight security at his Tampa gated community, I came upon the Boggs residence, a stately gray and gold stone mansion.

Boggs greets me at the door looking every bit the way he had as a player—with a full head of light reddish-brown hair and a goatee beard and roughly still at his playing height and weight of six feet two inches and 190 pounds. Although Boggs was a Hall of Famer like Rice, the interview with him would be wholly different. Whereas Jim was a naturally gifted slugger and a man of measured words, the loquacious Boggs was an intense student of hitting who considered it an art form and would prove to be more than happy to spend a good portion of the afternoon sharing his theories of his craft with me—as well as anything else I wanted to discuss with him. He was the same media-friendly person that I had interviewed decades before in his prime with the Red Sox.

Wade escorts me into his trophy room, which included a most impressive collection of his jerseys and awards for—

among other achievements—his five batting titles, eight Silver Slugger Awards, two Gold Gloves, and an elusive World Series trophy he won late in his career with the Yankees. It was an incredible display of his achievements that filled the room and would rival anything seen in the National Baseball Hall of Fame and Museum in Cooperstown. As we sit down on his couch to begin our discussion, it wasn't lost on me that I was in the presence of one of the greatest hitters of all time—the Ty Cobb of his era. Of all the Red Sox none had been as committed to learning and executing the art of hitting a baseball more than Boggs. Considering the talent they had in their lineup, his approach speaks volumes. The end result was 3,010 lifetime base hits and twelve straight All-Star Game appearances.

Wearing a Wharton High School T-shirt, Boggs was now in his seventeenth year as the school's assistant baseball coach.

"Do they have any idea . . . ?" I begin to ask before Wade cuts me off with a grin.

"Oh yeah, yeah, they know who I am. It's easy nowadays to go and watch my at bats on YouTube and read about me on Google. Back in the late '70s and early '80s, when I would coach at my alma mater, Plant [High School in Tampa], I had to always explain myself because there weren't search engines back then. But now the great part of it is that [the kids] just treat me like the other coaches. I think other teams are more in awe than [our players]. When they come in and I'm standing next to them, that's when it hits them. But our guys, they're impervious to it. They just go, 'Hey, there's Coach Boggs,' which is great."

"If I had a Hall of Famer as an assistant coach in school, I might be a little intimidated by that," I remark. "Did you find that some of the kids, at first, were a little bit in awe?"

"Oh sure," Boggs confirms. "The young kids, especially the freshman, naturally are when they come in. I'm sure they are prepped by their parents like, 'Do you know who the assistant coach is?' But they're like sponges; that's the great part about it. They absorb everything you're teaching them at that level. The thing we thrive on as coaches is getting them to the next level, whether it's college, junior college, or even professional baseball."

"Listening to you talk, I'm wondering why you aren't still a hitting coach or maybe even a manager at the Major League level—especially with the Rays right here in town," I say. "Why did you choose the high school level?"

"I was a hitting coach in Tampa Bay in 2001 after being an assistant to [general manager] Chuck LaMar in 2000 in the front office," Boggs answers. "I didn't like it. As a hitting coach in the big leagues, you can lead a horse to water, but you can't make him drink it. High school kids absorb a lot, and they're playing the game for fun—not for a paycheck. I'm sort of old school like Walt [Hriniak]. I'd yell at the player and get in his face and everything like that. Then I'd get called into the principal's office, and LaMar would say, 'You can't yell at the players.' I asked, 'Why? Whatever happened to motivation?' He says, 'You can't do that anymore.' I went, 'Really? Well, we're going to have a problem then.' We would go on the road and have the field in the afternoon for extra hitting, and not one guy would show up. So then I started assigning three guys on every road trip to show up for extra BP [batting practice], and they called their agents! [The agents] would say, 'You're overworking my client.' I'd go, 'Really? What's your client hitting—.220? I think he needs a little bit more work.'"

Despite his frustration with players at the big league level, Boggs is pragmatic about it, understanding how things often work: "They said Ted Williams couldn't manage because he was too overzealous about having perfection, that he didn't understand what the layperson was like," he theorizes. "And someone like Charlie Lau was never a good hitter, but he was a great teacher. I was a really good hitter, but I know how to explain hitting in simple terms as well as very complicated terms. I can get as complicated in astrophysics as you want, getting into the dynamics of the path of your bat as far as the direction of the ball goes and then breaking it down into zones, because I wrote a book on the modern techniques of hitting.

But I can also keep it as simple as ABC—as red fish, blue fish. I can go either way."

For the ensuing fifteen minutes Boggs breaks down for me which zones he preferred versus sluggers like Mark McGwire or Jose Canseco, going into great detail the reasons why. I liken listening to Boggs talk hitting to Albert Einstein discuss his theory of relativity. It is nothing short of mesmerizing.

By 1986 Wade had become one of the faces of baseball. Hitting over .360 in two of your first four seasons will do that for you. But he also had a star quality and charisma that would land him on some of the most watched television shows of the eighties.

"You became a part of popular American culture while with the Red Sox," I note. "Your appearance on *Cheers* and then on *The Simpsons* solidified that. Did it all seem kind of surreal at the time?"

With many ballplayers wanting to be actors or rock stars, Wade seemed delighted by the question: "The neat thing about the *Cheers* episode was that it was in spring training of '86," he says. "My agents had reached out to Hollywood to see if I could appear on any Boston-based TV shows. The first to get back to them was a detective show, *Spenser: For Hire.* They wanted me to take batting practice while Spenser was chasing bad guys through the park, but we got rained out and I had to go on the road, and we never rescheduled it. That would have been neat. But then, *Boom!*, they got me a spot on *Cheers*, which was great! Then a bit later I did *The Simpsons* when they had other [baseball] All-Stars. I was in a Red Sox uniform for that one."

Of all the shows on which he would appear, *Cheers* (which at the time was at the height of it's popularity) was the one that was clearly most memorable to Boggs.

"I got to play myself and ham it up," Wade says excitedly. "I went to John McNamara during spring training and said, 'Mac, can I get a couple days off?' He goes, 'Absolutely not.' I went, 'Well, I got this thing in Hollywood that I *really* need to go to. I'm going to be on *Cheers*. So then he goes, 'Get out of here!

I'll see you in a couple of days!' It was really neat. I went out to Hollywood and read the script like a thousand times. The day of shooting [the cast] went into wardrobe and makeup and then did sort of a rehearsal. The director came over and said to me, 'Just to make you feel at ease, there's probably going to be nine hundred people in the audience.' I said, 'That's fine. I play in front of fifty thousand people, so I don't mind crowds.'

"When we started filming, this time in front of about fifteen hundred people, it was probably close to 11:20 at night. Normally they'll film all the way through the night, just to make sure everything is right. [But in my scene] I come into the bar [and] start bantering back and forth [with characters Woody, Norm, Carla, and Rebecca] before [the patrons] chase me out. [After the scene] I come back into the bar, and I hear, 'Cut! Wrap! Put it in the can! That was great!' Since then I was known as 'One-Take Wade.' No one messed up their lines, and it was rated the number one episode of *Cheers* at the time. I wanted it to go on forever. I wanted to mess up and redo it and mess up and redo it again. But they were so pleased with everyone's reactions—from Cliff's and Carla's to Norm's and then Woody's responses to me at the bar."

"You mentioned that your episode on *Cheers* was the highest rated for the show at that time," I say. "It just dawned on me that when Keith Hernandez did *Seinfeld*, it was also the most watched episode of the season for that show. So what is it about you ballplayers? You're good actors!"

"The thing about ballplayers is that we have to get things right the *first* time," Boggs explains. "We don't have, 'Cut! Take two!' If a ball goes through your legs, you don't call time out and then say, 'Let's do the play over again.' We have to get it right the first time or it's on ESPN for the next two or three days. We have perfection in our makeup, where you get it right the first time or you're not around very long."

I remind Boggs that I had interviewed him at Fenway a couple of times in the mideighties and that I recalled that he would routinely hit balls halfway up the bleachers during batting prac-tice. "You probably could have been that thirty-five to forty home run guy in the middle of the lineup instead of the .360 hitter you were," I theorize. "I believe you could have gone either way. Why did you choose to be that league-leading hitter, seemingly year after year, as opposed to a slugger who could have com-peted for the home run title?"

While not outwardly showing any disdain at the question (which I appreciate), Boggs seems a bit put off by why I, like many others, assume he could have been a power hitter based on his batting practice prowess. "The definitive word in there is *chose*," he says. "That's the definitive word that all reporters use, that I *chose* to do it that way. In batting practice the pitcher throws fifty miles an hour. It's coming in at one speed, and it doesn't tumble with the forkball. It doesn't break with the slider. It doesn't break with the curveball. I hit by sight, by recogni-tion. In order to do that I'm at the last possible second of rec-ognition to put a swing on the ball. The majority of home run hitters hit the ball so far out in front of home plate in order to hit it out of the ballpark. At fifty miles an hour I can have that kind of swing. But at ninety-five miles an hour against a guy with a really nasty forkball or slider, I can't make that distinc-tion. Number one, I have to wait to see if it's going to break and then [number] two, put a pass on it. That's the God-gifted abil-ity I had—great eyesight. At 20/12, I could recognize a slider, a forkball, and various things to square up a baseball. It wasn't a matter of choosing this over that."

In his eleven seasons with the Red Sox, Boggs would have home run totals in the single digits every year except one—when he broke out with twenty-four dingers in 1987 while still hitting .363.

"It was just a different swing [that year]," Boggs says matter-of-factly. "I was hitting balls further out in front and not hitting line drives. I was hitting long fly balls that were carrying out of the ballpark. I came back in spring training of '88 and tried to duplicate that swing, and it was horrendous. I was hitting

.130 halfway through spring training, popping balls up to the infield and rolling over on balls because it was a completely different swing. It wasn't me. At one point in my career I once went 748 plate appearances without popping up to the infield, which tells people that I can't be fooled. But now my left hand was way lower than my right hand [on my swing], which creates elevation and loft. It's all about timing. I just couldn't figure out that same timing I had in '87. By the end of spring training the line drives started coming back. My hands were back in the right position. I wound up hitting .366 in 1988, leading the league in hitting again. Thank goodness the line drives came back, but the home runs disappeared [to just five] because of the type of swing, which was completely different from the year before."

"I'm sure you've had to explain this a hundred times," I say.

"*Five hundred* times," Boggs says emphatically. "But they still don't get it." By "they" Boggs is referring to the Boston media: "They write books, and it all goes back to the articles that they used to write—the commentary of Eddie Andelman and various other people on the radio," Boggs explained. "They'd say, 'Wade Boggs is selfish because he doesn't want to hit home runs.' Oh my goodness! Wouldn't I rather run a trot around the bases than try to hit one high off 'the Wall' and then go head first into second? It would be a lot easier to trot around the bases and wind up every year hitting .365 with forty home runs—*a lot* easier. If I had played at Wrigley, I would have averaged thirty home runs a year. But I had thirty-seven feet to conquer [with the 'Green Monster'], and my ball was going at an upward angle, hitting the top of the wall and consequently becoming a double."

"I always thought that Jim Rice would have hit more home runs had he played elsewhere," I say.

"*Absolutely!*" Boggs exclaims. "Jimmy would hit line drives in parks on the road that were home runs but that would have dinked three-quarters of the way off 'the Monster.' If they didn't play it right, it's a double. But if they did play it right, because

Jimmy hit it so hard, it's a single. He was penalized playing [at Fenway]. My goodness, if Jimmy had played at Wrigley Field or today in a place like Minute Maid Park in Houston . . ."

Boggs pauses to reflect, letting his imagination run wild, before saying slowly, "Boy, I would *love* to hit [at Minute Maid Park]. Oh gosh, that's a nice place."

"You just touched on the Boston media and how unfair they could be," I begin. "What the hell was it with them? You were a Hall of Fame third baseman, had over two hundred hits seven straight years, and you won five batting titles there."

"There they are," Boggs says proudly, as he pointed to his batting title trophies.

"You were always so gracious giving interviews, great with the media—even giving time to a kid like I was back then," I say. "Do you think the backlash was just a Boston thing where they're trying to rouse controversy to sell papers?"

Boggs sighs and then gives a thoughtful response: "It's probably my downfall—being so gracious with the media. They asked me a question, I answered it. I gave them what they wanted to hear. I explained how things happened. I took blame if it was on me, but I never threw guys under the bus, never saying, 'Well, the reason we lost was because of him.' I *never* did that. Instead I would say something like, 'You win as a team, you lose as a team.' But somehow I would make statements, and they would get convoluted, turned around and misrepresented a little bit and, *Boom!*, the next thing you know, you've got headlines in the *Boston Herald.*"

Clearly still flabbergasted, Boggs, a leadoff hitter for much of his career, is dumbfounded by how the Boston media also criticized him for not driving in enough runs.

"You'll never see another player with two hundred hits and one hundred walks in a season," Boggs predicts. "Those days are long gone. I did it four years in a row, which is the name of the game for a leadoff hitter. Now a leadoff hitter in, say, 158 games a season has 158 at bats with nobody on or in scoring position. *So how can I drive in runs?* But still all the people on the radio and the talk shows and in the print media would say, 'He never drives in any runs.' If 158 of my 600 at bats—almost one-third of them—are with nobody on, I can't drive anyone in. The one year, in '87, when I got moved to the third spot, I wound up with eighty-nine RBIS, but I had led off until the middle of May. Had I hit third all year, I would have easily driven in a hundred—*easily*!"

"You once wrote the introduction for a book on hitting by Walt Hriniak, your batting coach with the Red Sox," I point out. "I know that you two worked well together. What influence did Walt have on you as a player?"

Boggs, who clearly had great affinity for Hriniak, gives a pregnant pause before reflecting on the man who helped his career as much as anyone. "On day one, at the start of spring training in '82, I walked into the clubhouse at 6:30 in the morning, and the first player that I met was 'Captain Carl.' He was just getting out of the shower, and I said, 'Hello, Mr. Yastrzemski.' But he just walked right by me. I thought, 'Oh gosh, this is going to be fun.' So I went over to my locker, and Walt was nearby. I introduce myself to him, and he goes, 'I'm Walt Hriniak, hitting instructor. I expect you here every morning at 6:30.' I said, 'I'll be here.' Walt said to me my second day of my first spring training, 'Few dare to be great.' I took those words to heart. That was my badge of honor that I carried with me. Walt would yell at you when you needed to be yelled at and comfort you when you needed to be comforted. He was monumental in my mom's death in '86, being there for me. Every great prize fighter has a corner man, and Walt Hriniak was mine. Every day, every swing, every at bat, Walt would get the most out of me. That's why there are five silver bats [for each batting title] right there. I was always told I was too slow, no power, couldn't run, couldn't field—yet here I am now in the Hall of Fame."

Hriniak was a disciple of hitting guru Charlie Lau, whose theories were diametrically opposite to those of the greatest Red Sock in history, 'Teddy Ballgame' himself. "Ted was hips ahead of hands," Boggs explained. "Charlie was hands ahead of hips. Ted just didn't like his philosophy. The two didn't see eye to eye. They didn't like each other either. When I came to spring training in '82, I already had an inside-out swing, staying inside the baseball and hitting the ball to left field and left-center—that type of swing. Ted's style didn't work for me because I couldn't get out and hit the outside pitch and pull it to right-center like Ted could. I couldn't master that swing. [The result of such an effort] would be a roller to second every time for me. So why fight it when my strength was hitting the ball off 'the Wall' rather than trying to pull everything? Still Ted would come to spring training and walk around and teach his own [style of hitting]. It probably wasn't until after my second batting title that Ted finally said to me, 'You know, kid, you can hit!'"

Williams and Boggs may have had different philosophies when it came to hitting, but in addition to being two of the greatest hitters of all time, they had another thing in common: ridiculously cogent recollections of virtually every at bat they ever had.

"I've met Pete Rose a number of times," I say. "And I think he can remember every hit that he ever got off every pitcher he ever faced. The detail is incredible. Do you remember every hit you ever got?"

"Let's see," Boggs says, leaning back on his sofa. "There were 3,010 of them. I could probably give you about 2,850—maybe even 2,900 of them."

"That's good enough!" I exclaim.

"I could tell you what the weather was like that day and what the count was and various things like that."

"What is it about the great hitters who sometimes have that capability?" I ask.

"It's no different than being a doctor or a carpenter or a lawyer," Boggs explains. "Doctors know prescriptions. They have to recite them. They have to know what they're for. You learn your craft. A carpenter has to know measurements and how things fit precisely. We're no different. We're just at the top of our field. I feel that remembering hits [is just like having] stepping stones that [help you] progress through all the trials and tribulations of your life."

Boggs then gives me a rapid-fire example of a hit from decades ago: "'Saturday day game. It's 3:20. Scotty McGregor. Threw me a curveball. Sixth inning. 1-2 count. Home run.' You just remember things. It's like going through the Rolodex and someone mentions a pitcher's name. You start remembering your at bats off of the guy, and all of a sudden you're like, 'That was around April 14, freezing at Comiskey,' and *Boom!*, you start painting a picture. You're more or less like an artist. We have to paint a mental image if we're talking to someone. It's like you're breaking out a brush. Then you start painting and painting, and the room is your canvas. When I had a conversation with Ted at the end of his life, he could remember every at bat he had had off of Bob Feller—what the count was and what he did off him. He would captivate a room. But when someone walked up to him that he had met the day before, he would look at him and introduce himself again. His long-term memory was exquisite, but his short-term memory had completely left him."

"Despite your different approaches to hitting, it sounds like you had a very special relationship with Williams," I observe.

"*Wonderful, wonderful!*" Boggs blurts out without hesitation. "I've got a shotgun that he left in his will for me and a fly rod and reel and other various things. Ted's all over this house. I have pictures of Ted all over, and I read his book as a junior in high school. My dad made me read it cover to cover over a weekend."

"You are so entrenched with the history of the Red Sox," I tell him. "You should have been with the club forever—in the same way your contemporaries Tony Gwynn was always a Padre and Cal Ripken was always an Oriole."

"That's what Mrs. Yawkey wanted," Boggs laments. "When she offered me a contract at the end of the '91 season—a seven-year deal for $37 million—I said, 'Where do I sign?' She said, 'We'll get it done. I want you to follow in the same footsteps as Ted and Carl.' And I said, 'Mrs. Yawkey, I don't want to go anywhere else. I love it here.' Again she reassured me, saying, 'Don't worry; we'll make it happen.' Then February came, she [has a stroke and] dies. I go through spring training in '92 with back-and-forth negotiations before Lou Gorman and John Harrington took [Mrs. Yawkey's] offer off the table. The best they could come up with was a year and an option. But I wanted long term and told them, 'I guess I'm going to have to play the year out and see what happens.' At the end of the year they didn't offer me arbitration, which meant I couldn't resign with the Red Sox until after May. That wasn't going to happen, so I became a free agent. Then Mr. Steinbrenner, by the grace of God, offered me a three-year deal, and that's where I wound up. Mrs. Yawkey wanted me to be a Red Sock for life, but that wasn't the direction that John Harrington and Lou Gorman and all the rest of them wanted."

Aside from his obvious knowledge and talent for hitting a baseball, Boggs will go down in the annals of baseball history as one of the most superstitious players the game has ever known. Of all his superstitions none is more synonymous with Wade than his steady diet of chicken throughout his career.

"I believe it was Jim Rice who gave you the nickname 'Chicken Man,' right?" I ask.

Boggs nods his head in confirmation before giving me the genesis of his obsession with the poultry. "In 1983 a buddy of mine, Brad Gray, had come up with an idea of writing a chicken cookbook," Boggs began. "We would have all my grandmother's, mother's, and [Boggs's wife] Debbie's recipes in it. We'd call it *Foul Tips*. That was our little play on words. So I started eating chicken every day, whether it be at home or on the road at a restaurant. This went on into September of 1984, when Jimmy came out with the nickname 'Chicken Man,' which was kind of humorous. It stuck like glue because all the way through my career I ate chicken. Frank Perdue would send chicken to my house. It's even my Twitter handle."

"Was the magnitude of your chicken eating exaggerated at all, or did you really eat it *every* day?" I ask.

"*Every day.*"

"Throughout your whole career?"

"Whole career."

Boggs then touches on his "rituals" that went along with his chicken-eating superstition: "I would eat every day at 12:30 and then leave for the ballpark shortly thereafter. On the road I would find restaurants that really had good chicken dishes. I would frequent those places all the time. Eating chicken became an absolute superstition. I couldn't have anything else."

Boggs's obsession became national news. On the front page of *USA Today* there was once an article about it under the headline "Wade Boggs's Top Five Restaurants in the United States for Chicken." But the publicity had a down side, as now the perceived secret to some of Wade's success was out, and opposing fans were out to sabotage his daily routine.

"One year in Milwaukee, a radio station went to the Clock Restaurant, where I used to eat all the time, and bought up all of its uncooked chicken. Someone at the station had read that the Clock Restaurant was on my [top five] list. So when I went to the restaurant at 12:15 or so one day, the owner of the restaurant was there and said, 'Wade, I've got some bad news. We don't have any chicken.' I said, 'You're kidding.' And he goes, 'The radio station came in here and bought it all.' I was with Mike Greenwell at the time, so we walked back to the Pfister Hotel, and I had a chicken sandwich there. Then we got in a cab and went to the ballpark. Around 3:30 the security guard at the front door says, 'There's a gentleman out here to see you. He says he's from the Clock Restaurant.' The owner had gone out to the super market, bought chicken, cooked it at the restaurant, and then brought it to the ballpark!"

"So how did you do that night?" I ask, amused and impressed by the Clock Restaurant owner's efforts.

"I had a *terrific* game! Three-for-four, two doubles, drove in five runs. So one of the radio station guys comes up to me afterward and says, 'I see that your superstition didn't really hurt you.' I said, 'Au contraire! The owner of the Clock brought me the Clock chicken, so I did have a good night.' The Clock Restaurant took some heat for that."

Another part of Boggs's "diet" as a player, while admittedly pursued more out of boredom than superstition, was his occasional epic consumption of beer on cross-country team flights. It has become the stuff of legend, with different media outlets making a parlor game out of nailing down the exact numbers of his personal beer-drinking records. *Pardon Our Interruption* once claimed the number was 64 beers for a cross-country flight, while actor Charlie Day went on *The Tonight Show Starring Jimmy Fallon* claiming that Boggs told him, while filming an episode of *It's Always Sunny in Philadelphia*, that his record for one day was 107—and then added that Boggs went 3-for-4 the next night. Wade seemed to confirm Day's story, telling TMZ that he did indeed once drink over a hundred beers in a day, jokingly attributing this *talent* to a "hollow leg." Even if all of this is somewhat exaggerated, it's safe to say Wade likes his beer.

Opposing teams would come to learn about some of Boggs's other superstitions and rituals and would try their best to disrupt them.

"I would run at exactly 7:17 before games," Wade recalls. "So we're in Toronto one time, and they held the clock at 7:16 for an extra minute and then turned it to 7:18. Every opposing park began doing that. Another [ritual] I had since I played little league ball in Georgia was making a *chai* in the batter's box when I would come up to the plate. A *chai* means good luck and life in Hebrew. I'm not Jewish, but I like the sign, and I would draw it when I would come up to the plate to wish myself good luck. It was easier than carrying a rabbit's foot in the back pocket and then sliding on it. Anyway [Orioles catcher] Rick Dempsey kept wiping out my *chai* during this one game. He did that like six or seven times. I told the umpire, Ken Kaiser, that I wasn't getting in the box until he stopped doing it. Kaiser told Dempsey to stop and the game went on, but it was just one of many cat-and-mouse games that people would play to try to get in my head a little bit."

"I've heard that you're into numbers as well," I note. "You always wore number 26 with Boston. How did you deal with having to ultimately change your number to 12 after you were signed by the Yankees?"

"Great story," Boggs says enthusiastically. "My daughter had a school dance when she was fifteen years old, and we went over to Blueberry Hill on Harbour Island. My wife and I were waiting for it to end when a Yankees' clubhouse guy named Nick calls and goes, 'Boggsy, just trying to finalize the numbers here. Did you pick a number yet?' I asked, 'What's left?' He goes, '13.' I said, 'Well, that one's out.' Then he goes through numbers in the thirties and forties, but there weren't many to pick from at all. The majority were either retired or already assigned to other players. Then he goes, 'Steve Farr said by no means is he giving up 26. I said, 'Let me think on it and give you a call back tomorrow.' Three minutes later he calls back and says, 'I just talked to Jim Leyritz, and he'll take 13, so now 12 is available.' I said, 'Okay, Nick, let me think about it.' I left Debbie to go to the bathroom, and while standing at a urinal, I noticed the wallpaper had 'Coca Cola Pick 12' all over it. Everywhere I looked, I saw 'Pick 12,' 'Pick 12,' 'Pick 12'! So I called Nick back and told him I would take 12."

"But as a superstitious guy, you wore 26 all of those years you won batting titles," I note. "Weren't you a little, you know . . . ?"

Boggs knows where I'm going and cuts me off. "What's two times six?" he asks, with a gleam in his eye, looking for me to figure out the use of the two numbers in 26.

"Twelve," I say. "Ahhhh, okay!"

"Yup," he says. "Everybody usually adds numbers to try to get to their number. Like if I wanted eight, I would have two and six and add them together to make eight. But I wore 26, and 12 is just a by-product of 26—two times six."

"That's incredible," I exclaim.

"Well, that's how I picked 18 in the Minor Leagues once and 27 another time in Double-A," he says proudly. "I wanted to wear Ted's number 9, but it was retired by all accounts."

Perhaps the ultimate for Boggs and his obsession with superstitions, rituals, and numbers occurred after his retirement, when in 2005 he received a call to inform him he had been elected to the Baseball Hall of Fame.

"I heard you received the call at exactly 12:26 in the afternoon—your two uniform numbers," I remark.

"Yeah, I had friends and family over," Boggs says. "My dad was in the big chair in the front room. I was standing behind the couch. Our nanny from Boston had called two or three times, asking me, 'Have you heard? Have your heard anything yet?' Every time the phone would ring, it would be someone else asking the same thing—which is natural. But then 12 p.m. comes and goes, and I'm kind of panicking because I thought I was going to get the call before noon. So we're all sitting around when, all of a sudden, the phone rings; I look up at the clock, and it's 12:26, the two numbers I played with. I'm kind of 99.9 percent sure that that's how it was planned because I'm the only person in the Hall of Fame that has 'superstitions' mentioned anywhere on his plaque!"

Indeed the last line of his plaque reads, "Legendary for his superstitions."

"Everybody else has stats; I have 'superstitions,'" Boggs continues with a chuckle. "Anyway, I thought I was going to get the call from Jane Forbes Clark [Hall of Fame chairperson], but it was a man's voice on the other line that said, 'Hi Wade. Jack O'Connell, head of the Sportswriters' Association and Baseball Writers of America. Congratulations! You made it! You're on 91.86 percent of the ballot.' I looked at my father and said, 'I made it, Dad.' That's when the waterworks started for everybody in the room and the champagne popped. It was a gigantic celebration. It really was."

Boggs's 474 votes (out of a possible 516) represented the

third highest vote count ever at the time. He wouldn't just enter the Hall of Fame the following summer; he figuratively busted through it's doors. And there was nothing superstitious about that.

While many of the Red Sox dealt with the pain of losing the World Series in 1986, Boggs's agony that year was almost entirely placed with his mother's passing while he actually embraced nearly everything about the club's campaign—including the Fall Classic.

"What happened to my mother [Sue G. Boggs] was the number one thing that overshadowed everything else that happened that year," Wade says of the car accident that took her life. "And that includes going to the World Series. Man, everything was going gangbusters that season. Then *Boom!* June 17 we're in New York, and I get a phone call from my niece telling me [my mother] had been killed in a car accident. Basically your world stops, and I didn't really know how to handle it. But I came home, bought her a coffin on her birthday on June 18, and laid her to rest."

Still impacted by the shock of the tragedy more than three decades later, Wade takes a moment to compose himself before continuing: "I came back to Boston with my father [Winn Boggs] because I wasn't going to leave him home. We got off the plane, drove to my house, then drove to the park. I got dressed, and Mac looked at me like, 'What in the hell are you doing here?' I said, 'I'm ready if you need me. I'll pinch-hit, or I'll do whatever.' The next day I played in our game at Fenway, and the fans gave me like a ten-minute standing ovation. I apologized to the umpire, but he said, 'Take all the time you need.' The cheering wouldn't stop. That just solidified the reason why I wanted to stay in Boston—how the fans treated me during that time."

As for the World Series, Boggs believes the outcome didn't take anything away from the season or the miraculous ALCS victory over the Angels. "*Absolutely not!*" he exclaims. "People can say that this was the greatest World Series ever played—

we're *entertainers*! That's what we do for a living—entertain. People buy that ticket, they go and sit in a seat to watch entertainment, and we've got to give them a good show. For a World Series to go all the way to Game Seven with all the twists and turns—it took nothing away from our 3–1 comeback [in the ALCS]. Granted, we had a lead in Game Six, but we also had a lead in Game Seven that we let slip away. But in the end somebody has to be the winner, and somebody has to be the loser. Unfortunately in our case we wanted it so bad [in order] to get rid of '1918' and not have to deal with that and the previous articles that were written about 'chokers' and '25 players, 25 cabs' and all of that. But we weren't even close to being anything like that. We were all very close, and when we'd go out on the road, there would be eight to ten guys at the dinner table."

"You talk about being entertainers," I say. "The final two games of that World Series had the highest shares for viewership ever in the postseason. And both games were extremely entertaining, as you point out. But I'm sure it must have been draining for you as well. After the final out was made in Game Seven, the cameras panned over to the Red Sox dugout, where you had broken down in tears. What were you thinking about at that moment that made you so distraught?"

Boggs doesn't hesitate: "I thought about having to walk through that door and how my mom wasn't going to be there— that was about the *only* thing that crossed my mind," he says somberly. "I was kind of upset Jesse Orosco threw his glove up in the air, but I would say for me it was 75 percent about my mom. We wanted to win the World Series so bad. It was my first taste of playoff baseball. In fact I think Tom Seaver was the only one on the team that had won a World Series, but he wasn't even on the postseason roster. Anyway, we all wanted so badly to erase all that [negative] history and become the darlings of Boston and to say, 'Wow, we did something that nobody else could ever do up until that point.'"

"Right after the World Series ended, despite all the disappointment in Boston, the city threw the Red Sox a huge celebration downtown at Government Center," I remind him. "Hundreds of thousands of fans came out to cheer you guys on. But in the days, weeks, and years that followed, Boston was hurting from the heartbreak of that World Series. It was like a long hangover. Yet today all of that has changed: the '86 Red Sox players are honored and feted all the time at Fenway Park. What do you think happened to change the dynamic after all these years?"

Boggs's philosophical response stuns me. He obviously had given this much thought and had done some deep soul searching on the topic: "In simple terms it's about overcoming failure, moving on with your life, and not beating yourself up all the time," he begins. "It's about [the fans'] overall forgiveness of not only Billy Buck, but the whole '86 team and that there are bits and pieces that various players did during the course of the World Series that had an impact. Like I said, it's not just one player. They brought Billy Buck back and had a day for him, and it was well received. They've gone over scenarios about why Johnny Mac didn't put in [Dave] Stapleton and take Buckner out and various things like that. They've forgiven Johnny Mac. If you take their [recent] World Series [victories] away, would they still have the imprint of '86 on their minds—of coming that close and then having the carpet ripped out from under? Would they still have those same feelings? When I go back to Boston, I sense a total cultural change [by which] now they classify themselves as winners. They always had that sense of, 'We came so close, but we lost.' And then you had the sportswriters and talk show hosts saying things like, 'Oh, they've got a lead, but these guys will choke again.' Then you get the wrong player who believes all of this, it adds to the pressure for him, and he *does* throw one in the dirt for a wild pitch, or he *does* give up a homer to lose a game, and everybody says, 'See, I told you he was going to choke.' It's a mentality and stigma they put with that club. Then 2004 came, and it was like, 'Holy cow! They did it! They won it all!' Now there's no more bad stuff to write about. No more losers, no more chokers, no more 'Curse of the

Bambino,' and no more of the various things that people narcissistically adhere to when they want somebody to feel sorry for them. Well, you can't go through life having people feel sorry for you all the time. Do something about it. In 2004 they did. They won it. Then people ask me, 'How does it make you feel?' It makes me feel wonderful because it took [all the negativity] away from us. Now they can't write bad stories about '86 anymore because [the Red Sox] won it all in 2004."

Appropriately, despite his awkward departure from Boston and his finishing his career by playing five seasons with the Yankees and two years in Tampa Bay, Wade Boggs had his number 26 retired by the Red Sox, is a proud member of the team's Hall of Fame, and dons a Boston cap on his Baseball Hall of Fame plaque.

"You look at the players that are in the Baseball Hall of Fame representing the Red Sox," Boggs gushes. "Ted Williams, Carl Yastrzemski, Jimmy Rice later on, Joe Cronin, Pudge [Fisk], Bobby Doerr, and now me going in as a member of one of the historic franchises of all time. I had the opportunity to have a 'B' on my cap and represent an organization that is so rich in the history of terrific left-handed hitters like Ted and Carl, and I'm extremely proud of that. I got my start with the Red Sox when I was seventeen—played five and a half years in their Minor League system and then eleven more with them in the big leagues. I grew up with them; the only thing I had ever known was being with the Red Sox before going to New York and Tampa Bay, so it was really a no-brainer to have a 'B' on my hat for the Hall of Fame."

Some would say it was tragic that Boggs didn't finish his career in Boston like Williams and Yastrzemski did—Ted with his farewell home run and Carl with his victory lap around Fenway Park, high-fiving fans along the way. Aside from the fact that Gorman and Harrington had taken Mrs. Yawkey's long-term verbal offer off the table, the Boston media were making it increasingly difficult for him to stay in Boston, writing stories not just about what was occurring on the field but off the field as well. At best it was sensationalist journalism; at worst, downright cruel. There were sordid stories about his affair with Margo Adams, his perceived obsession with personal stats, and his putting himself above his teammates. Did it sell newspapers? Definitely. Had the media dismissed all the greatness and dedication that Boggs had brought to the organization? Absolutely. Did it have an effect on his play? Almost certainly, as his .259 average—unheard of for Boggs throughout his career—in his final season in Boston in 1992 would attest.

"When I was getting beat up in Boston with the talk shows and various columnists that shall go nameless, I would try to explain myself, and it was like it went in one ear and out the other," Wade tells me incredulously. "It didn't matter how much I explained myself. Articles making me out to be selfish were coming out. They didn't know the underlying things that were going on. I didn't know where they were getting their quotes. While I was going through those bad times, we were in California. Rod Carew was behind the batting cage with me [during batting practice], and he said, 'For people who know you, no explanation is necessary. For those who don't, none is possible.' I started dissecting that and went, 'That's my life rolled up in a nutshell because to all my friends and family who know me, I don't have to explain myself.'"

The move to the Yankees—which represented a clean slate for Boggs—jump-started his career after the hiccup that was his '92 season. But he had to win over the New York fans first.

"My first few games in New York in '93, I was booed, so it was sort of like playing in Boston at the end of [my time there]," Boggs says. "Most cities are passionate about their baseball, and they take great pride in who puts on their uniform, whether it's the Boston 'red' or the pinstripes of the Yankees. I was the dreaded guy when I came over. That was the thing that all the media in Boston told the [New York press]: 'You're going to love this guy because he'll be on the back page of the *Daily News* every day!' But the New York guys loved me because [the Yankees] began to win again in '93. In '94 [the baseball strike] pulled the plug on us. [The Yankees had the best record in the American League when play was stopped in August for the rest of the season.] In '95 we made the playoffs. And then we won the World Series in '96. In '97 we played Cleveland in the playoffs, and that didn't work out so well. But in the five years I was in New York, we won, and the Mets were losing. It took all the heat off of us, which was great. That's the problem in Boston. There's only one team. You're on the back page all the time—win, lose, or draw. If you win, that article is two or three pages inside the paper, but the bad stuff is on the back page. Players know that. It's part of the business, and it's part of having to sell papers. Nobody wants to read about the guy going 2-for-3 and driving in a couple of runs and what his outlook of the game is. They want to know why so-and-so smashed his thumb at 3:30 in the morning. Oh well."

Despite all the negative drama with Wade's Boston exit, he miraculously was able to turn it all around in his return to Fenway Park on May 21, 1993—becoming a conquering hero, so to speak. In his first game back he went 4-for-4 with a walk.

"Before the game [Yankees manager] Buck Showalter said to me, 'Boggs, you don't have to play today. I want you to just . . .' But before he finished, I said, 'No, I can't do that. I absolutely cannot run away from this.' He goes, 'Are you sure?' And I said, 'Yes, I am 100 percent sure.' So my first time to the plate I had thirty-five thousand fans booing me before I singled. My second time up I had around twenty-nine thousand fans booing me, and I singled again. My third time up I had about twenty-two thousand of them booing me, and I hit another single. By my fourth at-bat I had thirty-five thousand of them giving me a standing ovation, and I singled for my fourth hit of the game. As I stood on first base, the cheering continued, and I tipped my cap."

"That was beautiful," I say.

"It was like they were saying, 'Wow, he came back and put his bat where his mouth was!'"

Boggs had won the Boston fans back over—at least for one night.

While the Yankees had regained their place atop the baseball world after nearly two decades, the Red Sox floundered in the five years after Boggs's departure from the club, making the playoffs just once and failing to win even a single postseason game. And while Wade had finally won the elusive world championship in New York that he had come ever so close to winning with the Red Sox in '86, his heart was never far from Boston.

"After winning the World Series in '96," I begin, "you hopped on to the back of a police horse as an officer rode you around Yankee Stadium to acknowledge your adoring fans. What were you thinking about at that very moment?"

"It just kept running through my mind that we weren't going to play tomorrow," Boggs says with a grin. "We were the world champions, and this is exactly the way it feels."

Wade then pauses before saying something most telling: "Then I thought, 'I wish it'd felt like this ten years ago.'"

5.

Still Smokin'!

If I had started Game Seven [of the '86 World Series], I feel we would've been world champs. . . . Everybody on the team knew I would've beat the Mets—without a question.

—OIL CAN BOYD

It's a picture-perfect late April morning at Pawtucket's McCoy Stadium, home of the Triple-A Red Sox. Team employees and players begin arriving, food vendors prepare their stations, and the booming sound of air-blowers throughout the stands ready the park for an afternoon baseball game. Despite all the bustling activity and white noise, there is still a serenity about the place as the crisp spring air permeates throughout the old ballpark and morning dew glistens off the playing field grass.

But it won't be serene for very long. Oil Can Boyd, the alternatively brash, hilarious, colorful, and highly dependable former starting pitcher for the Red Sox, pulls up into a parking spot by the stadium entrance in a shiny gray convertible. As he gets out of his car, Boyd appears as slender and vibrant as when he took the mound at Fenway during the eighties. The only telltale sign of his age is the gray hair peering out the sides of his black flat cap and in the thin beard that lines his face.

As a young African American player in 1980s Boston who spoke his mind and at times displayed erratic behavior, Boyd sometimes got into hot water with the team, the fans, the media, and the American League office. But while he is just as loud and outspoken as he was then, I would find him to also be slyly intelligent, a contrarian to the accepted way of societal thinking, a master of code switching (depending on the topic), and exceedingly cordial. Getting to know him would be a delight.

"Call me Can!" Boyd says enthusiastically as we shake hands. "My friends call me Can. I live just down the street from here, so I come to McCoy quite a bit. I come over with friends and sign autographs for kids."

I remind him that he would regularly interact with children at Fenway during batting practice when he pitched for the Red Sox. "You really love kids, don't you?" I ask as we find a tall round table inside the corridors of the stadium to stand around and chat.

"Oh, quite a bit," Boyd says with a big grin as his eyes sparkle underneath his glasses. "There was a little league game last night I went to see. I put my time in with [little league players] and give them direction and focus—not just about sports but about life in general. The obedient child is a good child. The kid that listens is the kid that's going to prosper. I want to see kids get on the right track in life. I also focus my time on giving back socially by raising money for different foundations for people in need—like the homeless, women with breast cancer, or children born with cancer. I just want to help in some way by going out there and trying to give a little inspiration to their lives. It's my motivation. Those are the gestures that I feel really good about. And while it feels good to be acknowledged as the ballplayer I was, it was my personality that took me a long way. It made people remember me for many years after I was out of the game.

"With me baseball was good and bad, but I wouldn't trade it for nothing! All the people you meet along the way—from high school to college to the Minors and up to the Majors—those teammates become one big family. You feel like you're in a cult with baseball—an 'all for one, one for all' type of thing.

And that's what keeps me playing right now—a chance to play with people that love the game."

Yes, Oil Can is still out there pitching—in a men's senior league that travels to games as far away from Rhode Island as Arizona and Las Vegas.

"I tell my teammates every summer, 'I appreciate you guys loving the game, man,'" Boyd says. "'I can still play, but if I didn't have you guys, I wouldn't be playing ball.' I still love it. I love living out of a hotel, getting up and dressed, and going to the field. I'm just as motivated now as I was when I was playing ball for a living. It shows the passion I still have for the game."

Perhaps as much as any player who's ever lived, baseball is in Boyd's DNA. Much of his family, going back several generations, played in the Negro Leagues, including his father Willie, who was a baseball legend around Meridian, Mississippi.

"Throughout the whole Mississippi-Alabama region back in the day, my father and his younger brothers got a chance to play Negro League baseball," Boyd recounts. "After my dad got hurt in baseball, he went into the managing part of the game and got a chance to coach his siblings and cousins. They're legendary at home, man! People talked about them like they were the baddest cats that ever played. My whole family background in baseball was my inspiration to one day play in the Major Leagues—get a chance to experience the game at the highest level. I was the one in our family that got a chance to do it."

Boyd's family had a front row seat to the history of the Negro Leagues, and Oil Can was more than eager to share it with me: "My dad got a chance to see Henry Aaron and Willie Mays as young kids—fourteen, fifteen, sixteen years old—before they signed professional contracts. From the mid-1930s through the midfifties Negro League teams would come in from Birmingham or from Mobile and play semipro baseball. So they would barnstorm through different towns in the Southern region— from Little Rock to Memphis to Nashville to Birmingham to Montgomery and even down to the Carolinas and Florida. It was a period in time where the majority of Blacks were still playing baseball."

And then Oil Can drops a stunning statement: "The Majors only chose the 'most available best,' you know what I'm saying? My dad would say—even Mays and Aaron would tell you—that there were cats that *were better* than they were but didn't get an opportunity to play [Major League ball]."

"*Really?*" I ask. "*Better* than Mays and Aaron?"

"Of course," Boyd says, his voice rising an octave. "Somebody had to make Willie Mays and Hank Aaron the kind of ballplayers they were."

"You're one of the biggest advocates of the Negro Leagues I've ever heard of in today's age," I say. "Is it true that you once made an effort to bring the league back?"

"Basically what I'm more concerned about is not so much bringing the league back but rather bringing African Americans back to baseball."

"You're referring to the drop in the percentage of African Americans in the Majors—down from 28 percent in the early seventies to the 7 percent it is today. So what do you think happened?"

"People have to own up to what's going on," says Boyd, never one to believe ballplayers should simply play and keep quiet on social issues. "Society has changed quite a bit in the last thirty-five years or so. In the process the African American started to be extinguished through gangs, drugs, kids running astray. Poverty and crime are at a high in Black neighborhoods, so they're going to put away baseball. Baseball used to be an outdoor, inner-city community thing. There was a passion for the game of baseball in the Black community. Once that candle went out, you started seeing the kids go in different directions. You want to know where most of the Black ballplayers are today? They're in jails. I've been in there; that's where they are now."

Boyd then takes a couple of steps back. "Look at me, Erik," he says. "Look at my physique. Baseball players look very common. Today's ballplayer looks like a football player a little bit, but when we were coming up, players came in any size, any stature. They were just gifted athletes with their hand and eye [coordination] and fleetness and with a great passion for the game. If I had tried to play baseball today, I might've fallen to the wayside because the streets are calling the kids in abundance, and they don't really know how to say no. They want to live. When I go home [to Mississippi], I go to poverty-stricken areas. I go around my people quite a bit, and I see desperation in their eyes. I see their kids are not getting an opportunity to be kids anymore like I did. I grew up with a mom and dad in the house, with direction, and with siblings keeping me on the right track. There was no 'danger stranger' out in the streets. We didn't have to worry about being shot walking out the door or being accustomed to it. The seed has been sown, and now you're dealing with people that don't really understand that, people that don't believe that there's a life out there—and that's sad. I would say two-thirds of Black kids all over this country don't see a positive side. We're the elite to be a doctor or a lawyer or a professional athlete—almost like the chosen ones in this day and time."

"Can, I'm interested. We recently had an African American president for eight years. Did it change anything for people of color?" I ask.

Boyd doesn't hesitate. "Uh-uh. I didn't even get a chance to really acknowledge that we had one, to tell you the truth. Our lives were focused so much on individuality and survival mode. Look, I love New England. I love everything about how the people treat me and how special it is, but I want to go back home to Mississippi, where 85 percent of African American kids' lives are in disarray and try to do something about it. And I know baseball can help kids to stay focused. Black fans won't come to baseball games because there's hardly any Blacks playing. They want to see somebody that reminds them of themselves. Right now you probably don't have two thousand Black people in the whole United States that'll sit and watch a great player like Andrew McCutchen play baseball. I get very emotional when I see a Black baseball player today. It's almost like Christmas to me!"

"Let me throw two names out at you, and please give me your thoughts on each of them," I say. "Satchel Paige and Jackie Robinson."

Oil Can gives a pregnant pause before giving a most well-thought out yet—in the case of Robinson—unconventional response: "I love them both, but Satchel I *idolized*," Boyd says.

I can't say I was surprised by this revelation, as Oil Can's theatrics on the mound mirrored his idol's in many ways.

"As a kid growing up," Boyd continues, "I heard his name so much that it was like he lived in my house. I actually got a chance to meet him. All of my family knew him quite well. He would stop in Meridian when he was coming through, and they got to see him play ball in Hattiesburg, Mississippi, where he played most of his ball before getting a chance to play in the Major Leagues. He was just so well loved, so admired. You have to understand the legacy and the things he did to create baseball like it is today—the showmanship, the flair of the African American ballplayer, which they called 'hot-dogging' back in the day. Back then it was 'show time' because you played for the fans. You didn't play for endorsements, and you didn't play for the TV. You played for the people that came and paid for those tickets."

"You realize that you had a little bit of that Satchel flare in your game, right?" I ask.

"People used to say that all the time," Boyd says. "The Red Sox owner Haywood Sullivan got a chance to catch Satchel and told me I was the second coming of him. He said my demeanor, my talk, my walk, and our being from the same part of the country made me like a walking ghost of him."

"What about Jackie?" I ask.

"You would think that by [Jackie's crossing the color barrier] it would be grand [for Black players]," Boyd explains. "But I think Jackie would be sick to know that [Blacks] are not playing now. So in actuality he didn't do too much because they're not playing today."

"Do you think that other African Americans feel the way you do about Jackie and this issue?" I ask.

"In 1947 I would say that 75 percent of the African American ballplayers that were playing in the Negro Leagues didn't appreciate Jackie going to the Major Leagues," Boyd tells me. "They were already playing baseball, already had a livelihood from it. By his going to the Majors, the individuality was taken away from the African American player. The generation that would come after Jackie didn't feel that way. Hank Aaron, Willie Mays, Frank Robinson—those guys felt like Jackie gave us a chance. But he didn't. Like I said, the Majors took away our individuality, and now the African American player is obsolete. He's expendable for a lot of reasons. If Jackie was alive today, he would be sick to walk through neighborhoods and see windows nailed up and hear gunfire and pick up the newspaper to read about all the babies being shot and killed in gang violence, knowing that if they just had a baseball to throw around, a daddy to play catch with, siblings to take them to the park every day, things would be different. But now you've got kids that are walking around with $2,000–$3,000 in their pockets, no education, mad and angry, and they don't know why. A lot of them don't even know who Jackie Robinson was. My dad didn't have a big opinion of Jackie and didn't think we would benefit from him, and he was right. It may have taken thirty or forty years for it to take place, but Jackie became expendable too. Once they bought him, hey, they figured, 'We can do what we want to do.'"

"Did you ever express these opinions with other African Americans with whom you played?" I ask.

"Sure, and I would get into arguments with players I played with and [those] from different teams," Oil Can confesses. "I would tell them that I didn't feel like I was given an opportunity to play Major League baseball through Jackie. I'm a fifth-generation professional baseball player. My people were playing before Jackie was born."

"I know you had differences of opinion with Jim Rice and Don Baylor about it, right?" I query.

"Yeah, they were tokenized," Boyd says matter-of-factly, alluding not so endearingly to his opinion that Rice and Baylor put up with racial injustice so as to not make waves. "Even though they were good ballplayers, they still were tokens. I refused to be a token of any sort because I was very personal about the love and passion I had for something I could do as well as anybody. I wasn't there to fill no void. I was there because I could really play. Jackie didn't give me a chance to do that; my great ancestors did. My people have been playing ball since 1880."

Oil Can then gives his theory on why Jackie Robinson was selected by Dodgers general manager and president Branch Rickey to become the first African American to be signed by a big league club: "Jackie was chosen for very select reasons," Boyd opines. "He went to college, so I think his intellect had just as much to do with them signing him as his playing ability. During that period two-thirds of Negro League players were illiterate, including my dad. Blacks didn't believe in education. They were told there wasn't any reason for them to have an education. You were a mule, and that was it. You were a descendant of a slave, and there was nothing in the world for you. And if you hear that every day of your life—goddamn!—you'll start to think like that. My dad said Jackie was a good ballplayer but was by no means great. He said the [Major Leagues] missed all the great Black ballplayers. But when Branch Rickey made a proposal to Jackie, he definitely had alternative reasons outside of integrating baseball."

"Money?" I theorize.

"Of course!" Boyd exclaims, making it sound obvious. "The exact same thing took place with slavery. Ain't nobody gave a damn about no slave being beaten or being hung from a tree. It was all about the economy. It didn't have nothing to do with us being free, but you've got people around here hollering, 'Abe Lincoln freed folks.' Abe ain't freed shit! 'Emancipation Proclamation' means from one power to another one. That's all it means. Lincoln didn't do shit!"

"Legalized slavery?" I theorize.

"That's *exactly* what it was!" Boyd shouts. "That's *all* it was! But what was left out of the whole Jackie Robinson thing was the Black fan. Y'all brought in the Black player, but, hell, y'all left the people that love them on the outside. Then when we wanted to go to the ballgame and see Jackie, [we were told], 'You got to sit over there.' 'What you mean? I can't sit right here and see Jackie? Naw.' You see, the Black fan didn't come with the Black ballplayer, and that's what I'm upset about."

"This is a change from the serious topic of racial injustice we've been discussing," I say, attempting to lighten things up a bit. "You have one of the greatest nicknames in baseball history—'Oil Can.' I read it came from drinking rot-gut whiskey."

"That's it—*moonshine!*" Boyd says, smiling proudly. "I was a little boy drinking up the whisky, and, shit man, in the first and second grade I was drunk on the little league baseball field. In different communities and origins in the country at that time a slave mentality was still very strong. What you had learned from the master came into your house, so we learned about moonshine. Blacks started to think that they could make some money on bootlegging it. It was an illegal business that all the police in town knew about. Hell, some of the cops would stop by and get themselves a little swig too. In the South it was a whole way of life. Matter of fact, my mom died from drinking that bad whiskey—fifty-seven years old, same as I am now. It attacks your liver. All the drinking comes from oppression, from being a sad Black person. In the South, where life was just so hard for people of color, it created a demise like you've never seen. You felt worthless, so the way you drowned it and got rid of it was by getting drunk. When I was seven, I got caught drinking the rot-gut whiskey out of an oil can, so a friend started calling me 'Oil Can.' Soon everybody's calling me 'Oil Can,' and it really stuck."

"What do you think happened to all the great nicknames?" I ask. "You never hear any anymore."

"Again, that came with the flair of the African American player, which is now missing from the game," Boyd says. "A few white guys had cool nicknames, like 'Smoky Joe' Wood, Walter 'the Big Train' Johnson, or 'Boo' Ferriss, but those white ballplayers came from the South. You very seldom had a ballplayer from California or Massachusetts that had a nickname. In the South people usually have two things: a sense of humor and a nickname. Ain't nobody funnier than a person from the South. I don't care what kind of comedian you are. Two-thirds of Black comedians are from the South, or their mom is from down there. It's built into you. It's where the great nicknames came from. And it goes with baseball better than anything you could ever imagine."

"Like 'Cool Papa' Bell or Hank 'the Hammer' Aaron," I say.

"Exactly," Boyd says. "Aaron hammered the baseball. Or Willie Mays, who was a very gentle, speak-to-everybody kind of cat, would say, 'Hey, kid'—and he became the 'Say Hey Kid.' It's just one of the things that has been taken away from the game. When I taught little league baseball a number of years ago back in Mississippi, I gave all my kids on the team nicknames. Some of them are now in college—and that's what they're being called by. They get asked where they got their nicknames, and they'll say from Oil Can Boyd. One might say, 'Can called me "Moose" or something like that. It just needs to come back and be part of the game again."

"Nineteen eighty-six was, by all accounts, a terrific season for you and the Red Sox, but it wasn't without some rough spots," I say. "If not for getting suspended for twenty-one games, you would have . . ."

Oil Can quickly cuts me off and finishes my sentence: "Yep, I would have won twenty games," Boyd, who won sixteen, says. "And I should've won five of my ten losses. I'm not bullshitting."

Yet what could have been an epic season of personal accomplishments was stymied by a suspension after Oil Can went into a tirade following an All-Star Game selection snub by Kansas City Royals manager Dick Howser.

"It was personal," Boyd tells me, still clearly agitated over it. "It had *nothing* to do with baseball. If it was about baseball, I would've been pitching. It was my personality that got passed around baseball without certain people knowing me. I always felt shunned when it came to everything. It extends from me being 'pro-Black' opinionated. But if you grew up where I did, you had a lot to be upset about. And I don't just have opinions on things; I've got great opinions. So anything I heard that I didn't like, I had a problem with that—and that gets around. That didn't first happen in 1986 but happened when I first signed a professional contract. Right away I would hear things like, 'He's going to be hard to deal with.' And [coaches] would say to other Black players, 'If y'all become like him, you'll never play again, but he has to play because he's great, and we'll let him act like that.' And I did get away with it because I could pitch better than most everybody else. If I didn't, I wouldn't have played one hour. Shit that happened with other Black players wasn't going to happen with me. Still some of them would tell me, 'You can't say that, Dennis.' And I'd go, 'We can't be ourselves?' Well, that's why some people left me off the All-Star team. They were like, 'He's a great baseball player, but . . .'"

Oil Can reflects for a moment, then shows his rage over what he saw as outright bigotry: "If I was the brown-nosing-est, ass-kissing-est brother like I saw one of them be, I wouldn't have had any problems whatsoever! But I told them, 'Motherfucker, do you know where I grew up at?! Do you understand what I grew up doing?! Yeah, I'm old enough to name myself a 'water fountain fool.' I'm old enough to remember when a sign said, 'Colored right there—whites over there.' Do you understand that shit? Do you know I grew up hearing my dad called a 'boy' in front of his kids? When's he going to be a man? He's got seventeen children, and he ain't no man?"

Perhaps Boyd's outburst has something to do with a promise he made to his father years before: "I told my dad when I signed a contract, 'Dad, I'm going to make sure that everybody regrets that they did that shit with you.' But here's the thing: people that knew me have always understood me. A white man, probably about eighty, told me just last night in Taunton, 'You changed my whole life. I was the happiest man in the world just watching you pitch. You did it so special and so unique and with so much confidence that it was remarkable to watch you play.' Anyway, Howser and those guys didn't understand me, so I got snubbed from the All-Star Game."

"Despite the suspension and the controversy surrounding it," I note, "you finished the year strong—winning the division title-clinching game and then saving the season by winning Game Six of the ALCS with Boston one loss away from elimination—a lose-and-you-go-home scenario. So now it's the World Series, and you're slated to start Game Seven against the Mets. But it's postponed due to rain, and Mac goes with Hurst instead of you. How did you respond to the news, and in retrospect do you think about what could've been had you pitched and won the game to end the sixty-eight-year 'curse'?"

"Well, it changed my whole career," Boyd says rather somberly. "And it changed everything about how I felt about the game of baseball. First and foremost my ego got kicked in a little bit. I was thinking for that game, 'I'm the best pitcher on the staff—and that's including our Cy Young Award winner.'"

"Roger?" I ask quizzically.

"*Damn right!*" Boyd responds emphatically. "[Clemens] will tell you that. I ain't never been passed over for nobody to pitch before me. That's the first time that ever happened in my life. I've always been the one that they put in there to make sure things went well, so it really bothers me still to this day that I was passed over. That's hard to live with. I ain't second to nobody at this shit. Try being Black coming from Mississippi and being the only Black ballplayer in 160 years to pitch for the Boston Red Sox—so how good am I?! And you're going to take this shit away from me? No team had ever beaten me back-to-back games. I might've lost against a team, but then I'm beating you the very next game. If I had started Game Seven, I feel we would've been world champs. I definitely feel like that because I pitched well in my first start [in Game 3]; I pitched the last part of that ballgame like I should have pitched the beginning of it."

"Yeah, you had a rough first inning, but then after that . . ."

"After that I retired eighteen of the next nineteen hitters!" Boyd says, finishing my sentence. "That decision [to remove me from Game 7] didn't even come from John McNamara, and I didn't find that out until the next year. That decision came from the trainer, Charlie Moss. He told me personally that he recommended for me not to pitch. It was in early February in '87 at spring training, before we had to report. I was in Florida at the time, so I lived at the ball park. He came up to me behind the backstop and said, 'Can, can I talk to you?' I said, 'Yeah, yeah, what you need, Charlie?' He said, 'You know why you didn't pitch Game 7?' I said, 'What do you mean? What are you talking about?' Charlie said, 'I'm the one who told them I didn't think you were ready.' And that's all he said."

"Didn't think you were ready?" I ask rhetorically. "You had one day's rest more than Hurst did."

"Yeah," Boyd says slowly, with a dejected look in his eyes. "It's a goddamn shame."

Not buying Charlie Moss's reasoning, I bring up to Oil Can what I thought the reason could have been, knowing full well it might open an old wound.

"You don't have to answer this," I say delicately, "but do you think your not starting Game Seven had anything to do with your smoking marijuana before games?"

Boyd doesn't hesitate. "I smoked pot since I was five years old—every damn day of my life," Oil Can confesses. "And at that time I was fighting cocaine too. I was fighting it the whole year that I won sixteen games, so what the fuck? I wasn't just fighting it that day. I was fighting that shit from the time I put on a Red Sox uniform—from the first day I signed."

"Well, maybe that was the reason," I say.

"A mixture of that and a few other things—like me being suspended," Boyd theorizes. "And then the idea of me coming back to be the winner of the [decisive game] of the World Series was another. For me to be the hero after I done got suspended, didn't get picked for the All-Star team, had a fit, quit the fucking game, threatened to go home and not play no goddamn more, told the whole fucking Major Leagues to kiss my Black ass—this was the way not to let me be the hero. To me that's the reason I didn't start that game."

I offer another hypothesis: "What if they'd said to you something like, 'Hurst won the other two games he pitched against the Mets, so . . .'"

"They *tried* to say that," Boyd interjects. "They said he pitched so well against them. But in actuality Bruce would tell you that Dennis should've pitched that ballgame because I'm the man you put out there to take care of business. Bruce felt like that about me and Roger; they all did. Everybody on the team knew I would've beat the Mets—without a question. All of them that have answered the question, 'What do you think if Oil Can had pitched that night?' have said I would've won. Every last one of them. Marty Barrett was the first one who said it, saying, 'Dennis knows how to beat you. He's not pressured, nothing bothers him, and he's just too good of a pitcher.'

"Again, the real reason was that whole suspension shit and how it would've been the biggest redemption for me personally to come back and be the winning pitcher of the World Series. I come back and win that game, and I *own* Boston. I love Bruce. He was a good pitcher. He did well to beat them twice. He pitched his ass off to get those two wins. But that's the New York Mets, a Major League baseball team. It was going to be hard as hell to beat them three times. *C'mon!* They're going to make adjustments. It was going to be tough to get through that lineup with all the right-handed hitters and with Darryl

Strawberry and the rest of those cats, man. You're not going to be able to pitch them like you pitched in the first two games, and your shit ain't going to get no better than it was. They're going to hammer the ball, and they did."

"So how exactly did it go down?" I ask. "How did McNamara deliver the news to you that you weren't starting, and how did you react?"

"He told me at the hotel that I wasn't pitching," Boyd begins. "I said, 'I'm not *what*?!' And he didn't even tell me that if Bruce got into any trouble, I would be the first one in. As it turned out, I didn't even pitch that game—period. So after talking with [McNamara], I walked right out of the hotel in New York City, by myself, to a dangerous neighborhood and bought some drugs."

"Uptown?" I ask.

"Yeah, with a gun," Boyd says.

"You had a *gun*?" I inquire incredulously.

"I had a gun," Boyd confirms. "You could bring a gun in your luggage. It ain't like that today. When I think about it all, even today, it still makes me cry. It changed my career completely."

"How exactly did it change your career?" I ask.

"Well, that's the other part of it. Even though I played five years after that, I should've played ten more. But getting [snubbed] changed my whole career and personal opinions about me throughout baseball. Many people shunned me and didn't give me an opportunity to play no more just from that one Series."

"How did your teammates react to your outrage?" I ask. "In other words who were your allies on the club?"

"I loved them all," Boyd says, smiling. "But none more than Geddy—that's my brother. I had a special way with him from the first day—just something about him. He appreciated me as a person, and I could see it, I could feel it, when he talked to me. Shit, he knew he could come and talk to me no matter how I was. I could be in a fucking rage, and he'd come over, put his arm around me, and calm me down. He had that way with me. Yeah, Geddy's my man."

"I wanted to touch on your marijuana use," I begin. "You've stated that there wasn't a game that you pitched in the big leagues—214 in all—that you weren't on weed. Did you pitch better because of it?"

"No question," Boyd confirms. "But like I said, it didn't start in the Major Leagues. It started in eighth or ninth grade. I recognized the benefits when I was a kid. Some people might say, 'Well, shit, you was a great pitcher anyway.' And I'll say, 'Naw, man, you wouldn't believe what this shit made me think. When I got on the mound, I became invincible. My shit became the best shit that ever could be thrown up to the plate. I didn't just have control—I had *command*. The things I thought about when I was on the mound, whatever I wanted to do—I would do."

"It almost sounds like you're saying you may not have made the Major Leagues . . ."

"*Without it!*" Boyd exclaims, again finishing one of my sentences. "No question about it. In college that's how we got prepared. All my teammates in college—we all smoked. They weren't going up to bat unless they got 'blazed up.' Now they could hit shit all over the field because they were thinking, 'Yeah, man! I can do anything!'"

"I assume you've talked to Bill "Spaceman" Lee about this?"

"Oh yeah! Oh yeah!" Boyd says excitedly. "We talk about it the same way. He said, 'Can, they don't know what they're missing.' I said, 'I know, Billy. They don't realize how good they would've been!'"

"I've heard it can give you tunnel vision and better concentration," I add.

"When I was high, I didn't hear the fans," Boyd explains. "I didn't know they were there. I didn't hear them clap—didn't hear shit. I was so focused that it was like I was just out there by myself. Soon as I didn't smoke, I heard everything and didn't like it. I needed that quiet."

"I did a book with the '86 Mets and had a lengthy conversation with Doc Gooden that included a revealing talk about his cocaine use and how it affected his life," I say.

"Good man," Boyd interjects. "He's struggling now. I know. I've seen him."

"Did your struggle with cocaine ever reach the level that his did?" I ask.

"It did, but my mentality and how I grew up was different from his," Boyd confides. "I decided I didn't want this drug anymore and wasn't going to let it kill me. [Cocaine] is there to kill you. It's not for enjoyment. It's not for recreation. It's for incarceration and death. That's what comes with it. You might get incarcerated first and then die from it. Both of them are going to happen if you fuck around with it. I ain't going to say that Doc doesn't have things to live for. Yes, he does. He's got everything to live for. But you need a different mentality. When you get control of the way you go, then you're all right. Any time I had to fight with that, I had to worry. When I was in the phase that Doc is in, I was also drinking. You had to watch when you drank because once it got dark outside, you better be home. I started learning that, and that's how I started weaning myself off of [cocaine]. I knew that if I had a couple of beers, I needed to go home—*and I made myself go home.* The more you make yourself do that, the more you'll do it. That's how I got away from it. I wanted to live for me—not for my kids, not for my family. Now my family is so happy because I want to live for them, too."

"Is there still temptation?" I ask.

"I just make sure that I don't put myself in harm's way," Boyd says confidently. "I done learned how to [do that] over the years. When people out there say, 'Hey, you want to do a line, my man?' I've learned to tell them, 'Y'all knock yourself out; I'm good. I don't want to die. That shit'll kill you.'"

"Even now—people still offer you that stuff?" I ask.

"Yeah, but what I can do now is turn people down. I couldn't do that five years ago. You see what I'm saying? Now it's easy to turn them down, and it's actually fun. It makes you feel good about yourself when you turn it down."

"You're in control?" I ask.

"Yeah, yeah, I even laugh about it," Boyd says, grinning. "However, I make sure that I don't cross the line of being a hypocrite. But by telling them 'That shit will kill you' in such a way, I'm helping people without saying to a grown man or woman that they shouldn't be doing this. It's like being a psychologist or doing the Jedi mind trick or some shit. But it's working for me. I think about guys I knew like Otis Nixon and his struggles with cocaine. Ken Caminiti is another—dead from it. I think about a lot of people."

"Can, it's evident that through all the peaks and valleys in your life the one constant has been your love of baseball," I say. "So what do you miss the most about pitching in the Majors and with the Red Sox?"

"I still play the game," Boyd says enthusiastically, "so I don't miss the game. But I do miss the camaraderie of the fans that I met and the other ballplayers. I think about them all when I get a chance to reminisce. I also miss the smell of the grass and the red clay and eating Jolly Ranchers. All my teeth fell out because of that. It's a wonder any ballplayers got any teeth because of all the junk we put in our mouths. We'd be on the bench with a pocketful of Jolly Ranchers like we were two years old. Damned toothache's been hurting ever since then!"

Oil Can lets out a big chuckle, before continuing: "But there's a lot of great things I miss, Erik. I miss more than I don't miss, and that's why I stay around the game all the time. I teach the game, I like playing the game, and I like the benefits that come from the game—the little perks here and there to go to a Major League game. I go there as a fan—to watch the fucking game. The ambience is real good. I like seeing the young ballplayers and seeing how every generation has the love and passion for the game. A player like Dustin Pedroia makes you love baseball. I have to see Pedey play—not so much for his amazing talent, which he has, but the way he loves the game like I do. And I love the elements—the outfield wall, the ballpark smell. It's a very unique smell at a ballpark—the food that is being cooked, the sausages and burgers and the pizza. Ballpark food is the best food in the world. I love eating at ballparks. Then there is the feel of a Major League baseball. It feels different than any other. And at the Major League level everything is top of the line—from the gloves to the balls to the bats to the spikes that they wear and use. It's just different from anything else, and it reminds you how special it all is—and how baseball is the best shit ever invented."

Boyd then gives me a mischievous glance and grabs hold of my right forearm before making one exception: "The best shit invented *besides weed*! I think everybody in the league would agree!"

Oil Can howls with laughter. He's enjoyed our visit—almost as much as baseball and marijuana!

1. Bill Buckner in a Queens, New York, restaurant during the last major interview of his life. Despite a near Hall of Fame career and a life exemplified by great courage, Buckner was subjected to misguided blame by the casual fan and media for the Red Sox's losing the '86 World Series. The ridicule left a scar on Buckner that never completely went away. Photo by author.

2. Roger Clemens at Fenway Park, where his superstardom began. Many of his '86 Red Sox teammates point to the Rocket's twenty-strikeout performance early that season as the turning point that made them believe they could win a championship. Clemens won both the Cy Young and MVP Awards that year and would quickly establish himself as the greatest pitcher of his generation. Photo by author.

3. (*opposite top*) Hall of Famer Jim Rice at the Red Sox's spring training facility at JetBlue Fenway South ballpark in Fort Myers, Florida. In his prime Rice was the most feared hitter in Major League Baseball. After a long and contentious relationship with the Boston media, today he is one of them, working as a NESN studio analyst before and after Red Sox games. Photo by author.

4. (*opposite bottom*) Wade Boggs stands proudly in front of some of his personal baseball memorabilia at his Tampa, Florida, residence. A first-ballot Hall of Famer and one of the greatest hitters in baseball history, the superstitious twelve-time All Star won five batting titles and finished his career with a .328 batting average. Photo by author.

5. (*above*) Oil Can Boyd at Pawtucket's McCoy Stadium. His flamboyance—and success—on the mound for the Red Sox were reminiscent of those of his hero, Satchel Paige. Often misunderstood for his outspoken nature and countercultural ways, he was widely regarded as one of the most astute players on the club. Photo by author.

6. Rich Gedman at an indoor batting cage at McCoy Stadium. A local kid and Boston fan all his life, his dream of making the club was realized in the early '80s. Despite all the highlights of the '86 season, to this day he still carries pain because of the way it ended. Geddy now works as the hitting coach for the Red Sox's Triple-A club. Photo by author.

7. (*opposite top*) Spike Owen at Grainger Stadium in Kinston, North Carolina, where he recently managed the Down East Wood Ducks of the Carolina League. Owen was acquired with Dave Henderson from the Seattle Mariners in one of the greatest late-season trades in Red Sox history in 1986. Spike would lead all Red Sox hitters with a .429 batting average in the '86 ALCS. Photo by author.

8. (*opposite bottom*) Hall of Famer Tom Seaver at his beloved Diamond Mountain vineyard in Calistoga, California, where he produced his award-winning cabernet. His mentoring of young Red Sox pitchers like Clemens and Hurst after his midseason acquisition in '86 helped them immeasurably down the stretch. Photo by author.

9. Bob Stanley, who was recently the pitching coach for the Buffalo Bisons, in the visitors' dugout at McCoy Stadium. Despite a largely successful thirteen-year stint with the Red Sox, his wild pitch in Game Six of the '86 World Series was, unfairly, the focal point of his career. But a strong sense of humor and his young son's recovery from cancer helped put the importance of baseball into proper perspective. Photo by author.

10. Dwight Evans—with the right field of Fenway Park, which he manned for nineteen seasons, directly behind him—managed to have a superb all-around baseball career despite dealing with the serious health issues of his two sons. The youngest, Justin, would lose his battle with neurofibromatosis in 2019. The Evans family's strong faith and spirituality have helped navigate them through the most difficult of times. Photo by author.

11. Marty Barrett at his home office in Somerlin, Nevada. In a Red Sox lineup loaded with stars, it was the reliable, situational-hitting Barrett who would tie a World Series record for most hits in a Series. A brilliant baseball man, he was everybody's choice on the club to one day become a big league manager, but instead he traded the grind of travel during the season to stay close to home with his family. Photo by author.

12. Steve Lyons outside of his Hermosa Beach, California, townhouse. The versatile Lyons, a Red Sox fan while growing up in Oregon, was traded for Tom Seaver midway through the '86 campaign, missing out on his dream of playing postseason baseball for the Red Sox. But it was as a color analyst at the network level that Lyons would make his biggest mark on the game. Today he's a studio analyst at NESN. Photo by author.

13. Bruce Hurst near his home in Phoenix, Arizona. After mastering a split-fingered fastball five years into his big league career, Hurst became an outstanding pitcher for the Red Sox. In '86 he went 5-0 in September, then earned a victory over the Angels in the ALCS before beating the Mets twice in the World Series. Photo by author.

14. Calvin Schiraldi in his Austin, Texas, home, standing alongside his Red Sox jersey and a framed *Boston Herald* trumpeting him in the pennant-winning game he closed against the Angels. Schiraldi established himself as a dominant closer down the stretch in '86 but couldn't get the final out in Game Six of the World Series, a setback that would overshadow an otherwise stellar campaign. Following his playing career, he began coaching high school ball at St. Michael's Catholic Academy in Austin, where he still manages today—and where he has won over three hundred games. Photo by author.

6.

The New Englander

There's pain that I carry. . . . I'd just really appreciate this game so much more if I hadn't gone through the pains of '86.

—RICH GEDMAN

T he popping sound of batted balls reverberates inside a batting cage within the bowels of McCoy Stadium. Young Red Sox hopefuls take their swings in preparation for that afternoon's game. Standing to the right side of the cage and studying intently the hitting tendencies of his Triple-A Red Sox pupils is Rich Gedman, the bespectacled Pawtucket hitting coach and former Red Sox catcher throughout the entire decade of the eighties.

"The guys are treated somewhat like automobiles," he tells me. "I'm like, 'Here's what you need. This is the gas you need to put in. This is what needs to happen, and this is how it's going to happen. This is the workout. You have one of your hips that has to do this, and you have to strengthen it so that you have better balance in your body.' I take care of them. I make sure they're doing the things they need to do to have the best chance to get to the big leagues."

Called "Geddy" by most every player in the facility, he resembles the kind of coach any Triple-A player would die for: a two-time All-Star and postseason hero with an approachable, mild-mannered nature used in teaching the right way to play the game.

As I would find out on this early summer morning, Geddy is an uncharacteristically sensitive soul for a catcher of his era, in which collisions at the plate and the occasional calling of a purpose pitch were part of the game. And it's perhaps in part for this reason that he still carries a special kind of pain from the '86 World Series and then from sitting out the beginning of the following season in a contract dispute, a period that began the slide of what had been a stellar career to that point.

But then there is this: Gedman, more than any other of his '86 teammates, "got" what it meant to be a Red Sox player, having lived and died with the club throughout his youth.

"You know, I always compared [playing at Fenway] like it was Disneyland," the Worcester native tells me with a gleam in his eye, as we sit down and begin chatting at a nearby table. "You watch Disney [shows] as a kid, and you go into that fantasy world. It's not real life. It was the same with the Red Sox. In the backyard as a kid, you're Carl Yastrzemski, you're Carlton Fisk, you're Reggie Smith, you're Rico Petrocelli, you're Jim Lonborg, and you're Luis Tiant. You try to be like them; you emulate them. You have their stances, their windups. Baseball with the Red Sox means a lot in New England, and it was so wonderful to grow up following it."

Growing up a Red Sox fan during the period he did meant knowing all too well the Game Seven World Series losses in '67 and '75. It meant enduring the pain of watching his Sox blow a fourteen-game lead to the Yankees in '78. But all the grief and disappointment only fueled his desire to be a part of a Red Sox club that would one day win it all.

"You've traveled around the country," I point out. "Having grown up in the Boston area, can you speak to the passion the Red Sox fans have that might be different from other cities?"

Geddy doesn't hesitate, bringing up perhaps the most heated rivalry in American sports: "I think you either loved the Red Sox or you just hated the Yankees," he says with a grin. "Growing up a Red Sox fan, I thought *everybody* around me was a Red Sox fan. If one of my high school teammates said they liked the Yankees, I would be like, 'Screw you! I'm not even sure I want you on my team.' It was a hate—a misguided hate—or a misunderstanding of what the rivalry meant. Then as I grew older, it wasn't hate; it was respect. The Yankees had a different way of doing things and did it over and over again to win all those championships. But even when both teams had losing seasons, Yankee–Red Sox games always meant something more for a New England kid. If you didn't grow up here, you don't really understand quite what it's like."

Thus it was a great twist of irony that Geddy's first big league manager with the Red Sox was the legendary Yankee catcher and three-time World Series skipper Ralph Houk, who compared Rich with an iconic Yankee backstop: Thurman Munson, who Rich rooted strongly against as a kid.

"You grew up with that whole bitter Munson-Fisk rivalry," I say. "How did Houk's comparison to Thurman make you feel?"

Appreciating the greatness of Munson, Gedman takes Houk's assessment of his abilities to reminisce about the encouragement his former manager gave him early in his career: "Ralph was a man I didn't appreciate as much as I should have when I was with him," Geddy says with a sigh. "He was so good to me. One of the most important things he said to me was in 1981 after a series at Yankee Stadium. My batting average was .059. While walking in the airport to our plane, he put his arm around me and said, 'You know something, kid? You're going to be okay. Your hits are going to come in bunches like bananas.' I looked at him and was so relieved. It was like I got a new breath of fresh air—that I wasn't going to be penalized for struggling offensively. I really took off and hit well after that. That's all it took—nothing complicated. Just three sentences from somebody I held in high esteem saying that I was going to be all right. Obviously the vote of confidence had an impact, or I wouldn't remember it word for word all these years later."

At that very moment a young player—maybe only twenty-one or twenty-two—comes over and asks Rich if he has a minute to talk. The two walk a few steps away—out of earshot—and it looks just like a father talking to a son, with the player nodding and then grinning as he walks back toward the cage as Gedman yells over to him, "Have some fun today!" Perhaps it was Geddy giving the kid some reassurance, much in the way Houk had given some to him more than three decades earlier that day at the airport.

When Geddy comes back to the table, I convey my observation about his father-figure image around the players.

"They're actually at the age of my two sons," he says.

"Well, you're obviously very approachable," I observe.

"I would say more times than not," Geddy remarks, before volunteering what it takes for these kids to make the jump to the big leagues: "I don't think this game is black and white. I don't think you can judge a book by its cover. Some of the guys with a lot of talent that you think are going to get to the Majors, don't—or they get there but don't stay. Then with others with lesser talent, there is just something about them that you think, 'He's going to get there and stay there for a long time. He may not have what these other guys have, but there's a mental toughness there that's going to get him through. I'll take him in a heartbeat because he's dependable, he's reliable, he listens, he's smart, and he's tough.' Baseball is a tough, grinding game. You have to be hard-nosed.

"As for my job," Geddy continues, "I try to make things seamless. I give them whatever they need to work, however much work they need, and tell them what their approach should be. I continue to recognize their strengths but work on their weaknesses."

Listening to Geddy talk, I think he would be a natural to manage or coach at the Major League level. First and foremost, former catchers tend to do well as managers in the way they handle pitching staffs and call games. In Rich's case, since he previously managed independent league ball before his current decade-long stretch in the Red Sox organization as a coach, it would at least seem feasible. I bring this possibility up to Gedman, and his initial response is quick and dismissive.

"My years are short," he says, acquiescing to the idea that it's become a younger manager's game. "I realize that fifty-seven is a lot younger than it was twenty years ago, but I don't know if I'm made for that. I try to see things fairly simply. When I make it complicated, it gets a little blurry for me. I really enjoyed managing independent baseball—it was fun—but one of the things I don't do is talk enough. It's partly because I'm always worried about what I might say wrong as opposed to what I might say right. When I talk baseball, it seems very clear to me until somebody rebuts what I just said, and I go, 'Wait a second; this is how I feel, so I'm right.' A few years back it was something I thought I would like to do, but now I really find myself in the trenches. I think that's where I'm best, where I can share some of my career, my thoughts, and my understanding of what it's like to go through what the person I'm talking to is going through."

And perhaps there is no one in the Red Sox organization who can convey the highs and lows of baseball better than Gedman. He experienced it all first hand—on a historical level—in 1986.

Rich Gedman had a premonition that he couldn't explain. It was Opening Day, 1986, and the Red Sox were coming off a disappointing fifth-place finish. They were about to start the season before a sellout crowd in Detroit against a Tigers team just a year removed from one of the most dominating championship campaigns in baseball history. The starting pitcher for the Tigers that day would be their future Hall of Famer, Jack Morris. The odds were stacked against Boston.

"Before the game," Geddy recalls, "I was sitting on the warning track, waiting for a cage underneath the center-field stands to be opened. It's almost like I saw the season happen right before my eyes, and I'm thinking, 'I don't know how we're going to do it, but I just have a feeling this could be something special.' And then Dewey [Dwight Evans] hits the first pitch of the game for a home run off Morris, one of the great pitchers of his time. We hit four home runs off him that day."

One of those home runs would be hit by Gedman himself, and despite the Sox's 6–5 loss that day, Rich had an epiphany: "I thought, 'If they're one of the best teams and that's the best they've got, we can play with them. We can play with anybody.' And as the season went along, we obviously did pretty well. It seemed like in every series we'd take two out of three or three out of four. Then we put together a streak in early September, winning eleven in a row, and put it away. It was one of those magical times where everything you thought could happen, did."

"That was also the year that Roger Clemens broke out 14-0," I say. "And of course that included his twenty-strikeout game against the Mariners. Now I know you're a modest guy, but as his catcher, you certainly had a lot to do with his success in the way you called games. What was it that made Roger so special during that marquee season of his magnificent career?"

Gedman, still very close with Clemens to this day, doesn't hesitate: "One, I think when he first came on the scene that year, people already had high expectations of him. And then when you start off 14-0 and you strike out twenty guys in just your fifth start of the season, people are going, 'This is a Red Sox pitcher who we need to come watch!' Roger was magical. It was incredible what he was doing. Here's a young kid who had the poise and determination of a wily veteran. He had this great competitive edge that he would find every time he was out there. And you knew not to mess with him on the day he was going to pitch because he was so focused."

Gedman then pauses and begins reflecting on the importance of how he and the three primary starting pitchers came up through the Red Sox organization: "Clemens became the leader of our pitching staff, with everybody following in behind him because we'd all been in the organization, and there was a wonderful bond that was created together. Bruce Hurst and Clem were very friendly. Oil Can as well. Us four guys plus some of the infielders and outfielders—all organization guys. They knew the aches and pains of the team's history. They knew the stories about the failures that we faced in September. But we would turn out to be different in '86, and it was wonderful. We had a really special group with a tremendous amount of talent."

"What about the personalities on that staff you had?" I ask rhetorically. "You couldn't have had any three more different types of people than Clemens, Hurst, and Boyd."

"Each was driven by different things," Geddy says. "Bruce felt that he had a responsibility to uphold the standards of being a Mormon. Oil Can was fighting for the rights of the Black man in Massachusetts, driven by the pains of his childhood. And Roger, a kid from Texas, came to Boston with a 'me-against-the-world, I've got something to prove' kind of mentality. All three wonderful people in their own way."

It would be those three pitchers with their battery mate Gedman, along with a deep, punishing lineup, that would lead Boston to its first ALCS in eleven years.

When baseball historians evaluate the greatest games in post-season history, Game Five of the 1986 ALCS between Boston and the California Angels would have to be near the top of everyone's list. Without much fanfare no Red Sox player played a bigger role in that epic game than Gedman.

"Everyone remembers the home runs by Donnie Baylor and Dave Henderson," I begin. "But you reached base *all five times* you came to the plate, including a two-run homer in the second inning and a hit-by-pitch in the ninth to set up Hendu's two-out home run. You're a guy who had hit for the cycle in '85, driving in seven runs in that game. But that Game Five may have eclipsed the cycle game, wouldn't you say?"

"For what was on the line, sure," Geddy says. "Lose that game, and we were done. We somehow had to find a way to stem the tide—win a *tough* game that allowed us to keep a series going to get home. And that was the thing: let us get home because if we could, we knew we could win [the series]."

Ever humble, Gedman downplays his contribution to the epic Game Five comeback: "It wasn't any *individual* performance," he says. "It was a *team* performance. It wasn't, '*I* had a good day.' It was, '*Everybody* on the field did something to make a difference in that game.' It was just one of those days where you're going, 'It could have gone either way, and the guys who could have made it happen, did.' Certainly the brightest light of all on that day was Dave Henderson. He had the ability to grab hold of the moment. And of course Don Baylor and his home run in the ninth, as well. If you look at the pitches that they both hit for home runs, [those pitches] had no business going out of the ballpark. They were just big, strong gentlemen that made a miracle happen."

"Numerous times I've heard other ballplayers say that when you win a game like that one, momentum shifts strongly to your side," I say. "What about you? Did you think to yourself, 'The series is ours now'?"

"Only if you execute," Geddy explains. "There is no question there is such a thing as momentum. But what happened is the Angels never got a chance to get back in it. Our guys never let up. We were not ahead of ourselves. When we got back to Fenway, it wasn't like, 'We got to win the series.' It was, 'We got to win the next game. Stay in the moment.'"

The Red Sox never let the Angels back up off the mat, winning consecutive blowout games in Boston to capture the American League pennant. But it was that comeback-for-the-ages in Game Five that proved to be the turning point in the series and easily the most devastating defeat in Angels franchise history. Little could anyone imagine that just thirteen days later Boston, in an almost eerily similar circumstance, would suffer the same fate against the Mets as the Angels had to the Red Sox.

"Painful to think about," Gedman says with a degree of sadness when talk turns to Game Six of the '86 World Series.

"Did losing the way the Red Sox did in the World Series take anything away from the euphoria you felt less than two weeks before from the Angels series?" I ask.

Geddy gives a pregnant pause to ponder the question. "No," he says. "It gave perspective. You're going, 'I can't imagine what it was like for [the Angels], only to have it turn around and have it happen to you.' So now there was empathy for their side. Getting there and being on the verge of winning—to be so close. I'm still dealing with it today."

"You're still dealing with it after all these years?" I ask.

"Yeah, and it's partly because of where I grew up," Geddy says, now even more somber. "There's pain that I carry. My personality's changed because of it, but I think for the better. It's made me a better person in a way too. Maybe a little too subdued because I wear it. I carry it with me. Some people are different; they can get over it. I'd just really appreciate this game so much more if I hadn't gone through the pains of '86. It took me a long time to even be able to talk about it. I didn't even want to talk about it because I watched how it fractured teammates. How people were ruthless. It's like, 'Whoa. I know it means something to you, but you're reacting to this the wrong way.' Like the hatred toward Bill Buckner. He's a human being; if you watched him get on the field every day, you'd understand the love that he has for this game. We played for each other. We did not play to fail."

Geddy looks away toward the batting cages to gather his thoughts before making another point: "People will tell you today, 'You got to the seventh game of the World Series, and that's a great achievement.' But if you don't get through it and win, it's not the same. It's nice to be a part of it. It's nice to say that I was there. And some great players never get a chance to get there in the first place. But if you don't win it all, you'd rather finish last because of the shit you carry with you. You don't know if or when there will be a next time you're going to be [back in the World Series]. I wish I could express it to these guys here the way I'm talking to you because it's inside of me, but it's hard to get out."

"You bring up Buckner, someone I have really gotten to know well," I say. "The guy had 2,715 career hits. A batting title. A great glove at first base. And for many fans who don't know any better, the error at first in Game Six is all they remember about him."

Geddy doesn't think my take is so simple. "It's not that they don't know any better," he exclaims. "It's just how things get dramatized. They need this reason to blame somebody. But we didn't win or lose because of an individual. We lost as a group. Even then it became a fracture within the team. You sit there and you go, 'If he'd done this . . . If he'd done that . . .' But time out! That's the beauty of this game."

"To your point," I begin, "a number of things went wrong or were a bit off in Game Six for the Red Sox—and not just in that fateful tenth inning of Game Six. McNamara pulling Clemens after seven innings—Clemens was pitching a gem but nursing a blister—was one of them. As his catcher, did it seem like the right call to you at the time?"

Before answering, Geddy addresses all the controversy that McNamara's action raised in the time after that game, and he seems torn between his loyalty to McNamara and his friendship and admiration of Clemens, ultimately giving two views that basically contradict each other: "What I do recall is that it seemed like [McNamara's action was] something people used to fracture our club," he begins. "It was really kind of weird. In the weeks, months, and even years after the World Series the question continued on whether Roger opted out or if Mac pulled him. I don't know what happened in the decision. Mac said Roger asked out. I believe him. Mac said that Roger's finger was bothering him. I don't know really what to believe, except in my heart of hearts I know that Roger is the type of guy that wouldn't opt out. I know he wouldn't. And I love Mac to death because he's the one who gave me the opportunity to play every day."

Geddy leans back in his chair and sighs, trying to reconcile it all. "So I'm sitting here thinking, 'Well, knowing Mac, he's trying to protect Roger, but then he wasn't expecting Roger to say, "Oh yeah, I was fine."' Who do I believe? After it's all said and done, it really doesn't matter. In my opinion Mac was the man at the top and made the decision. And that's the way I was taught as a kid: if you're not the leader, you listen to the leader. You don't question him. He's doing what he thinks is best for the team."

"Again, if Clemens had stayed in that game with the way he was still throwing, do you, as his battery mate, believe the Red Sox would have won the World Series that night?" I ask.

"I'd like to think so, but we'll never know, right?" Gedman responds pragmatically. "It was a pretty magical year for Roger Clemens and the Red Sox. And he was our leader—the leader of our pitching staff, if you will. So you think there's no way that Roger's technically going to lose that game. But it's easy to say after the fact."

"I want to ask you about another bit of misfortune that night: the wild pitch that Bob Stanley threw to tie that game. I've talked to Marty Barrett about this, and he contends that Stanley got crossed up with what you were calling: an outside pitch that Bob threw inside. Was that what happened?"

"No, it was supposed to be in," Geddy says. "It was supposed to be in, but he went in too far. I'm not sure exactly what it did, but I couldn't get to it. I did get a glove on it. But you want to know what bothers me more than anything? If I had picked that ball up clean after it got away from me, [the runner, Kevin Mitchell] is out of there. I bobbled it just a hair. If I don't bobble it, I throw home, and he's out at the plate. No doubt in my mind."

"Marty also told me there was a pick-off play on with Ray Knight way off of second base—Knight represented the winning run—but that Bob didn't pick it up," I say. "And because of the pick-off play, Marty shaded over toward second and Buckner had to move a few steps away from first to cover some of Barrett's ground. Because of this, Buckner didn't have as much time to set himself for Mookie Wilson's ground ball, which ultimately went through his legs. Do you recall what happened there with the missed pick-off play?"

"I didn't see it," Geddy says. "With everything going on I wasn't focused on that. I was more concerned with the pitch at hand. But if Marty says [there was a play on], I believe him because that's the way he played. He could do a pick-off with just Steamer too, but I wasn't looking at [Barrett]. I was more concerned with Steamer [Bob Stanley], making sure he was okay. His dad had passed away earlier in the year. His dad. Boggs's mom. My dad and my sister both passed away during the '86 season as well. So there was emotion. There was serious emotion between me and Steamer. I said to him during that game, 'Our dads are watching this.' It was an emotional moment, and I was concerned it might be too much [for him]."

This is precisely the human element that fans miss or don't know anything about. While the untimely death of Boggs's mother was well publicized, the personal sorrow and heartbreak of Stanley and Gedman were relatively unknown to the public at large. The Mets, a team that had won a startling 108 games during the regular season, evidently weren't the only obstacles some of the Red Sox had to deal with during that World Series.

With everything on the line in Game Seven the Red Sox seemingly were able to put the heartbreaking Game Six defeat behind them, breaking out to a 3–0 lead with the help of second-inning home runs by Dwight Evans and Geddy. They were facing Ron Darling for the third time in the Series, a pitcher with whom Geddy had a particularly long history.

"We played at rival high schools in Massachusetts; I was a senior at St. Peter's, and Ron was a sophomore at St. John's," Gedman explains. "And here we were in Game Seven. It was unbelievable."

"Darling pitched a great Game One in a losing effort and then won the fourth game," I say. "But Game Seven was a lot different; the Red Sox hit him hard. Did seeing him a third time in a little over a week help you guys?"

"Pitching three times like that is hard for anybody to do," Geddy says. "It was the same with Bruce Hurst. They were seeing him for a third time too. It's not like [winning three games in a series] has never happened, but it's just hard to do. It's the mental part of it more than anything. It's almost like you feel as if you're playing against your buddies in the neighborhood now because you see them so much."

"Hurst really came on late in that '86 season through the postseason," I note. "He went from being the number three pitcher to number two behind Clemens and was arguably the best down the stretch. What do you think clicked for Hurst that maybe he didn't have in his first few years with the Red Sox?"

Geddy doesn't hesitate. "*Maturity*," he emphasizes. "Everything that happened up until [the end of '86] he had never experienced. But in the heat of the moment, in the most stressful of games, he was calm, cool, and collected. His feathers never got ruffled. He never looked nervous and never looked concerned. He was a pillar of strength, if you will. And that's the way he acted on the mound."

Listening to Gedman talk about Hurst, I couldn't help but make the comparison to Clemens. And like Clemens had been pulled in the previous game, I believed that Hurst may have been pulled too early in his Game Seven start.

"Rich, as you know, Bruce was terrific through his first five shutout innings of the final game," I begin. "So it still surprises me today that after he gave up three runs in the sixth, Mac went to the bullpen. I'm not second-guessing anyone here, but as his catcher, do you think he could have gone another inning or two?"

"Looking back—and I don't know if I'm right or wrong—I think he probably could have gone longer," Gedman says. "But I think with the strain of the Series, he gave us more than enough. He carried us to that point. But it's tough to say. I know he would have tried though."

After the Mets beat up on the Red Sox bullpen to pull away with an 8–5 victory and the world championship, Geddy and

Hurst walked over to the victorious Mets' clubhouse to congratulate their former teammate and friend Bobby Ojeda on winning his first title. Ojeda once told me it was 'the classiest move he ever saw in baseball.' I bring this up to Geddy, and he only recalls how happy he was for his comrade in arms.

"Oh, I guess since we couldn't win it and rejoice on our own, I was just so happy for Bobby," Gedman says. "It just sort of happened—a gut thing for both Bruce and me. It was something similar that Bob Boone, a player I really looked up to, did for us after the Angels series—and I didn't even know Bob that well. So to me it seemed like it was something you were supposed to do."

Things weren't supposed to turn out the way they did for Gedman. Perhaps no player in baseball deserved his fate less than the Boston catcher, who nurtured the club's splendid young starters in the rotation and who, from childhood, had always bled Red Sox red. But 1987 was an odd year in baseball, and there was a lot of head scratching going on that spring.

"You were one of the players who tested free agency at probably the worst possible time, a period when owners were colluding against their own players," I say. "Was there any bitterness with the unfairness of how all that went down for you that year?"

"It was more the mixed messages, the confusion of understanding how it was all happening," Gedman begins. "It was a trying time in the game and certainly was not something I ever expected to go through."

Geddy would rejoin the team after a holdout, and he struggled mightily to get back on track. He went from being an AL All-Star the previous two seasons to dropping off significantly in the '87 campaign and through much of his remaining four years with the team. Like the '86 World Series defeat it's an episode in his career with which he still seemingly battles today.

"I was probably trying too hard," Rich says introspectively. "But you asked if I was bitter. Actually I was angry. I don't know who I was angry at. Some of it was being angry at myself. My responsibility to my teammates became fractured. It looked like I was a selfish player. Sometimes, I guess, that's the way this game is. You are selfish, but you're not. When you're on the field, it's not about a contract; it's about relationships. It's about competing together. It's about being the best you can be for the guy next to you. And with [the holdout], it appeared like I was everything I was not. I guess I got embarrassed and got angry and didn't know what to feel or how to think. I felt all these emotions that I didn't even know the words for, and I couldn't explain it myself. And when I was out there on the field, I couldn't perform; I was distracted. I wasn't me. I could never find myself getting back to me either. I felt overexposed and didn't know what to do about it."

"In retrospect, is there anything you would have done differently?" I ask.

It was clear by his answer that Geddy had given this very question a good deal of contemplation: "Now when I talk to players and see them getting like I had gotten, I tell them, 'What you have is good enough. Don't look for more. Just play. Play and have fun. It's a game.' I know we're playing for a lot, but it's the other stuff that's just distracting. The game is pure. It's beautiful. It's a great game to play. You bust your hump, and it rewards you. You play with an edginess and you do things out of character. You overswing. You try to do more. Then, all of sudden, you're back watching baseball players play, and you notice a fluidity to their actions, especially the really good ones. Then you see that the difference between being really good and being so-so in this game is very small. And that's what happened to me. I wasn't a .220 hitter. I usually wavered around the .260–.270 area all the time. But all of a sudden you feel like you're in a hole and can't dig out of it. I'd think to myself, 'Gosh, what the heck's going on here?' That's the mental part of what was going on with me, and it wasn't pretty. And then I broke a foot and pulled a groin. I had never had a substantial injury before. And then you start thinking, 'I deserved this; I put it all on myself.' You start thinking crazy."

I try to assure Geddy that his teammates wouldn't have thought any less of him for testing the free agent market or holding out, as every ballplayer, no matter how much he loves the game, wants to do what's financially best for his family. After all, for most of them, time is so limited in baseball. But Rich seemed to infer he was different from others because of his devotion to the Red Sox organization.

"I wasn't going anywhere, and everybody knew it," he explains. "There's more to this story, but I wasn't going to Oakland. I wasn't going to Houston. I wasn't going to St. Louis. My thinking was I was going to be with the Red Sox my whole career. And why would I not want to be? It's like leaving your perfect job. It was an exercise of an option, my knowing that for the first time I may have leverage in the contract. But then, a year later, I lost on salary arbitration—something I wouldn't wish on anybody. My whole life had been in baseball, and I was so grateful and thankful for the opportunity the Red Sox gave me. So it was really hard on me."

Gedman would ultimately finish up his baseball career in the National League—a year in Houston and then his final two seasons in St. Louis. He has been out of the Majors since 1992. I ask him what he misses most from 'the Show.'

"I think what Willie Stargell used to say about playing for the Pittsburgh Pirates: that it's like a family," Gedman says with a smile. "Through thick and thin with the Red Sox, we were there for each other. You picked each other up; you watched over one another; you took care of each other. It was like you could do no wrong; your teammates, even the veteran players, appreciated your abilities and talents, your flaws, and your character. They loved you for who you were and understood you too. When we see each other for the first time in a long time, it's like we haven't skipped a beat. There were plenty of magic moments together that you remember and can sit and talk with them about. And you remember their faces, the way they were, how they acted, what you liked about them. That's the stuff that I miss."

Gedman then hints at why he believes the '86 team never returned to the World Series: "Aside from the players, we had some people on our coaching staff that were really special," he says. "And that's why I get so irritated when people tried to fracture us. That's why we probably never got to be what we were supposed to be. And we let it happen. Shame on us; shame on us. John McNamara, Bill Fischer, Rene Lachemann, and certainly one of my favorite people, Walter Hriniak, were there when we needed them and made us better."

Then, being the New Englander who has lived and died with the Red Sox his entire life, Geddy sums up how so many Boston fans feel about 1986: "Any team that gets that close like we did, it's disappointing. I guess now, looking back, you can see where the game's bigger than itself because of how many people it affected in New England. It's really a strange dynamic when you look at it. It's absolutely mind-blowing when you think about it. And, gosh, I was a part of that. It's really amazing to me. I have to pinch myself. At the time I didn't realize how big it was. Thank God I didn't know it as a kid. I would have been in real trouble!"

As the interview, which clearly was difficult for Geddy at times, concludes, he seems both relieved and thankful for getting so much off his chest. "I think you probably helped me be a better coach today, Erik," Gedman tells me, "because I said some things here that I haven't said to a lot of people. It really makes me appreciate what I get a chance to do every day and maybe even make an impact on someone else."

I smile at the comment and with all sincerity tell him, "For what it's worth, Rich, to me you will forever be that twenty-six-year-old catcher playing in the '86 World Series."

With that Gedman makes his way inside the cage to toss some batting practice to his guys. He needs to get back to making an impact on the next generation of Red Sox.

7.

For Love of the Game

....

With the Red Sox, you were totally mentally and physically exhausted
after every game, and it was awesome. It's the way it should be.
—SPIKE OWEN

With a laid-back Texas manner and easy smile,
Spike Owen is a happy man—and he should
be. He played shortstop in thirteen big league
seasons—including three in Boston from '86 to '88—has a loving family, and is the proud owner of a magnificent mansion
on thirty-nine acres of property on Barton Creek just outside of
Austin, Texas, that is valued north of $10 million. His sprawl-
ing estate features every modern convenience one could think
of—six bedrooms, five fireplaces, four living areas, three din-
ing spaces, a master study, a pool, a hot tub, and an outdoor
kitchen with a bar and grill. Spike lives the proverbial life of
Riley in his own Shangri-La.

But on this early spring morning we met far from the type of
luxurious living—in terms of both distance and decadence—
that Owen enjoys back home. As I drive through the neighborhoods of Kinston, North Carolina, to our meeting at Grainger
Stadium—the home ballpark for the Down East Wood Ducks
of the Carolina League—it is immediately apparent that the
town has seen better days. There are rows of abandoned homes
on several streets, and on another, four houses double as tiny
churches, perhaps offering spiritual hope to those struggling

below a poverty line that had recently climbed to 30 percent. A nearby school appears shut down, as tall weeds have sprung up between its pavement crevices. Many store fronts in the business district are either empty or in disrepair. And across the street from the seventy-year-old stadium itself, a fire station is regularly sounding its sirens (four times on average during games, according to Spike) to attend to various crises. All of this, however, doesn't even begin to take into account the hard life of a Minor League manager in even the best of environments—the long bus rides, the low salaries, and the countless hours under a hot sun working with young players.

Despite all of this, Owen, the manager of the Wood Ducks, approaches the table where I am waiting for him along the first base side of the grandstand, with a hop to his step, a smile on his face, and bottles of cold water in his hands, appearing like a man who wouldn't want to be in any other place than Kinston that day. It may not be Fenway Park, but it is, after all, still a professional baseball setting. And for Owen, now in his late fifties and trying to ultimately make it back to "the Show" as a coach or manager, that is good enough.

"After I officially retired in '96, I went back home to Austin to my wife and kids, and everything was great," Spike explains. "Being there for my kids when they were eight and nine years old in Little League, I would tell them to just go play and have fun. I wasn't trying to teach them to become Major Leaguers. And it was great being a dad and spending quality time with the family. But then after so many years of that, I was like, 'There's gotta be something more. I want to see if I can have an impact on people that I can help.' So I decided to get back in while I was still young enough. I just got tired of sitting at home, and it got easier [to leave home to coach] when the kids got older; it allowed me to branch out. Plus I was very fortunate that my first stint in coaching was with the Astros' organization in Round Rock, about forty-five minutes from my house. We went on the road obviously, but at least when we were home, I got to be with my family. And then I spent four years in the

Rangers' organization, which was also at Round Rock, as a third base and infield coach. So I haven't been roughing it that bad."

Spike would go on to point out that his greatest satisfaction has been seeing a bunch of the players he has either coached or managed make it to the big leagues. But he stops short in taking too much of the credit. "Players get themselves to the big leagues," Owen says. "As coaches and staff and managers, we want to try to facilitate [their gifts] as much as possible. But their talent gets them [there]; I tell them that all the time. We've had so many guys up there, and that's the fun part of being in the Minor Leagues. Take a guy like Ronald Guzman. I had him in A Ball in 2015, and three years later he's in the big leagues. That's obviously everybody's dream that's out here."

"You've had your own taste of the Major Leagues as a third base coach," I point out to Spike. "A few years ago in Texas Tony "Beas" Beasley began chemotherapy treatment when you managed the Rangers' A Ball team in Hickory. That was when you were called up to replace him for a period of time. Did that experience further drive your career aspirations in becoming either a full-time coach or manager in the big leagues?"

"Yes, absolutely," Spike says without hesitation. "But number one, I'm very thankful that Beas is back and healthy and doing good. That's not the type of situation that you want to necessarily make your big league debut in as a coach. But it was a really fun year, and I enjoyed coaching third base. It's intense, man; it's a lot more intense up there than it is here. I've now coached third for ten years—one year at the big-league level and nine years in the Minors. Obviously in the Minors when you're managing, you're still coaching third. But going back to what you were saying, I'd certainly like to get back there either as a coach or as what I'm doing here: managing. I'd love the opportunity to do it. But it seems like organizations are going in a little bit of a different way now as far as hiring managers [an allusion to the trend of appointing skippers lacking in managing experience]. I'm still down here in the 'bush' [leagues] banging it out. But you never know."

I then ask Spike if, of all the managers he's played under, there was one who had the greatest influence over how he manages today. Leaning back in his chair, he smiles and gives me a long, "Oh, man," an obvious expression that this is a tough question to answer, especially considering that he's had around twenty-five managers. He then proceeds to name many of them out loud: "Rene Lachemann, Del Crandall, Chuck Cottier, Dick Williams, Marty Martinez as an interim manager, John McNamara, Joe Morgan, Buck Rodgers, Tom Runnells, Felipe Alou, Buck Showalter."

But of all of the managers he had in the big leagues and giving special nods to Cottier, Rodgers, and Alou, he wants to talk about the one he went to the World Series with in 1986: "McNamara, in his own way, in his quietness, came up and talked to you, and he would do so in such a subtle way," Spike says. "He would just walk up to you, look at you, take his finger and point at you, and go, 'You can play.' Just something as little as that. And then he'd turn around and walk away. It wouldn't be like we're gonna carry on a conversation. But it was so important for him to build you up, especially in that Boston market. So from a standpoint of really just trying to instill confidence in my players, just a little ten-second deal telling them, 'You can play' or, 'You can do this' helps get their minds focused and confident. It makes them feel like you believe in them as a player."

Listening to Spike's passion for the game and for managing, and developing young players, I wonder aloud if there is anything he *didn't* like about managing.

"It comes with the territory, but the travel gets old real quick," he tells me. "That's the *one thing*. I think everybody around here appreciates the sacrifices that our wives and families make to allow us to do what we do; you can't overstate that. My wife is home in Austin, and there are times I wish I was back there."

Owen's Austin roots represent so much more to him than the area where he and his wife live today. The city is where teammate Don Baylor was born and raised and where Spike first played ball with fellow Texas University teammates Roger Clemens and Calvin Schiraldi. The four would come to be referred to as "the Austin Red Sox."

"Spike, early in the '86 season, before you were traded to Boston, your former teammate at Texas and future Austin Red Sox teammate Roger Clemens struck out twenty of your Seattle Mariners to set the all-time mark in a single game," I say. "What was it like facing your buddy Roger Clemens that night?"

"I was leading off, and when you're facing a former teammate and buddy, it kind of amps you up," Owen says enthusiastically. "His first pitch—the first pitch of the game—came up and in. Then [with] the second pitch he puts me on my back. So I was like, 'Okay, all right. Here we go!' But the thing that really hacked me off is that he comes back [from a 2-0 count] and punches me out. That kind of sent a little wake-up call to our dugout: everyone knew we were friends, but he *still* came up and in and knocked me down on the first two pitches."

Despite Clemens's dominance, Spike says he hardly realized it: "I had no idea he had that many strikeouts," Owen recalls. "That's because it was such a good ballgame. Mike Moore was pitching for us, and we were in a tie ballgame into the seventh inning and took a 1–0 lead until Dewey [Dwight Evans] hit a three-run homer into the net. So we were battling and trying to win the game. You hear how many strikeouts Roger had, and you're like, 'Oh man, they killed us.' But it was a very good ballgame."

"You were actually having a nice career in Seattle by '86," I say. "You had been there for four years by that point and had just been named team captain. Did you think you'd be a Mariner forever, or did you sense a trade was a possibility?"

"I was kind of in the mode of just being in Seattle my whole career," he says. "Like a lot of guys, you kind of want to be with the team that drafted you. But I'm very thankful that the Seattle organization gave me the opportunity it did. I was the first guy [the Mariners brought up] as part of a youth movement they had going on in '83. By '86 we had some really good young players, with an infield of Alvin Davis, Harold Reynolds, myself, and Jim Presley and outfielders like Hendu [Dave Henderson] and Phil Bradley. And our pitching—we had some good arms. If they had hung with us—the core of that team—for a few more years and added a few pieces, I've always wondered how good we could have become. But we went through so many managers during my first few years that when Dick Williams came in '86, I did kind of see the writing on the wall. As things happen in the game, rumors start swirling around, like, 'Hey, something's going down.' On the day of the trade my wife was waiting on me outside [the clubhouse] when, sure enough, [Williams] called [Dave Henderson and me] into his office and said, 'We've traded you both to Boston.' Afterward some of the guys were saying things like, 'Man, I wish I got traded. I want to play on a winning team.' But I always thought that you never really knew if the grass was greener somewhere else. But in this particular case it was really a blessing. It afforded me my only opportunity to play in a World Series. To go from last place to first place [in a trade] is pretty exciting."

"When Boston made that trade for you and Dave Henderson with just six weeks left in the season for shortstop Rey Quinones and players to be named later, everybody I knew in the Boston media who was following the team felt this was a pretty one-sided deal. After all, the Red Sox were headed to the playoffs and needed an upgrade at shortstop and a center fielder for the injured Tony Armas. In this one deal the Red Sox picked up two solid everyday players to fill those voids. Did you see it as one-sided, like, 'Wow, this is a steal for the Red Sox'?"

His answer surprises me: "No, I didn't look at it like that at all," he says matter-of-factly. "Obviously you know who you're traded for. In that arena, as a professional player, I don't think you get there unless you have a lot of self-confidence. So, yes, I felt like I was the better shortstop. That's no disrespect to [Quinones]. That's just the nature of the beast. But I also wasn't thinking, 'The Red Sox really got away with something here.' Because the other guys named later were good players too."

While Owen wasn't surprised he was traded in what was another losing season in Seattle, he seems somewhat astonished by the irony in going to Boston at that point: "Earlier that season we were playing Boston in the Kingdome," Spike explains. "Al Nipper's pitching, and Don Baylor's playing first for the Red Sox; I'm on first base, and Phil Bradley's at the plate. So Nipper hits Bradley with a pitch—I think in the head. Well, [Bradley] gets up and charges the mound. I go from first base straight to Nipper. While Al is watching Phil coming at him, I spear him in the back like a football tackle. I hit him and then go down. All of a sudden I look up, and Don Baylor picks me up off the ground and just throws me over the pile. I was like, 'Thanks, Groove, I appreciate it!'

"So now I get traded, and me and Hendu meet the Red Sox in Minnesota at the Metrodome. I walk into that clubhouse, which was long and narrow. I'm looking for Roger or Calvin because I don't really know any of the other guys. Well, [I was] coming off that brawl hitting Nipper, and sure enough, I hear Roger go, 'Hey, Nip, here he is! Here he is, Nipper! Here he comes!' I started laughing and said to Roger, 'Hey, I'm on this side now! Whatever you need!'"

We both have a good laugh at his story.

"How did Nipper react?" I ask.

"Ahh, he was great," Spike says, waving his right hand while smiling. "He didn't give me a hard time at all. It was all good."

And with Nipper's seal of approval Owen would begin the most memorable ten-week ride of his career.

"In just your third game with the Red Sox you tied a Major League record by scoring six runs in a game," I note. "You obviously were very comfortable and confident in your new Boston surroundings. Did you thrive off the intensity of the Boston fans as opposed to the atmosphere in the more sedate Seattle?"

Owen doesn't flinch: "Oh, no doubt about it," he says. "Seattle is much more low key. Boston was just so intense. 'Thriving' is a pretty strong word that I wouldn't use here, but I hadn't played baseball like that in a while—and never to that level of intensity and pressure. When I was young and playing at Texas [University], though it's not relatable [to Boston], in a sense that's the only thing I can draw to. Because at Texas—and again, there's such a huge separation from that and the big leagues—we were *expected* to win. So that's the similarity, even if it's at a totally different level. I owe a ton to the University of Texas and to Coach Gus [Cliff Gustafson] and [Assistant Coach] Bill Bethea for helping me achieve my dream of playing in the big leagues with that intensity and mindset of winning, like everything's on the line. It's why you play. Of course you never know how you're gonna react till you're thrown into it. Nobody does."

"So it sounds like playing at Texas prepared you for Boston as much or even more than your time in Seattle," I say.

"It certainly helped," Spike exclaims. "The fun part in Boston was how I wasn't playing for individual stats—they no longer mattered. It was just win the game and what can I do to help us win this game. Make a play, move a guy over, get a guy in—do whatever it takes. That wasn't always the focus in Seattle when we were twenty games out of first place and it was like, 'Man, I gotta get my arbitration numbers up.' And rightfully so. A lot of times in this game you've gotta be selfish for certain reasons. But with the Red Sox, you were totally mentally and physically exhausted after every game and it was awesome. It's the way it should be. The intensity of it was pretty special. You don't get to play in those types of environments a lot. There are guys who played their whole career and never got to play in that environment. So, it was really cool."

The intensity of playing in Boston that Owen kept alluding to moved into high gear that October in the most drama-filled postseason of all-time. And Spike rose to the occasion throughout.

"You had a remarkable '86 postseason," I note. "Batting out of the nine hole in the ALCS, you hit .429 to lead the Red Sox. Then, in the World Series, you hit .300. Everybody knew how solid you were defensively, but you weren't known for your hitting, batting .246 lifetime. Yet you performed so well on the biggest stage against some really outstanding opposing pitchers. Looking back, what do you attribute your offensive surge to?"

Like some of his other teammates, Owen gives much of the credit to batting coach Walt Hriniak. "Walt really helped me out once I got to Boston," Spike says. "What he taught me even helped me as the years went by and I was with other organizations. [That postseason] I was just really comfortable in the box—I can't explain it. It was almost like I was more comfortable in the box than I was at shortstop. Like in the second game against Gooden, I got three hits and was just seeing the ball so well. There were even several balls I hit in the World Series that guys made pretty good plays on that could've been hits. It was crazy."

Owen, along with his teammates, rode a wild ride of ups and downs in the ALCS and the World Series. Spike shakes his head when reminiscing about the bizarreness of it all.

"You could put Game Five in Anaheim in the same file as Game Six in the World Series," Owen theorizes. "There were a lot of similarities with the exception being the Mets didn't hit the home runs like Baylor and Hendu; their hits were bloops and then the error. After we came back against the Angels in that game, I remember the feeling in our clubhouse. There was obviously excitement of what had just happened, but we were all like, 'This is over! We've got them!' I had never felt that before. And this was the playoffs against a really good team in the Angels. When I tell people this, they might go to me, 'Oh yeah, Spike, really?' But I'm telling you, Erik, the entire clubhouse was like, 'This is over! We're going back to Boston and we're gonna defend our home turf, so to speak!'"

Not surprisingly, there was a far different feeling after losing Game Six of the World Series. "In my short time after the trade to Boston, it was definitely the quietest I'd ever heard our clubhouse," Owen recalls. "We had a real veteran team and, usually after a loss, someone like Baylor, Dewey, Buck, or somebody would speak up and say, 'Hey, we'll get 'em tomorrow' or, 'Hey, don't worry about it.' But that loss was gut-wrenching. I remember standing out there with two outs and two strikes looking at the Shea Stadium crowd and just thinking, 'Man, we're about to be world champions.' Then I kinda got back into the pitches—and then bloop, bloop, hit, you know the story. There's no doubt I wish we would have been the first team to bring Boston a World Series since 1918.

"I'm sure after Game Six the Mets felt they had it, just like we did after Game Five. But we came out and dropped three runs on the board [in Game Seven] to get the lead. But it's just baseball—it's crazy. You've gotta get twenty-seven outs. Looking back on it, I think every one of us believe it was a great Series and we played the best we could. It just wasn't enough."

"Do you still think about it?" I ask.

"Not on my own," Spike says. "Only when I'm doing interviews or when some fan at an autograph or card show says something about it, like, 'Hey '86!' So, it's always out there. But no, I don't really sit around and think about it."

I tell Spike how well received his '86 Red Sox are up at Fenway nowadays—how it feels like the fans have largely dismissed the outcome of the World Series and, instead, now focus more on the nostalgia of his team. Owen seems to understand how this dynamic came about.

"I think the character of our club, the overall makeup, and some really good players appeal to the fans," he says. "There was also a lot of drama, never knowing what would happen with Oil Can over there, and Clemens and Hurst and our bullpen. I'm really happy to hear you say this. I've been out of the loop in Boston for years, so I wouldn't know that. The last time I was back was for a Joe Morgan night a few years ago when I was coaching Triple-A for Texas. The Rangers were nice enough to let me go. But with managing, I can't pick up and take off very often."

Owen reflects on his time as a Minor League coach and manager—with Kinston now being the third team he's piloted in the Rangers' system since 2015. "They've all been memorable in different ways," he says. "Coaching at Round Rock [the Rangers' Triple-A team until 2019] and being close to home obviously was a dream. That organization was first-class with everything they did. And then you look at the year I was in High Desert [the Rangers' Advanced-A team in Adelanto, California], and you just gotta laugh about it and go, 'Wow, what an experience that was!' It was just a totally different deal from Round Rock. Then last year at Hickory—year by year, it's always something different. Some good, some bad."

"So how much longer do you see yourself in baseball?" I ask.

"Well, I'm fifty-seven," Spike says with a telling sigh. "I think I got until my midsixties, probably, hopefully. And then we'll see how it's going then. Now with all the kids out of the house, if I'm still enjoying it and if the [Rangers organization] still wants me around, then yeah, I'll still be doing it then."

And with that, Spike graciously offers me tickets to that evening's game. I'm traveling with my wife and daughter, and I tell Owen that we would have enjoyed the experience, but we had to continue a journey down to South Carolina that day.

"I understand," Owen says with a sly grin. "The big metropolis of Kingston doesn't have a whole lot to offer."

Except, for Spike Owen, it may offer a possible stepping stone back to the big leagues.

Some hang on in the game because they have to after their playing careers are over. Spike Owen is not one of those guys. He's in it for the love of the game.

8.

The University of Seaver

It was a shame [Seaver] couldn't pitch in the ['86] World Series. It would
have been amazing. I think we would have won if that'd happened.

—MARTY BARRETT

It's easy for the casual fan to downplay, or even forget, that Tom Seaver, one of the greatest pitchers of
all time, actually played a prominent role on the '86
Red Sox. Not that one could decipher this just from looking
up and finding his 5-7 record or his 3.80 ERA for that year. But
when he was acquired by the club from the White Sox as part
of a midseason trade for Steve Lyons, with Boston already holding an eight-game lead in the AL East, it was a sign to the Red
Sox and their fans that the organization was all in.

"It was just another piece to the puzzle," Marty Barrett told
me. "I thought, 'How good can this team be now?'"

When I spoke to Seaver—who has since died from complications of Lewy body dementia and Covid-19—about the
trade while I was out at his vineyard on Diamond Mountain
in Calistoga, California, on a pristine spring day in 2017, he
downplayed his impact in the classiest of ways: "That club was
set—with Jimmy Rice, Roger Clemens, Bruce Hurst, and the
rest of them—really good guys," he said. "But I was thrilled to
be back with Mac [John McNamara], who's one of the sweetest
guys in the world, and Fish [Bill Fischer], who was my pitch-

ing coach in Cincinnati. And I thought I could help the team stay in front by doing whatever Mac asked of me."

When Seaver took the mound at Fenway Park to pitch his first game as a Red Sock on July 1, it was pure theater. There was electricity in the ballpark, and it wasn't just limited to the sellout crowd in the stands. Even the Red Sox players on the field and in the dugout—veterans and younger players alike—were in awe.

"I had goose bumps out at first base at the start of that game," Bill Buckner once told me.

"I couldn't stop looking at him," marveled Roger Clemens, who was 14-0 at the time and was often viewed as the "New Seaver," as he described his first game as Seaver's teammate.

Added Don Baylor, who told the throng of media that night, "When I look at him, I don't see a pitcher. I see a *living legend.*"

Seaver, then forty-one years old and well past his prime, was still effective enough to maneuver through a tough Blue Jays' lineup and toss seven complete innings of four-run ball en route to a Red Sox victory.

Red Sox reliever Joe Sambito was as excited as a boy on Christmas morning: "I grew up on Long Island and I was a Mets' fan," he told me. "Tom Seaver was one of my idols, and I was pumped when we acquired him. In Seaver's first start with us he got the win and I got the save. That was special!"

But much more important than Seaver's performance on the field that night was the impact he would have on the team's young pitching staff.

"It was special for me to watch a guy at his advanced age go out there and *really* pitch," Clemens told me. "He was a power *pitcher*, not a power *thrower*. There's a *huge* difference. It was a poignant situation watching Seaver work. He would start a game throwing eighty-six to eighty-seven [miles an hour]—just messing around. But then by the fifth or sixth inning, all of a sudden, at his age, he's throwing ninety-one to ninety-two, popping that outside corner with pinpoint control. I would go to myself, 'Okay, I get this now. He's got a little bit [of heat]. I see what's going on here.' And Seaver could pitch inside for strikes too. I mean, intimidation is winning. I would normally sit with Fish on the bench while watching Seaver out there doing his job. It was really fun to watch."

While the media gushed over the similarities between the young Clemens and the elder Seaver in a passing-of-the-torch kind of way [their lockers were conveniently side by side], far less attention was paid on the influence Tom Terrific had with Hurst. But for the left-hander the experience was nothing short of an education.

"I got to spend three months at the University of Seaver," is how Bruce described it to me. "It was the best. He would fill my head with some of the most beautiful thoughts during a game that I pitched—just kept me grounded and focused. His impact was tremendous. Even though he didn't get to pitch the whole year, he still won games for us with his presence, his understanding, and his experience. Those were things I really relied on."

Perhaps it was no small coincidence that Hurst's strong second half and postseason in 1986 was helped by having a legend by his side.

Bruce then leaned back in his chair and grinned before reminiscing about how Seaver, a master of his craft, still utilized resources like his coaches: "It was phenomenal to watch his work ethic and how he worked with Fish, a prince of a man. Fish would sometimes let him know if he should throw a fastball to a hitter; or tell him, 'He's on you'; or whether he should throw something else. That was the relationship they had. It was really fun to watch one of the greatest pitchers of all time still relying on coaches [and] depending on another set of eyes. That was wonderful. I mean, he's Tom Seaver, for crying out loud. Look at his body of work. He's arguably one of the top five pitchers of all time. He doesn't get the credit because the 'baseball geniuses' of today have taken his delivery and how he pitched and poo-pooed it as something that can't be done or is a bad thing. But his delivery was *flawless*—just beautiful.

He wrote the book *The Art of Pitching*. He understood the science and the physics and all the things that go behind delivering a baseball. But he understood the art form of it as well."

For Hurst, Seaver's influence wasn't just limited to the young pitcher's mental and physical approach on the mound, but extended to his mental capacity off the field as well.

"I'll tell you one story that just mesmerized me about him and is kind of sad now because of how he has memory loss," Hurst, who admitted to having a poster of Seaver as a kid, told me. "After like a two-week road trip three large diaper boxes are on top of his locker filled with fan mail. I mean *full* of fan mail. Now think about how big those boxes are when they can fit twenty-four Pampers or whatever. So while he had three boxes, I had like five letters. We had these little square tables in the middle of the locker room at Fenway, and after we'd done our work and had a little time, I started signing a few autographs. Seaver looks over my shoulder and goes, 'What are you doing?' I look at him like, 'It's pretty obvious—I'm signing autographs here.' He says, 'Let me see that,' and he grabs a note that read something like, 'Dear Mr. Hurst, You're the greatest pitcher in the history of mankind. Can I have your autograph?' So Seaver goes, 'It's a collector. I get letters like this all the time from this guy.' So I say, 'You don't know who this guy is.' And he goes, 'You wanna bet?' So he pulls up a chair; thumbs through one of his boxes; grabs an envelope with the same address; reads the letter, which was written verbatim to mine; wads it up; and throws it in the trash. I was stunned. The guy had a photographic memory. So now he starts thumbing through another box and comes up with another letter from a collector and says, 'This guy's got his *sister* writing to me now because he knows I won't answer him!' Then finally he comes to one and goes, 'This is a lucky kid. This is legit.' So he signs his autograph, seals it up, and puts it in the mail. Aside from his physical strength and delivery, his memory and the way he saw things was remarkable. That's the one story that, for me, has always stood out about who he was."

The Red Sox would have their ebbs and flows in July and August, but they never faced a significant challenge to their title dreams the rest of the season. Seaver's performance on the field was as a serviceable fifth starter, but it was the quiet confidence he brought to the club that was immeasurably important.

"He just brought a ton of professionalism to our team," Barrett told me. "He showed us how to act and how to carry ourselves. He had a calmness about himself. There was never any of the rah-rah stuff. It was always like, 'We've got this. We're going to get this done.' And you knew he meant it, and you knew about the vast amount of experience he had from so many years of playing in big games and series. For the little bit that I knew him he became one of my favorite guys—just wonderful."

Oh, what could have been.

The Mets, the organization in which Seaver grew up to become the biggest star in club history, would run away with the National League Eastern division title. The Red Sox, while not as dominant, would ride a long September winning streak to build a lead as high as ten and a half games in the AL East. While the other two division leaders, the Angels and Astros, would prove to be more than formidable opponents in the postseason, the Mets and Red Sox had the best records in their respective leagues and seemed to be on a collision course to meet in the World Series. Aside from this being a potential dream match-up for the networks, the high drama of Seaver pitching against his old club in a World Series was practically unfathomable.

But with just two weeks remaining in the regular season, this absolute fantasy scenario would be taken away by the baseball gods when Seaver suffered a sprained ligament on the outside of his right knee while pitching in Toronto. Tom would attempt to throw off the mound the next week, but his knee was simply too weak, and McNamara was left with no choice but to remove him from the postseason roster.

It's mind blowing to ponder how Seaver may have affected the outcome of the World Series had he been active. Surely he would have gotten a start—most likely in Game Four at Fenway—and would have been used in relief to try to stymie Mets rallies in the historic Games Six and Seven at Shea Stadium.

"It was a shame [Seaver] couldn't pitch in the World Series," Barrett told me. "It would have been amazing. I think we would have won if that'd happened."

Hurst took it a step further: "It would have been a *mess!*" he exclaimed. "I can tell you right now: the Mets were a great club, but Seaver would've pulled out all the past and laid it on the table. I would've loved for his last game of his Major League career to have been in Shea Stadium in a World Series. Even though it would have been in a Red Sox uniform, it still would have been phenomenal."

Over lunch with Tom and several of his '69 Mets teammates later that same spring day at a local restaurant in Calistoga, Seaver downplayed the significance of how throwing his last pitch during a World Series game at Shea could hypothetically have changed history: "The point was, Erik, I was new to the Sox," he said. "I could have essentially gotten in the way. Even though I was injured, I was asked [to be in uniform and] be there at the World Series. But I stood out of the way and didn't get in the middle of it. I was going to be on the periphery. John McNamara asked me to go. He was my manager, and if he asked me to go, I was going to go. But there was nothing I could really say. I remember thinking, 'This isn't about me; it's about them.' If someone wants to ask me a question, fine. But just leave it to them. Don't screw it up for them. It wasn't about me one *i-o-ta*. Period."

Maybe so, but his calming influence and effect on Hurst, who nearly won all three games he started against the Mets, can't be overstated. "He'd keep reminding me to get the first out every inning, get the heavy hitters out, and to keep throwing strikes," Hurst would tell me. "He kept reminding me of those three things. He was always in my ear, giving me advice. He really was immense for me."

Back at the restaurant, unprompted after a sip of wine, Seaver couldn't help but recall how Game Six ended, even showing some serious emotion while recollecting the fateful final inning: "And Billy Buckner—the *cripple*," Tom remarked, shaking his head from side to side. "He had a prior injury. Usually Stapleton would come in, but [Buckner] talked Mac out of it. But they should have taken him out. *Absolutely*. I love Mac, but this is three more outs, and the World Series [is ours]. *How can you not?* The game's *over*! And then, of course, the ball found the first baseman and went down the line. *Out! Take him out!* But he wanted to be in the celebration."

Buddy Harrelson, Seaver's old Mets teammate, could only smile at his best friend and remind us all of how quickly fate changed hands that night: "I was the third base coach for the Mets," he said gleefully, turning his head toward me. "I'm in the coaching box and [Tom's] right there at the end of the Red Sox dugout. He's standing up and mouths to me—because they were winning by two runs and we had two outs—'Call ya, call ya,' with his hand to his ear [like he was holding a phone]. I mean, you guys weren't quite up to the top steps but were right there."

"Ready to run up," Seaver confirmed. "Champagne was on ice."

"I mean, they put up on the goddamn scoreboard, 'Congratulations Red Sox,'" Harrelson continued in disbelief. "And then it all changed. After it was over, I looked over at [Tom], and I went like this [putting his hand to his ear], 'I'll call ya.'"

The two enjoyed a laugh, Buddy's understandably a bit more pronounced than Tom's, even after all these years.

After an aborted comeback attempt in the spring of '87 with the Mets, a club that was desperately seeking pitching help with Dwight Gooden in drug rehabilitation and a rash of injuries to their staff, the man the folks in Queens referred to as "the Franchise" called it a career with the dignity that eludes so many other legends. And while I join the countless numbers of his fans who will have lasting memories of his 311 career wins, his three Cy Young Awards, and his overall dominance as a pitcher in his prime and then as a mentor to the young Red Sox pitchers in his final season, I will also envision something else. I will forever picture him on a sun-splashed Saturday morning, making his daily rounds up and down the hills of his vineyard—clippers in hand, dogs by his side—talking emotionally about the baseball life he happily exchanged for a second act of growing the grapes to produce his award-winning cabernet.

9.

What Truly Matters

You can take that '86 World Series—and my whole career—and throw it out the window. I got the health of my son and that's all that counts for me.

—BOB STANLEY

The tall, middle-aged man with a light blue golf shirt, khaki shorts, and casual loafers strolls into the visiting Buffalo Bisons clubhouse in Pawtucket on a steamy July afternoon, as instantly recognizable as when he was the longtime relief pitcher for the Red Sox. Gone was much of the hair atop his head, but what remained was his long-structured face, deep monotone voice, and the reserved demeanor of a businessman you might see riding home on a commuter train. But the truth is that Bob Stanley is one of the *funniest* men you'll ever meet in baseball. *Seriously.*

Moving into the dugout of an empty stadium to chat, he starts right in with a rich, condescending, dry humor—much in the same vein as another famous yet self-deprecating former Major Leaguer, Bob Uecker. "Boston fans," Stanley deadpans, reflecting back on his Red Sox days. "They love you and hate you. I'll never forget this one fan by the bullpen. He said, 'Hey, Stanley, you're worth every penny you make. It's the *dollars* I'm worried about.' I started laughing, looked at him, and said, 'That was a great line. I'm gonna use that probably the rest of my life.'"

Caught off guard by the totally unexpected humorous tagline, I roar in laughter as Stanley gives me a sly grin. Admittedly I had no idea how funny a person Stanley could be during much of our talk. Win or lose, he had always been a stoic figure out on the mound and during most interviews. "You see," he says proudly, "here I am still using that line—*with you.*

"Anyway, in Boston, they're big baseball fans and want to win," Stanley continues. "You've got to understand that when you go out there and have a bad game, they're gonna let you know it. But if you have a good game, they're gonna definitely let you know that too. In the beginning [of my career] it was always good. Then at the end I signed the big [million dollar] contract, and . . ."

Stanley doesn't finish his sentence, his voice fading at the end of it. For anyone who knows Red Sox history, he doesn't have to. He went from being one of the most successful, versatile pitchers in baseball as a starter, middle reliever, and closer from the late seventies through the mideighties to somewhat of an outcast during the second half of the '86 season with the emergence of Calvin Schiraldi.

"I thought about changing my name from Bob to Lou," Stanley quips, "so I wouldn't know if the fans were saying, 'Looo,' like they did for Lou Piniella, or booing me."

His career would never be the same. But it certainly didn't start out that way. Stanley was one of just three players—along with Rice and Evans—who played for both the great '78 Red Sox team and the pennant winner in '86. On a team full of stars on the '78 team, arguably the best team in baseball that lost to the Yankees in a one-game playoff, it's easy to overlook that "the Steamer," who got that nickname for "steaming down" opposing hitters, was 15-2 with a 2.60 ERA that year. I remind him of his remarkable season, but instead of gloating about it, he answers modestly.

"I had another nickname back then too," Stanley says. "'The Vulture' because I would come into games and get the win, you know? I'd come in to relieve, say, Luis Tiant, with a man on second, break a [hitter's] bat—that'd tie it up; then we'd score five, and I'd get the win. Tiant said to me just the other day, 'If it wasn't for you, I probably would have made the Hall of Fame, but you blew about twenty of my games!'"

Stanley looks out at the playing field and wants to get something off his chest before we continue: "That '78 team," he says, now looking straight into my eyes for emphasis, "we had a big lead, then everybody got hurt, and the Yankees got hot—end of story. But here's the thing. If we had played that playoff game against them in Yankee Stadium, we would've won because Bucky Dent's home run would have been a can of crap!"

"Right," I say. "And don't forget about Rice's deep drive to right field in the ninth. It may have been out at Yankee Stadium because of the short right-field porch. How dramatic would that have been? As it was, that may have been the greatest game of all time for pure drama."

Clearly still bothered by the outcome, Stanley quietly murmurs, "Yeah."

"I want to read you a quote from Ted Williams from back in September of 1980," I tell him. "He goes, 'I don't think many people know it, I'm not sure if Stanley knows it, but he's the best relief pitcher in the game. Check the stats.' So Ted Williams was saying that at that time you were better than Rich Gossage, better than Bruce Sutter, better than Dan Quisenberry. How did a quote like that, coming from the great Ted Williams, make you feel?"

"It's unbelievable," Stanley says. "He was the greatest hitter ever in the game, and for him to give you a compliment like that was something. I was on Cloud Nine. I'll never forget it."

In 1982 Stanley was voted the most outstanding pitcher on the Red Sox staff by the club—winning twelve and saving fourteen—and was the pitching equivalent of a Swiss Army knife for all the different ways he was used.

"Your versatility was valuable for the Red Sox, but were you at all bothered that your saves total didn't add up to those of the Gossages of the world, maybe hurting you at contract time?"

"Not at all," Stanley says. "Nowadays saves are usually one inning. But it was different back then. I'd go three innings—sometimes more. I think the greatest accomplishment I ever had was pitching 168 innings out of the bullpen in one year. That's a Red Sox record that will never be broken. I talk to these kids here and they go, 'I pitched ninety innings last year.' I go, 'Really? I had ninety innings in July.' So it was crazy back in '82. I remember Ralph Houk bringing me in in the second inning, when we were down 3–0 to California. I went four innings, we came back, and I got the win. Somebody else got the save. Reporters asked Houk why he brought his closer in in the second inning. He says, 'Because I wanted to save the game right then and there.' Like I said, it was a different time."

The following year Stanley saved thirty-three games—a career high and an especially impressive total during that era of multiple-inning save opportunities. He was still very effective through the 1985 campaign, despite pitching with a ganglion cyst on a right throwing-hand finger that put painful pressure on it whenever he threw a slider. But then came '86.

"You were terrific in your first nine seasons in the big leagues," I say. "You did whatever was asked of you and pitched through pain. Did the fans' turning on you—after everything you achieved—bother you when you began to struggle a little bit?"

"Yeah, a little," Stanley says, at last showing some emotion. "I mean, I busted my ass for all those years, and after '86 they didn't like me anymore."

"If you recall, you had an outstanding spring in '86," I note. "You looked ready to resume what was a great nine-year career to that point—the greatest relieving stint in Boston history. But then, just as the team was on it's way to win the division title, Schiraldi steps into the closing role. How does a guy who's been a winner his whole career, like you were, deal with a situation like that?"

"I was upset," Stanley says without pause. "I had fourteen saves at the All-Star break. Then that first game back I blew the game, and Schiraldi came in, opened up people's eyes, and they just shoved me in the back. I only got two more save opportunities the rest of the year and got 'em both, but that's the manager's decision. You pitch whenever they call. But I wasn't real happy about it."

That leads up to the fabled Game Six, when Schiraldi couldn't get that final out that would have given the Red Sox their first championship in sixty-eight years. How ironic was it that Stanley, pushed aside for the young Schiraldi in the second half of the season, was now called upon to be the savior out of the bullpen as he had been for all those years?

"When they opened the bullpen door and you came trotting onto the field, needing just one out to end the 'curse' for generations of Sox fans, what was going through your head?" I ask.

"Just trying to get a ground ball to get Mookie Wilson out," Stanley says. "And it didn't work. I threw a pitch that went to the backstop to tie [the game]. Some people say it was a passed ball, others say a wild pitch. Geddy and I are good friends, and we don't want to take that away and lose our friendship by watching it again and bringing back bad memories. In my mind it doesn't matter. It's the same outcome. Game's tied."

"So all the other stuff—one out from a championship, the end of the 'curse'—didn't enter your mind?" I ask.

"No," the Steamer says flatly. "I was supposed to start that inning. It was tied, and then we scored two runs to go ahead. Then the phone rang, and they said from the dugout, 'Schiraldi's going back out there.' So who knows what would have happened if I'd started the [bottom of the inning] with a two-run lead? Nobody knows."

"I know from the books I co-wrote with Mookie Wilson and Davey Johnson that the Mets, having had Schiraldi on their club the year before, wanted to get one last crack at him," I say. "The last thing they wanted was to see you come into the game."

"That's what Keith Hernandez told me after I got a job with the Mets," Stanley quips. "He said, 'When we saw Schiraldi go back out there, we got rejuvenated.'"

"The Mets felt Schiraldi had great stuff but didn't have that 'x-factor' in the big games," I say. "But they knew that with all your experience, you did. Plus you had that vicious sinker."

"Yeah, and my sinker was pretty good in that Series," Stanley exclaims. "I pitched in five of the seven games of that Series. But it was McNamara's decision not to bring me in [earlier]."

"Five of seven games?" I ask rhetorically, not immediately recollecting that fact. "All of that work is really good for a sinker, right?"

"Oh yeah," Stanley confirms. "The more you work, the better it is."

Wilson of course would hit the slow roller that went through Buckner's legs to win Game Six for the Mets.

"What do you do after a game like that ends?" I ask. "I think it was your wife's birthday too, right?"

"Yeah, it was," Stanley says. "I took twelve beers and put 'em in a paper bag and walked into our room at the Grand Hyatt. She's sitting on the bed and goes, 'We had it!' Then she started crying and all that. I'm like, 'Hey, don't worry. We've still got another game.' I was upset, but that's baseball."

"You were really able to compartmentalize things," I say.

"Yeah, we still had one more game," the Steamer says. "I was thinking, 'Okay, [Game Six] is over. Let's move on to the next game. You can't dwell on a good performance or a bad one. The next day is a different day."

"Effective relievers like you have to have short memories, I suppose," I say. "It's almost a job requirement. How long did it take you to get over that loss once the World Series was over?"

"It took a while because of people reminding me of it, you know?" Stanley says. "That winter my kids—who were four and five at the time—were playing in the driveway, and somebody came driving up, got out of the car, picked up one of my kid's bikes, threw it against a basketball pole, and said, 'Tell your father he sucks!' When I came home [in Wenham, Massachusetts], I called the cops and said, 'A guy in a yellow car just came up my driveway,' and I finished telling him what happened. So they went looking for him. About fifteen minutes later this yellow car comes up my driveway, and I'm like, 'Oh my gosh!' But it was my buddy, and he wanted me to sign a card for him. I said, 'You're lucky you didn't get your tires blown out.' It wasn't the guy."

"I've gotten to know Buckner well through my association with Mookie," I say. "Bill had a baseball career that would be the envy of most players—nearly three thousand hits, a batting title, a great defensive player. But as unfair as it is, he is best remembered by the casual fan for that error. Your career numbers were also terrific, and you're an inductee in the Red Sox Hall of Fame. And also as unjustly, the casual fan also remembers you most for Game Six. How do you deal with something as unfair as that reality?"

Stanley exhales and is pragmatic in his response: "You know in Buckner's case it is unfair because of the career he had. He almost had Hall of Fame numbers. You've heard the old saying, 'They remember the last thing you did.' Well, that's what they remember with Buck. But there are a lot of things in that game that we blew. We blew a rundown that cost us a run, but no one remembers that; [fans remember] only the last thing that happened. So that's that."

In a sign of true class and how deeply invested Stanley was in both the Red Sox organization and its history, it is telling that he was the *only* player to attend the unveiling of the '86 team highlight film at Fenway Park. In other words, he "gets it."

"A lot of guys were great players—even Hall of Famers—and never made it to the World Series, so I was fortunate to do that," he says earnestly. "But the outcome was not the one we wanted."

Bob pauses and then speaks about what is truly important in life—and what he's learned from some harrowing experiences over time: "In '86 I prayed to God that I'd be the hero," he said. "But He didn't answer my prayers. But in 1990, when my nine-year-old son got cancer, I prayed to Him to cure my son, and that prayer *was* answered. I was telling everybody,

'You can take that '86 World Series—and my whole career—and throw it out the window. I got the health of my son, and that's all that counts for me.' And that's the way it is."

Stanley's son, Kyle, was diagnosed with cancer in the sinus area the year after the Steamer finished his thirteen-year career with the Red Sox. The little boy is now a man—with a baby—and, according to Stanley, "is doing great."

"There are more important things than baseball," Stanley says earnestly. "What happened in '86 bothers a lot of other people, but it doesn't bother me at all."

"Wasn't there another boy who had a similar type of cancer whom you knew and tried to comfort back in 1985?" I ask, recalling a story I had read.

Stanley knows immediately to whom I'm referring, and I can immediately tell how emotionally invested he had been with this other sick little boy.

"Yeah, Devin," he says. "I used to do work for the Jimmy Fund all the time and visit [sick] kids. I'd always bring the young [players] that had come up from the Minors when they were struggling. I'd have them meet me at Fenway, and I'd bring them over to Children's Hospital and show them these kids—bald, some of them dying—and it would open their minds up, and they'd say, 'Wow, this game isn't that important.' So that's the way I look at it.

"One day I got a call to come see this kid that was terminally ill. I went to see him and brought him a bat, my jersey, and a couple of balls. He wouldn't come out of his room because they had taken his right eye out. He was embarrassed. So I came in and gave him my jersey, and we talked for like a half hour. The kid was nine years old—same age as my son [when he was sick]. The doctor called me later and said, 'I don't know what you did with Devin, but I'll tell you right now, he's running down the hallway in your uniform top. Thank you very much!'"

Stanley pauses and, choked up, finishes his story about Devin: "I was with my wife one day, and I saw [Devin's] father, a security guard. I went up to him and asked, 'How's Devin doing?'

He says, 'He passed away.' I said, 'Geez, I'm really sorry.' He says, 'No, you gave my son his last week of happiness, talking about baseball. We buried him in your jersey.' I just started balling my eyes out. My wife and I both. Five years later the doctor said, 'You remember Devin?' I go, 'Yeah.' He says, 'Well, Kyle has the same tumor.' I go, 'So what do you think?' He says, 'We've done a lot of research. We give your son a 50-50 chance. Devin didn't have that.'"

Understandably the Steamer has to take a moment to compose himself before saying simply, "Kyle beat it."

Caught up in the moment—as a father myself—I tried to reconcile in my mind how I could possibly ask him any more baseball questions.

Baseball is filled with delicious ironies, and one of them is that after the heartbreak of the 1986 World Series, Bob Stanley was the Opening Day starting pitcher for the Red Sox in 1987. I bring this up to Stanley, and he is quick to answer why.

"That was a mistake," he says. "Clemens [who was sitting out due to a contract dispute] didn't show up, and they made me a starter. It was the most miserable season I ever had. Then, right after the season, I cut the tendon of a finger in half. I fell on a bottle after falling down the stairs at my home. I was on my way to working out with Geddy at Fenway. I missed half of '88 because of that. The doctors at the hospital said I'd never pitch again, but I did. Some Red Sox fans probably wish I didn't, but I did."

Stanley would actually finish his final season and a half by pitching pretty good baseball for the Red Sox before calling it a career and eventually moving into coaching.

Again—more sweet irony was to follow.

"One of your first Major League coaching jobs was with the Mets' Pittsfield farm team in '97," I say. "What was it like working for the team that brought so much pain in that '86 Series?"

"When they called me, I thought it was a joke," Stanley says, grinning. "I thought someone was joking around because I sent my resume to everybody. But then Jack Zduriencik, their farm director at the time, got on the phone. I went for an interview and got the job. I just wanted a job; I didn't care who it was with."

Stanley smiles before recounting a related story: "I'll never forget this little old lady. One winter day at a mall up in Boston, she walks up to me and says, 'Can I have your autograph? You're one of my favorite pitchers *ever*!' And I said, 'Yeah.' So I sign it, and she goes, 'What are you doing now?' And I said, 'I work with the Mets.' And she just took [the autograph] and ripped it up! It was funny."

"So what happened with the Mets?" I ask.

"I got fired. So I thought, 'Now I can go back to hating them!'" he says, chuckling.

"I'm wondering, Bob, after your story about that little old lady, do you still receive letters from Red Sox fans, and do people still come up to you wanting to talk about your career?" I ask.

"Oh yeah, they like me *now*," he says. "I haven't blown a save since '89! And they still bring up Game Six, but I always tell 'em I got Alzheimer's right after that game and don't remember *anything*. You know, after the Red Sox won a few World Series recently, I figured they'd get rid of that tape [of Game Six], but no, that thing still plays."

Stanley and I share another laugh over his latest example of self-deprecating humor. Laughter—and faith—have truly been his best medicine.

10.

The Passion of Dwight

There were many nights that I was out there after having just come from the hospital and wasn't having a good game. And you know what? I just had to eat it.

—DWIGHT EVANS

Conventional wisdom has it that professional baseball players live a life of fortune and fame and are generally immune to the common and sometimes extraordinary struggles that beset the average person. In my own mind an encounter with the former Red Sox star right fielder Dwight "Dewey" Evans—he of the easy smile and Hollywood looks—wouldn't do anything to dispel that notion. That is, until Dwight began talking openly with me on a September morning in 2017 in the Fenway Park stands behind first base about the toll that NF—neurofibromatosis—has taken on his family for more than four decades.

"'Neurofibromatosis' is hard to say, and it's even harder to live with, but since the seventies we've been dealing with it," Evans says of the genetic disorder of the nervous system that causes tumors to grow on nerves and that has profoundly afflicted both of his sons.

"My younger son [Justin] right now is fine," Dwight continues. "He's had issues as well as surgeries. It hit him in his pituitary area. And then he had [a tumor] on his spine on the cerebellum, the lower part of the skull. They almost lost him once on the table, but he's fine. He's doing well right now. The older one, Tim—we had some pretty good news with him three weeks ago. The chemo is doing its job. The MRI they showed eight weeks ago had some cloudiness. They couldn't get all the tumors from the cerebellum, the part of the brain where a lot of balance and speech are regulated. If the tumors go too deep, then you lose a lot of that. His quality of life is not there. But the [tests] from three weeks ago showed that the cloudiness was gone, meaning the cloudiness was from radiation, and it caused some swelling in that area. It's the first good news we've had since March. In chemo they give him anywhere from six to eighteen months. But we don't live by that. We don't."

Some background: Evans and I had tried for several months to get together for our talk, but so delicate a situation had it been with Tim, who was battling stage four brain cancer, that this late summer day was our first opportunity. But all along Dwight stayed in touch with me, telling me we would make it work. Conversely I would tell him his family was in my prayers.

"Thank you for your prayers," he once wrote back to me. "We take that very seriously."

If there is an All-God team in baseball, Dewey is on it. He and his wife, Susan, have leaned heavily on their Christian faith to keep their family strong and intact. And it was Dwight's coming to the ballpark every day that served as a temporary escape from his life away from it.

"From 1977 through 1983, a period in which Tim had to endure twelve operations to remove tumors around an eye, you would sometimes tell him as you left his hospital room that you would hit a home run for him," I note. "And often you actually would! In fact you hit 131 home runs during those six seasons. Did Timmy and his condition inspire you to play at a higher level?"

Dewey grins as he reflects on a particular circumstance involving one of Tim's home run wishes: "I will tell you a true story," he begins. "Tim once had a twelve-hour surgery. We had to get there very early in the morning for it. It was right after a night game, so it was exhausting emotionally. So he comes out of surgery, and of course he's all groggy. He finally comes up to his room at around four o'clock, and I've got to get to the ballpark. [The ballpark] was kind of my safety zone. Once I walked into it, because I've played so long, I could take that stuff and leave it outside the stadium. But that one day as I left his room, I said, 'Tim, I love ya. I've got to go to the ballpark.' And he goes, 'Dad, will you hit me a home run tonight?' And I went, 'Oh, I'll try, Tim. I'll try.' And then he goes, 'Dad, Dad, will you hit me two home runs tonight?' And I said, 'Okay, okay, Tim; I'll try.' And that night I hit two home runs! Honest to God. I only wish he'd ask me to hit about four hundred more!"

Dewey smiles, looks me straight in the eye, and, as if he still feels the need to convince me, says, "*True story*, Erik. My wife was right there."

Not only did I of course believe Dewey, but I also remembered that night well. I was actually in the ballpark for that game while on a Ted Williams Baseball Camp field trip—August 30, 1982.

"It was unbelievable," Evans continues. "When I hit the second one, I'm rounding the bases, looking up to the sky, and going, 'Thank you.' I knew Tim was watching the game on TV. And you could actually see the lights of Fenway back then from Mass. Eye and Ear [Hospital] from his room. It was kind of a miracle moment."

"I absolutely love that story," I tell Dewey.

"I have another one like that," Evans says excitedly. "Dick Bresciani, who was the PR guy here for years, asked me back in 1982 to say hello to this very sick boy named Dan. Dick goes, 'Dwight, he's got liver cancer, and he's dying. He's stopped chemo and doesn't want to live.' So I bring him into the clubhouse, sign a bat and some balls for him, and introduce him to some of the guys. Afterward I take him out to his parents, and he says, 'Dewey, would you do me a favor?' I said, 'What's that?' He's quiet for a second and then finally goes, 'Would you hit me a home run tonight?' I said, 'Well, if I hit one tonight, it will be for you.' And I did!"

"That's incredible, Dewey!" I exclaim.

"It gets better," he says, holding up his right index finger. "After that night I never knew what happened to that kid. But then twenty years or so later, Dick calls me and says, 'Do you remember Dan, the boy who had cancer? He's still alive!' I said, 'You're kidding me! He's still alive?!' 'Yeah, and NESN's shooting a thing up here about it, so they want you to come up to Boston.' So I come up to Fenway, and Dan is standing with his brother right over there [Dwight points to an area near the Red Sox dugout]. They've got cameras set up. Batting practice is going on. Dan, now in his late thirties, looks directly into the camera, and says, 'Hey, Dewey, hit one over the net!' He doesn't know that I'm in the park; I'm not in the picture. Then I walk on to the set, and Dan looks up at me, does a double take, and starts crying like a baby. He gets up and gives me a hug. It's a tearjerker of a spot. Like I said, I wish I had more people ask me to hit home runs. But I hit one for Dan; it inspired him to live and go through treatment, and he beat it! I wish I'd known years before because it would have inspired me to do so much more."

"I'll bet," I say with a grin. "Your home run helped save that boy's life in a way."

Evans nods knowingly, seemingly incredulous at the thought of what a ballplayer's influence and encouragement can sometimes do to help people in need.

"Getting back to Tim," I continue, "with kids being kids, would he have to deal with some teasing from other children because of the way he looked from the illness?"

"Yes, and it was hard because along with the teasing and all that, when he was around four years old, his hat went from being on square to covering his left side. We tried to get some therapy, but it was difficult. The manifestations of NF go from hearing loss to learning disabilities to death by cancer. The manifestations come so fast. NF afflicts three times as many people as are afflicted by muscular dystrophy and cystic fibrosis combined. What we try to do is get the name out. In fact the

Yawkey Foundation gave a lot of money but not for NF research. They said all that money has to go to get the word out and try to educate people [about the disease]. That was really an awakening for us because no one had ever said that."

"You know, Dwight, to excel at playing the game of baseball like you did while keeping your family struggles with NF private, even among your teammates, is amazing to me," I say. "Every player goes through a slump now and then, and the Boston media showed they could be very hard on you guys. Did that make it even tougher for you to not make excuses, which you never did?"

"You know what?" Dewey responds, his expression revealing he had just recalled a perfect anecdote to my question. "It's funny. I'm going to tell you a story because, yes, I did hold everything tight. Jimmy Rice and I and my wife Susan were up in the Legends' Suite [at Fenway], which I do about ten times a year. Jimmy had just played in the NF golf tournament and read some things about me [and my sons' struggles with NF]. If you know Jimmy, [you know] he's even more sensitive and passionate than most people think, and he started weeping in front of everybody. He didn't know what we had gone through because we never talked about it. He looked right at me and said, 'I didn't know any of these things.' And then he broke down. But I never liked making excuses. There were many nights that I was out there after having just come from the hospital and wasn't having a good game. And you know what? I just had to eat it."

Instead of accepting what would have been undying support from the fans, media, and his teammates for having to deal with what he did off the field, Evans still chose to keep his struggles private.

"The one thing that I did find after having played here long enough," Evans, a nineteen-year Red Sox veteran, explains, "was that the New England fans are passionate. If you're bad, they're going to boo you. If you're good, they're going to cheer you. It's not that they're fickle. They're just emotional. You make a great play, they're jumping up, screaming. I remember how [former Red Sox teammate] Rick Burleson described it after getting traded to the Angels. He said, 'I miss New England fans because in Anaheim if I dive in a hole, make a great play, come up throwing, and throw the guy out, you've got twenty thousand people going just, "Wow." Whereas here they're jumping up, they're going crazy . . . just off the charts.' What's sad is I see players that don't get that. Some players don't have the makeup to play here. It's too tough for them. What they don't get is that once you're accepted by them, you're accepted for life. Then you just fall in love with them. I *love* emotion."

Among the greatest and most legendary Red Sox players of all time, Dwight Evans would have to be in anyone's top ten list. For nearly two decades he manned the right-field position like few had in the history of the game—a perennial Gold Glover in his prime with a rifle for an arm. At the plate he amassed career totals of 385 home runs and 1,384 RBIs. From a historical context he was the only Red Sox player to have played in both the 1975 and 1986 World Series. But while his big league career officially began in 1972, Evans's coming-out party on the national stage truly began on a cool October evening in 1975 about 270 feet from where we sat.

"In the eleventh inning of Game Six of the '75 World Series you made what Reds' manager Sparky Anderson called the greatest catch he ever saw, adding, 'We'll never see any better.' Would you talk about that catch and what it was like playing in what many believe was the greatest game of all-time?" I ask.

Evans smiles, recalling something the all-time hits leader, Pete Rose, said to him during that game: "I'm at third base, and there's Pete Rose," Dewey says. "Now I'm only twenty-three years old, and Pete, looking around at the fans, goes, 'Dewey, isn't this the greatest game you've ever played in?' And I go, 'I guess it is.' Finally at that point it dawned on me that it's a great game. Before Rose said that, I was too young to [be able to] look around and realize how great it was. And Bernie [Carbo] still hadn't hit his [game-tying] three-run homer yet."

Dewey then shifts gears to the catch: "The game was tied, with Ken Griffey Sr. on first base, and I'm in right field. With Joe Morgan, a left-handed batter, at the plate, I always tried to line myself up with the foul pole. Every time a left-hander hits a ball, whether it's down the left-field line or the right-field line, the ball tends to curve slightly toward the lines. With Morgan up, I'm not only anticipating a line drive base hit to me, but a ball in the gap, a ball down the line, a ground ball in the hole, and a ball hit over my head to my right or to my left. And since there's no tomorrow, I've got to be willing to go into the stands too. All these things are just going through your mind between pitches, and every pitch is different. I've always said that I guarantee that Ozzie Smith made plays in his mind before they happened. It's harder to do in the outfield, especially right field, because you might only get one ball a game. But you've still got to be ready for every pitch and anticipate where the ball could be hit. So before Morgan hits the ball, I'm thinking about all of this.

"Anyway, Morgan hits the ball, and my first instinct was to turn to my left. I'm running that way because the ball's gonna curve. But as I got closer to the warning track, the ball didn't curve; it stayed straight. This was because Morgan hit down on the ball, so he didn't hook it and it didn't have any spin on it, which it normally would. When I get to the warning track, not knowing where the fence is, I'm trying to drift back to get in line with the ball. I lost the arc of the ball. You always want to see the ball coming into your glove when you catch it. But I jumped up, arched my back, and it landed in my glove. I lost it but caught it. If you look at the replay, [you see] it's an awkward catch. I was amazed that I caught it. With Griffey all the way to third, I threw it to almost where the grass meets the dirt in the coaching box [near first base], where Yaz catches it, and Burleson—who was following the play—came to first base, where Yaz threw it to him to complete the double play.

It wasn't the greatest catch I ever made, but it was the most important one I ever made—no question. I mean, a couple of inches either way, it's off my glove and I'm not 'the guy.' Instead *we lose.*"

"And then there's no Fisk home run," I point out.

"Yeah, and if Bernie doesn't hit his home run, I don't make that catch," Evans counters.

Ahhh, so many "what ifs."

Dwight then comments on how losing the '75 World Series did nothing to dispel everything the organization had accomplished: "Nobody gave us a chance against Oakland [in the ALCS]," Evans says. "We beat them three straight. Nobody gave us a chance against Cincinnati, the Big Red Machine. We took them to the seventh game—a bloop single by Morgan to center field in the ninth, and they win it, 4–3. My biggest regret was not winning a World Series with the team we had then—nineteen home-grown players through our system. But I remember thinking, 'In the next five years we'll be in three or four more of these.' But we didn't play in another one for eleven years."

"Eleven years later, of course, takes us to 1986," I say to Dwight. "And you start the season off in Detroit with a bang—a leadoff home run off of Jack Morris on the very first pitch. It was somewhat rare to see you, a slugger, lead off a game, and to lead off the season with that home run was incredible. What do you recall about that leadoff home run, and did you get a sense that it might serve as an omen for the season?"

"True story—again," Evans starts off. "There's two or three weeks left in spring training. McNamara calls me into this office. He says our leadoff hitter didn't want to lead off. So McNamara says to me, 'Would you lead off?' And I said, 'Whatever you want me to do.' Within a couple of days I have a dream that I'm going to start the season off with a home run. I told Susan about it. I told Marty Barrett about it. And then I told Walt Hriniak, our hitting coach, about it. Walt walked away and then came back toward me, hit me in the chest, and went, 'I don't want you thinking home run.' He said that because when I thought home run, I got too big. If I just thought base hit, home runs would happen.

"So we're in Detroit in the old ballpark, fifty thousand in the stands, the national anthem is being played, and while there was never a time in my over ten thousand at bats that I didn't have butterflies or some anxiousness, coming up to start the season against Morris, I was really flying, jumping up and down trying to keep calm. The national anthem ends, and Walt goes to me, 'What are you going to do?' And I said, 'Walt, I'm going to hit a line drive to right center.' He goes, 'Dynamite! That's what I want to hear.' But just before going out onto the on-deck circle, knowing that Morris is going to want to get the first pitch over to get ahead in the count, I look over at Marty Barrett and say to him, 'I'm going deep on the first pitch.' And sure enough, I hit it just to the left of that pole they had in center field [by the four-hundred-foot sign]. I'm running around the bases, thanking God. I'm thinking, 'This is unbelievable! No one is ever going to believe this story. No one!' I had this dream; I told guys about it. And it happened! I actually floated around the bases. I don't even remember hitting the bases. It was just so special."

"You mentioned earlier how it would be eleven years between postseason appearances," I say. "So on September 28, on that sunny Sunday afternoon, Oil Can pitches the Red Sox to the division title against Toronto. What do you recall about how that moment felt for you?"

"I was twenty-three in '75, and now I was thirty-four years old," Dewey says. "It was a well-awaited dream, if you will, a dream I yearned for over those eleven years. It just shows you how tough it is to get back. So it was pretty spectacular when we won that [division-clinching] game."

I move on to the epic ALCS against the Angels, and Evans, now speaking fast and excitedly, takes over the content of the interview: "Erik, you know we're talking about some great games," he starts out. "Remember when Joe Carter hit the home run for Toronto to win the [1993] World Series? That was probably another of the most exciting games as well. But I have to tell you, in the ninth inning with two outs in Game Five of the ALCS in Anaheim, people were ready to pour out onto the field. City cops were on the field, holding people back and making sure nobody interrupted the end of the game. Then a lot of the cops came into our dugout, standing on the steps. Some of our guys had to go down into the runway because we couldn't sit on the bench and watch [Dave] Henderson hit. Others watched between the police officers' legs!

"After fouling a couple of balls off, [Henderson] hits one out [of the park], but all I could see were his feet leaving the ground. We still didn't know what happened! We wouldn't see the whole home run until we saw it later on instant replay. But within a few seconds those cops were out of the dugout, so by the time Henderson came around third base, we had him in full view. I've seen some pretty big home runs, but Henderson's, for me, was the greatest, most important, and most dramatic I ever saw. I'm not taking anything away from Carbo's or Fisk's or Carter's home runs; I'm not saying that. I'm saying [Henderson's was the greatest] for me as a player because we're down three games to one, and they're one strike away from going to the World Series and [already] hugging each other on their side—which we could see. It was *incredible*."

Then suddenly Dewey's face goes from being lit up from reminiscing about the Game Five comeback to a look of genuine sadness: "You know what's sad, Erik?" Dwight asks rhetorically, then pauses for effect. "It was a *day* game. You don't see too many of them anymore—and never in the World Series. I loved day games. The first two games of the '75 World Series were day games. I wish they would bring them back for the World Series—especially on the weekends. Start it at one o'clock on the West Coast. I'd love to see another World Series day game. I mean, who's watching a World Series game at two o'clock in the morning? I would love to, but I just don't have it in me anymore. So I turn off the game, and that's when all the excitement happens."

"And what about the kids?" I ask. "They're not up watching these games either. It makes you wonder if this next generation of fans will be as ardent as ours were toward baseball."

"Yeah, it really does," Dewey answers, while shaking his head slowly.

"So getting back to the ALCS, you're heading back to Boston with this seismic shift in momentum," I say.

"Yep, back for some home-cooked meals!" Dwight exclaims with a grin. "But I think what we learned after Game Five, as a unit, was not to go one game at a time, not to go one inning at a time, but to go one *pitch* at a time. That to me is the ultimate in a game—to not get ahead of anything, to have total mental concentration at its peak one pitch at a time. And we were doing that as a team."

"After winning the sixth game easily, you find yourself in a Game Seven," I say. "What I found fascinating—and even poetic—was that in this pennant-clinching game the two home runs were hit by the only remaining Red Sox from the '75 team—you and Rice. After all those years between pennants and all the team had to do to win that epic Game Five and to reach this point, did you have more of a feeling of euphoria or one of exhaustion?"

Dewey doesn't hesitate: "Oh, after we had played 169 games—not counting spring training—we're exhausted physically. But when you're winning and you're playing well, you overcome that exhaustion with euphoria. It's a time that the body hurts, and there are injuries you play through. I would have to have surgery on both of my knees after the World Series. We were *all* banged up, but it doesn't come into play what kind of pain or physical strain you're going through. It's pretty magical. To be in that moment, to have that feeling, is really neat. And, honestly, to be talking to you about it right now, it still gives me goose bumps."

It was clear from listening to Dewey, observing his emotions, watching his body language, and acknowledging all those years he endured between pennants that he, perhaps more than any of the other '86 Red Sox, relished and appreciated the opportunity to play in the upcoming World Series against the Mets.

Evans's anticipation of a return to the World Series would be matched only by his performance. He homered off of Dwight Gooden to put away Game Two and hit another off of Ron Darling in Game Seven to give the Red Sox an early lead in that contest. His nine RBIs were tied for the most in the Series—equaled only by those of Gary Carter. But while he talked to me about his disciplined approach in facing Gooden, whom he referred to as a "very special pitcher," and Darling, whom he described as "outstanding," Dewey's humility took our World Series conversation right to Game Four, when he allowed Lenny Dykstra's two-run homer to glance off his glove before going over the right-field fence at Fenway.

"We're up two games to one, we all know it's been sixty-eight years since the last Red Sox World Series championship in 1918, and we have a chance to come to within one game of winning it," Evans says. "The Mets are leading 3–0 in the seventh when Dykstra hits one toward the fence. I was there to make the catch, but when I jumped, my left hip hit the wall and stopped me from going any further. I should have had it easily, but I just couldn't get my arm [fully extended] above the wall. That wall [by the 380-foot sign] is higher than you think; it's about five feet high and comes up to my armpits. So the ball just tipped off my glove and into the bullpen for a two-run homer."

The Mets would knot the Series up that night before Boston would retake the Series lead the following game to set up the epic Game Six.

"I saw Clemens just the other night," Evans says of the Red Sox Game Six starter. "We connected, and it was great to see him again. What a pitcher. What a gamer. I don't know why he came out of that game or whose decision it was. We didn't really have pitch counts back then."

"Clemens had a batting helmet on and told me he was ready to hit in the eighth, but McNamara was apparently really concerned about Roger's blister on his throwing hand," I say. "To this day their stories differ on who decided to ultimately remove Clemens from the game. But after the Mets tied it against Calvin Schiraldi in the eighth, the Red Sox did take a 5–3 lead and were just one strike away from winning it all. What were you thinking, up two runs and needing just one more out to win Game Six and the World Series?"

"I had a feeling of gratefulness and was thanking God for that moment," Evans says. "But I was also thinking it was Schiraldi's third inning of work, and I don't believe he had done that all year. And Bob Stanley had been our hottest reliever for the last month to month and a half of the season and into the playoffs. So I was thinking I probably would have started Stanley [in the bottom of the tenth]. I almost said something to John [McNamara]. I had that kind of relationship with him. Of course I can say it, but he's going to do what he wants to do. But I thought it would have been better to let Stanley start and finish the inning instead of coming in with a mess. Still Schiraldi was throwing great. He had two outs on them before a line drive and two bloop singles. So that's not on him."

Stanley would enter the game, of course, to face Mookie Wilson, with a 5–4 lead with runners on the corners. After Stanley's wild pitch tied the game, Evans reflects on the fateful "Buckner play" and his unique vantage point in right field: "I'm looking at Stanley as the whole play is evolving," Dewey says. "Mookie was so quick, especially hitting left-handed, because he was already a step and a half closer to the first base bag. When he hit the ground ball, I look at Buckner and I look at Stanley, and it looked like Mookie was going to beat Stanley to the bag. It's no fault of Stanley's—Mookie was just so quick. So Buckner sees that situation, and when he went down for the ball, he was going for the bag. But the ball, as sure as I'm talking to you right now, was bouncing and bouncing, and then it hit something like a piece of dirt, causing it to stop and not bounce again. It stayed low on Buckner; it didn't have the hop.

The hop came out of it right before it reached his glove. I will never forget that as long as I live.

"A lot of people ask me, 'What did you do with the ball when it rolled into right field?' I'll say, 'I walked off the field because the game was over.' I don't even know where it went. I don't know if the umpire picked it up or what. [The ball recently was sold at auction for $418,250.] But, anyway, I love Buck. We wouldn't have been there without him. He'd had over two hundred hits and a great season. I disagree with people who say, 'They could have put Dave Stapleton in there,' which is something [McNamara] did a lot of times. But I know John wanted Bill out there because he deserved to be in that moment if we won. It was no fault of Bill Buckner's. Besides, the game was already tied when the ball went under his glove to allow Ray Knight to score. I heard one of our guys had already opened a bottle of champagne before the last pitch. I'm not superstitious, but that's just something you don't do."

Dewey then harkens back to an encounter he had with the Angels' Bob Boone that offseason: "I'll never forget seeing Bob that winter. We were a part of this group that would go to Hawaii or on hiking trips along with Wade and a few others from each league and our wives. So Bob looks at me and goes, 'I'm watching on TV, and when that [Buckner] play happened and you guys lost, I jumped up in front of my TV and said, "How does that feel?! How do you feel now?!"' And I got it. It wasn't that he was saying it in a bad way but rather in a way where I now understood what it was like for [the Angels in the ALCS]."

"From your vantage point what was the feeling in the clubhouse after that game?" I ask.

"They had pretty much put everything away—the plastic to protect the lockers, the champagne, and this and that. It was a tough moment," Dewey says with a sigh. "But we were not giving up. We knew we had already been through a lot [that postseason]."

"You certainly didn't give up," I say. "You homered off of Darling in the second inning to get things going, and then Gedman followed with a home run of his own for a 2–0 lead. Later in the frame Boggs singled home a run to give you a 3–0 lead. So really, despite the heart-wrenching defeat in Game Six, you guys were able to pick things back up and turn the page pretty quickly—as you certainly needed to."

"Yeah, there was no hangover; it was business as usual," Evans says. "Like I said about us, we were able to go one pitch at a time. We were very professional in that game and how we approached it. The Mets just outplayed us."

"But it's easy to forget how much fight the Red Sox had in them that game," I remark. "The Mets tie it at three, then go up 6–3, but then you guys pull to within 6–5 with a man on second and nobody out in the eighth."

"Who was the runner on second?" Dwight asks playfully with a straight face.

Before I can respond, Evans gives me the answer: "*Dwight Evans!*" he says gleefully. "I had just hit a double to right-center to drive in a couple of runs. And then I remember that Gedman came up after me and hit one of the hardest line drives I've ever seen at their second baseman [Wally Backman]—right at him. So I couldn't advance. Then Dave Henderson comes up, and if I'm on third base, that's an easy run to pick up with a fly ball. Could have tied the game. No fault of anybody's, but after Henderson and Baylor couldn't drive me in, I was stranded."

The Mets would then tack on a couple more runs in their half of the inning and hold on to win the game and the world championship.

"After the World Series, when I would be in an airport or some place," Evans volunteers, "I'd have people come up to me and say, 'What a great World Series.' I would look at them with my head cocked and be like, 'Really? What a great World Series? We lost.' But then I began to understand that if it's a Mets fan or just a baseball fan that had no skin in the game, to them, it *was* a great Series. As a fan of the game myself, putting myself outside of my team and our organization, I now understand how great it was. Unfortunately at the time it wasn't so for the Red Sox, our fans, the front office, and others involved. We were the bridesmaids—eleven years earlier and now again. And being a bridesmaid isn't fun. It was hard. It's taken me a long time to talk about it. In fact I have never talked this in depth about that World Series."

Dwight then turns to the tremendous success the Red Sox have had since the beginning of this century: "I'm so glad I still work with the Boston Red Sox," Evans, who has been a player development consultant since 2003, says. "I was able to be there in 2004, 2007, and 2013 [when the Sox won the World Series]. I'm shocked when people go to me, 'How do you feel about that?' I'm always like, 'What do you mean? I feel awesome.' Hey, we couldn't get the job done [in '86], but [the Red Sox] did it in '04—down three to nothing to the Yankees, who were just bombing them, and then coming back to win four straight. Then they go to St. Louis and win in a four-game sweep over them. They got it done; that's the bottom line."

"The '86 Red Sox were still a much-celebrated team, despite the World Series result," I say. "People forget about the huge rally at Government Center the city of Boston gave you guys after it was over. And today you and your teammates are treated like royalty when you return to Fenway."

Evans smiles as he listens to my take on his club and what it accomplished. "For a long time throughout New England history it was, 'The Red Sox will always break your heart,'" Dewey tells me. "But the die-hard fans are emotional, and they respect the spirit of giving all the human body can do and hustling and doing your best. They also know when you're dogging it, know when you don't care. They can feel that. They knew we cared. That's the difference with New England over other places. I understand why the '86 team was so special to them. It's because we did it all. The playoffs and World Series meant something to them. They flew me up to Boston in 2008, and Bill Buckner threw out the first pitch—and I'm catching it. The fans gave Buckner a standing ovation like I couldn't believe. I go out and meet him half way, give him a hug, and he's crying like a little kid because it meant so much to him. The fans knew [the World Series loss] wasn't his fault. They knew he always gave it his all. They knew the heart of Bill Buckner and that he was a gamer."

Evans then looks out at the field, pauses, and says with a sense of satisfaction, "They knew that we were *all* gamers."

Some time had passed since our memorable and revealing talk when I was deeply saddened—and somewhat shocked—to hear that Dwight's younger son, Justin, always an inspiration in the face of adversity, had succumbed to NF at the age of forty-two on an Easter Sunday. It was surprising to me because all throughout my communications with Dwight in setting up our interview, it was seemingly Tim who was going through the toughest period with his own complications from NF. Dwight had glowingly regaled me with examples of Tim's tremendous sense of humor despite having undergone forty-four surgeries throughout his life. Then, just ten months after Justin, Tim would indeed also lose his battle with NF at the age of forty-seven.

At this somber time I recalled a message Dwight had conveyed to me when we had sat and talked at Fenway Park: "Our issues with the kids, it's hard," he had said. "But with everything, God is in control. God is the same yesterday, today, and tomorrow. We believe God heals. Why He chooses to heal some and not others, I don't know. I'm not God. But we will continue praying. And that's how we stand until God shows us differently. It's called faith—and that's where we are today, Erik. That's where we're at."

In the days that followed the passing of both Justin and Tim, glowing tributes were given and written about them both, with the common theme being that despite their lifelong illness, their faith, which was passed down from Dwight and Susan, led them to serve and help others. The boys were, like the rest of the Evans family, an example to us all.

11.

Bubble

I went into the playoffs and the World Series seeing the ball like it was coming in slow motion. . . . Boggs said, "This guy's in a bubble. Don't walk near anything sharp or it's going to burst your bubble!" So it's been my nickname ever since.

—MARTY BARRETT

Marty Barrett and I have some history together. Back in the eighties he was one of the most approachable and baseball-savvy of all the Red Sox—everyone's pick for "Most Likely to Become a Big League Manager"—and we had several insightful interviews together. Then, three years after his playing career ended, we attempted to collaborate on an '86 Red Sox book. Ultimately, however, we couldn't land a publisher. Despite eight years having gone by since the World Series defeat—the thrilling regular season and ALCS notwithstanding—the primary reason for rejection given by editors was that Boston fans were still hurting from it. Still Marty and I had worked well together and got along famously. So when I emailed him to request an interview for this book, it was like reaching out to an old friend, and he graciously invited me to come talk to him at his home in Summerlin, Nevada, an affluent Las Vegas suburb.

I was especially excited about seeing him because I knew that Barrett, perhaps as much as anybody, always kept his finger on the pulse of everything to do with the '86 Red Sox and that he still kept tabs on many of the players. In addition, he was always one of the most widely respected players, not just on the Red Sox but in all of baseball. In fact Bill Buckner once told me Barrett was the smartest baseball player he had ever played with in his more than two decades in the game. His insight would be invaluable.

So on an impossibly beautiful late autumn morning in Las Vegas under bright blue skies, I drove the roughly ten miles from the Strip to Barrett's gated community, which was situated alongside Bear's Best, one of the area's most scenic golf courses. I then came upon Barrett's beautiful, ultra-modern home, impeccably designed by his wife Robin, and tastefully landscaped with a vertical garden of flower beds, trees, bushes, and stones. But there was something else that was eye catching in front of the house. In the only exterior sign that a professional baseball player might live there, near the entrance was an endearing sculpture atop a mantle of two young boys looking up adoringly at a teenager with a bat, all three attired in baseball uniforms.

Barrett, neatly dressed for a Saturday in a pressed button-down shirt—instantly recognizable as the player who once manned second base for the Red Sox—greets me warmly at the front door. As we walk through his spacious, immaculately clean home toward his office, he comments that I look more like a Floridian or Californian than New Yorker with my longer blond hair. I tell him I hear that a lot. I tell Marty, who is an avid golfer, how much I appreciated his taking a morning off from the golf course to speak with me. Ever cordial, Barrett says he appreciates my coming all the way out to see him and talk a little baseball.

As we enter his home office, it instantly strikes me as one you might expect of a former ballplayer. The shelves behind his large, stately desk are adorned with signed baseballs; books on the game; a framed poster from the first World Series match-up between Boston and Pittsburgh in 1903; and, what certainly is one of his most prized possessions, his Red Sox Hall of Fame plaque, which sits atop a thick *Baseball Encyclopedia.*

As we sit to talk, his son, Kyle, who attended Stanford and now works in Palo Alto, stops by the office with two glasses of water for us. By the way Marty introduces him to me, with a gleam in his eye, I can tell he couldn't possibly be prouder of him.

"I have a daughter, Katie, as well," Marty says.

"Two Ks," I note. "Just like Clemens and his four sons, whose names start with 'K.'"

Barrett laughs and says, "That's right! I never made that connection."

Perhaps from hearing the laughter and noticing a stranger in the house, a Norfolk Terrier named Finnegan comes into the office to pay a visit.

"He'll hang out with us for a while," Barrett says with a grin. "The other one will probably come in here too. He's Hank—another Norfolk Terrier but one with a rusty color, which is the more normal type that was chosen by dog breeders as Dog of the Year three years ago. Anyway, Katie played golf at Long Beach State and is now a golf pro at La Jolla Country Club. Kyle and my wife and I might all actually move to La Jolla too. We'll be with the kids then. We enjoy being with them so much, and let's face it, my wife and I are both going to be sixty, so what do we have—another twenty, twenty-five years left?"

"Sure, but do you still *think* like a kid?" I ask, smiling broadly.

"Oh, sure I do," he says. "My brain does, but my body goes its own way!"

Many of the '86 Sox still seem to gravitate toward Barrett, both directly and indirectly.

"Roger [Clemens] and I are always texting together," Marty tells me. "I don't see [Wade] Boggs quite as much, but if the team holds events or celebrations for us, he's always there."

"I do have messages from a couple of your good friends who knew I was coming out to see you," I say. "Buck said you were his favorite player that he ever played with. He wanted me to be sure to tell you that."

"That's really nice of him," Barrett says with a smile.

"And the other message comes from Dewey," I start off. "Unlike Buck's, it's not good news. I was on the phone with him last week, and while he wanted me to send you his best, he also wanted me to let you know that his son Tim now has stage four brain cancer."

"That family has gone through some tough stuff," Barrett says somberly. "You know, Dwight, Buckner, and I always ate together on the road. They had this thing back then called 'Eat to Win,' with a lot of chicken and pasta and stuff like that. Everywhere we went, we would eat lunch together before every road game."

"And I know you came up the same year with Oil Can," I say. "What a character he is."

"He's real funny!" Barrett says with a grin. "Get him going, and he'll let you know about *everything*."

"And a really bright guy," I add.

"He's *very* intelligent," Barrett notes. "That's the mistake you can make with Oil Can. That's why he was such a great pitcher. He just knew how hitters were thinking, had a good feel for approaching them, and knew the game really well. People didn't understand that about him. They thought that because he was from Mississippi, he probably was uneducated, but he was very bright then and still is now."

"Today it's so rare that the core of a ball club comes up through the system like so many of you guys did," I say. "In addition to Clemens, Boggs, and Oil Can, there were others like Hurst, Gedman, Stapleton, and so on. Did that make winning the pennant together in '86 extra sweet?"

"Oh, absolutely!" Barrett exclaims. "To know everyone for so long and to know they've been through the system and know our philosophy, you just kind of bond together as an organization. That's not to mean that you don't pick somebody up like Tom Seaver or Don Baylor or Billy Buckner to come over; it's always good to put the pieces together. But the core group we had always made us very proud that we were able to win it with home-grown guys. I do think that nowadays teams are going back to being more developmental, trying to bring guys up through the system, instead of how the Yankees did things back then [with free agent signings and trades for veterans]. Even the Yankees now have a strong Minor League system, so I think everyone's realizing that's just the way to go."

"So that old perception of the Red Sox—twenty-five guys, twenty-five cabs—doesn't sound like it pertained to your Red Sox team," I say.

"No, not at all!" Barrett exclaims. "We were a very close-knit group, always rooting for each other. What you're alluding to may have been the case beforehand because they never had a ton of success. They made a couple of playoffs, but they hadn't been there in a while. We were a different group, the guys born in the late fifties and early sixties."

"How do you think history sees this club?" I ask. "After all, they seemed destined to break the "Curse of the Bambino," and despite falling just short, it's a team that is still iconic in the annals of baseball lore."

Marty leans back in his chair to give the question some thought: "I think we were a once-in-a-generation type team," he remarks. "We didn't get it done. The '04, '07, and '13 teams—they got it done. But I still think we had a better club than those teams. Just the overall people on our team; we were very strong. And our lineup was amazing. Boggs was a .360 hitter and is in the Hall of Fame. We had another Hall of Famer with Rice and another guy, Buckner, who *should* be in the Hall of Fame. You had Dewey [Dwight Evans] and Baylor hanging around then. And believe me, Spike Owen could wrap it around too. I remember they called me, Boggs, and Buckner the 'Killer Bees.' Everyone was a *very* tough out. My point is that I think we were probably one of the better teams the Red Sox ever had in their history. Thank goodness for the teams that have won it—especially the '04 team, which took the monkey off of every-one's back. I root for the Red Sox to win it every year. Dustin Pedroia's been my favorite player ever since he's been on that team. I love the way he plays and how he brings out the best in everyone else. And the way Big Papi [David Ortiz] ended his career with one of the most amazing feats you'll ever see in baseball was just incredible. Classy guy. But I do think Red Sox fans still see us as champions and wish we could've won it all."

When you look up Marty Barrett on *Baseball Reference*, his regular season statistics, while certainly solid for a second baseman, don't jump off the page. In ten seasons in the big leagues he had a batting average of .278, had eighteen lifetime home runs, and never drove in more than sixty-five runs. But anyone who watched him play every day would know that his value to the Red Sox was immeasurable: a consummate team player, the take-charge 'quarterback' of the infield, and a perennial league leader in moving runners over with a sacrifice bunt. In the two hole his primary role was to move Boggs up a base or get on for the big boys like Rice, Evans, and Baylor to drive him in. Thus prior to the 1986 postseason, if you were going through the rosters of the virtual galaxy of stars from the Red Sox and their two opponents, the Angels and the Mets, you would be forgiven if Barrett, in comparison to many of the other players, didn't immediately strike you as the guy who could take over a series. Yet as it would turn out, in that greatest of Octobers for baseball drama Marty Barrett was the best player on the planet.

"You had a postseason for the ages in '86 by collecting twenty-four hits," I tell Marty. "First you were MVP of the ALCS, hitting .367. Then you hit a World Series high for all players with a .433 mark; your thirteen hits tied a record. When looking back now with more than thirty years of hindsight, how do you explain this feat?"

"For sure it was the high point of my career," Barrett says with a grin. "It's interesting, but it all went back to '84, when I hit .303 after really working hard preparing for that season. Jerry Remy got hurt in the first couple of weeks; I stepped in and had that great season. But then I made the mistake of my life. The next spring I went to spring training like I was

Dewey or Jimmy, thinking I could go there to get in shape, and as a result, '85 turned out to be a tough year. I lost my job for a week or two to Dave Stapleton. I ended up hitting just .266, my lowest average of my prime years. So after that season I said to myself, 'That will never happen again!' I worked my ass off that offseason, and the '86 season for me was proof to myself that I learned from the mistake of the year before."

Marty would end the '86 regular season with a .286 average and a career-high thirty-nine doubles.

"All my hard work culminated with the postseason," Barrett continues. "I went into the playoffs and the World Series seeing the ball like it was coming in slow motion. The timing was just so fortunate, with the big lights on you and its being New England's first World Series in a while. To be able to come through like that and win the playoffs like we did was amazing."

"Did it give you added satisfaction that nobody saw you coming?" I ask.

"I've always said it was like I was hiding in the weeds," Barrett remarks. "But I did hear during the playoffs that the Angels were saying stuff like, 'Everyone forgets about Marty Barrett' and, 'He's the glue to that team. He sets the table, and you cannot take your eyes off of him.' That was nice to hear because mentally I'm thinking, 'They are not even paying attention to me. They're going to give me a lot of pitches to hit. They don't want to face Boggs in front of me or Buckner after me. Let's make him hit the ball to get on; don't walk him. He's not going to take you deep, so let's give him something to hit.' Maybe that wasn't true, but by my thinking they weren't paying attention to me, I felt like I had an advantage. That's the mental part of the whole game."

"The comeback against the Angels was nothing short of stunning," I note. "Earlier you mentioned that the postseason was the highlight of your career. Was Game Five against California the most thrilling victory of your life?"

"Yeah, it really was," Barrett says. "We thought we were so good that year, yet the game before, when Clemens was throwing and we thought we had the game in hand, the Angels came back to win against our bullpen. So you're down three games to one, and then Mike Witt is pitching great against us in the fifth game. Gedman and I had played against Witt in winter ball the year before, so we knew how good he was. But then when they took Witt out of the game during the ninth inning, my antennas went up, and I thought, 'Hey, what's going on here? Whoa! This is such an odd move! Now we have a real chance.' Gedman was having a big game against Witt, so Gene Mauch brought in the lefty, Gary Lucas, to face him. Personally I'd have just let Witt pitch to Gedman and take my chances—or walk him. Then Lucas hits Geddy with a pitch and Hendu follows with a home run off of Donnie Moore, and, as they say, the rest is history. I can still see the Angels' left fielder, Brian Downing, kind of just fall into the wall with dead weight like, 'Oh my God. Did this just really happen?' It was such a great victory."

"And a real momentum shift, right?" I ask.

"Yeah, [the series] was over; it really was," Barrett says matter-of-factly. "We just went back to Boston flying high, and it wasn't even close. I mean, we were out of it and came back to life. We killed them in Game Six, and now we were like, 'Oh, we've got them. Things are really on our side.' Like you said about momentum, I think [the Angels] were like, 'Oh my God, we had this. We gave it away. We shouldn't have had to even fly back to Boston.' So they start thinking negatively and lose the series. The psyche is crazy."

Marty leans back in his chair, shakes his head, and with a sly grin finishes his thought: "But, Erik, that's what makes baseball the greatest game; it really is."

"Had your Red Sox finished the job against the Mets, it would have been remembered as the Marty Barrett Series," I remark. "It's been said that the voting media near the end of Game Six had picked Bruce Hurst as the MVP of the Series, though you had twelve hits through that game, on your way to a record-tying thirteen."

"Yeah, that's how I got my nickname," Barrett says with a smile. "Boggs started calling me 'Bubble.' He said, 'This guy's in a bubble. Don't walk near anything sharp or it's going to burst your bubble!' So it's been my nickname ever since."

We share a laugh over it before I reiterate that he easily could have been MVP of the Series: "Through those first six games you hit .480, had the most assists of any fielder, and played flawless defense," I say. "So let me throw this out there. Ten miles down the road from here, at some sports book on the Vegas Strip, what kind of odds would they have put up on the board, with all due respect, for Marty Barrett winning the MVP of the '86 World Series?"

Barrett doesn't hesitate: "A hundred to one—or something like that," he says. "It was the furthest thing from my mind. All I knew was how to play solid baseball and do my part by setting the table for the other guys. But despite being lucky enough to be as locked in as I was, winning [the MVP award] wasn't on my mind at all."

I knew from our past discussions that Barrett had as much insight as *anybody* regarding Game Six—one of the most historic games in baseball history by any measure—and I start right there when discussing the World Series.

"You once told me that one of the reasons the Red Sox jumped ahead on Bobby Ojeda was because he was tipping his pitches," I recall.

"He definitely was," Marty confirms. "We had a report from our advance scout, Frank Malzone, that said [Ojeda] would flap his fingers before throwing a changeup. And if he didn't do that, then we knew he would throw either a fastball or curveball. Personally I'd rather hit a fastball, so when I knew a changeup was coming, which was Bobby's bread-and-butter pitch, I just automatically took it unless I had two strikes. I told myself, 'If I see that little flip, I'm not going to swing at it.'"

"Did the knowledge of knowing what was coming contribute to your success against Ojeda, or were you just so locked in during those three weeks in October that it really wouldn't have made much of a difference?" I ask.

"Although I got four hits off of him, it actually might not have made a difference," Barrett believes. "But a great changeup—I'm telling you!—can put a hitter in a slump because it can force him into making funky swings. But in my case it may not have made a difference to know it was coming because I could usually sense when it was and hold up [my swing]. Still I was glad I knew."

Barrett then makes what I feel is a remarkable statement: "Back then, quite honestly, I would say we probably had *half the pitchers* in the [American] league tipping their pitches," he confides. "It's rare that it happens today. Nowadays pitching coaches set up cameras and watch everything. As their pitchers wind up, they put pictures together between the fastball, the breaking ball, and the changeup. Opposing teams do this too, to see if there are any changes in what the pitcher is doing—whether it's opening his glove a little bit, tilting it, or bringing it above the belt or below it, things like that. But pitchers do a great job of not tipping their pitches anymore."

"Ojeda was pretty fortunate to get out of there just giving up two runs over six innings, despite yielding eight hits, two walks, and some screaming line-drive outs," I note. "Did you feel like you may have let him off the hook a little bit and squandered some opportunities?"

Barrett lets out a sigh before admitting it was likely the case: "Yeah, it's probably true," he says. "And maybe we let our guard down a little bit when we had a guy like Roger Clemens going out there. You think, 'Okay, Roger, a couple of runs should be enough for you. Now go ahead and finish this thing off for us.'"

But after Clemens left the game after seven innings, Calvin Schiraldi would allow the Mets to tie the game at 3–3 in the eighth. The game would eventually head into extra innings.

"Hendu would again play the hero, just like he had in the ALCS, with a tenth-inning home run to put you up, 4–3," I say. "What were you thinking as he rounded the bases?"

"I'm thinking, 'Boy, we can win this thing. We can be World Series champs.' Then after that Boggs doubles, and I single him in to give us a two-run lead. I advance to second as they throw the ball home to try to get Boggs out. I'm standing at second base, and I remember Ray Knight looking at me, saying out loud, 'Great job, Marty. Nice hit.' Ray Knight of *the Mets* said that. It was pretty cool. And then I looked over at Keith [Hernandez], and there was this look of almost resignation on his face. Then he gets up in the Mets' half and hits one pretty good to center for their second out. We get two very quick outs."

"So you're one out away with a 5–3 lead," I say. "You told me some time ago that all you could think of at that moment was how Jean Yawkey, the elderly owner of the Red Sox, was going to feel after the Red Sox had won their first World Series in sixty-eight years and how proud she would be up there at the podium. Of all the things you could have been thinking about, why Mrs. Yawkey?"

Marty reflects on that very special moment when he stood at his second base position at a deadly quiet Shea Stadium: "It's funny. Mrs. Yawkey came to a lot of games and was a *huge* fan," he begins. "There had been a lot of heartache for her and the fans, so I thought how great this was going to be for her. It was going to be so cool that the curse was going to be lifted. I don't know if anyone else was thinking about Mrs. Yawkey at that moment, and maybe it was unnatural to do so when my mind should have been completely focused on the game. But after we got those two quick outs, I was thinking, 'Okay, this is going to happen!'"

And then for a fleeting moment Barrett recounts how he *thought* it was over: "Gary Carter gets up and swings at the first pitch," Marty tells me. "It looked like he popped it straight up, and I thought Geddy was going to have a chance to catch that foul ball. But it just went over the backstop—*just a little bit.*"

"They say that baseball is a game of inches, and that was a prime example," I say.

"Yeah, for sure. And then Carter just hung in there and blooped one into left," Marty recalls. "Now, with a man on, you're shifting to like, 'Uh oh.' Now you're locked back in, blinders on like Roger Clemens, blocking everything else out. But then a bloop into center, another bloop into center, a wild pitch—or passed ball, whatever you want to call it—and a slow grounder to first. *Game over!*"

More than three decades later all Barrett can do is shake his head: "It was like, '*What happened?*'" he asks rhetorically. "Just crazy! How crazy is this game?"

Marty's recollections of the events leading up to the "Buckner play" are as thoughtful as they are riveting. As the unofficial captain of that Red Sox infield and an astute baseball man, he had, in my view, the best perspective of anyone.

"Let's start at the beginning," I say. "Mac takes out Schiraldi and brings in Stanley to face Mookie [Wilson]. You once told me that you believed there was a better chance of retiring Wilson with Calvin out there. Why did you believe that?"

"Bob Stanley is a sinker ball pitcher," Marty begins. "Mookie's left-handed, so the ball is going to sink away from him, and he's going to be able to put the bat on the ball quite easily. I thought the chance of Steamer's [Stanley] striking out Mookie was far less than with Schiraldi. Mookie might not have struck out against either guy, but there was a better chance of it happening with Schiraldi."

"So," I say, "Stanley comes in, gets the count to 2-2 on Mookie before Wilson fouls off a bunch of pitches. Then the wild pitch occurs. You had the perfect view into home plate, and this is why guys like Dewey and Buckner have always told me, 'Talk to Marty about what happened.' So what happened, Marty? Gedman's such a prince of a guy, and he told me it was his fault. But did they get crossed up a little bit?"

"I know that Gedman set up away," Barrett recalls. This would be different from Gedman's recollection of setting up more inside. "He set up away, and then the pitch ended up being down and in. But I don't know. Quite honestly I don't know if it was a call for a fastball in or a fastball away. But I would think that as you're looking in there, if he's set up away and you thought it was going to be in, you'd step off [the rubber]. But it's tough because you never think a sinker's going to be in that area. You think, worst case, it might start over the middle and drift toward you, or it might start outside and you have to reach for it. But it's rare that you have to go to your right and get it. It's really tough. That's why I don't even know if it was a wild pitch or a passed ball; it was so borderline. I think all of us wish we had a crystal ball to know what would've happened if that hadn't happened and see what Mookie would've done if not for the wild pitch. With Knight on first, Mookie may have gotten a hit, he may have lined out to me, he may have popped out, or he may have struck out. I really would have loved to see that result. But it's tough; it's tough. It was an extreme change of momentum right there."

"It's interesting that Mookie Wilson almost never had at bats like that one," I note. "He was such a free swinger that most of his at bats went a handful of pitches at most. So, yes, it would be interesting to know what would have occurred had it not been for the wild pitch.

"Do you still believe that the wild pitch, which only tied the game, was bigger than the 'Buckner play,' which won it for the Mets?" I ask.

"Well, you hate to give them the tie," Marty reasons. "And I think that's why Rich and Bobby feel just as badly about that play as Bill did of his—and I would feel horrible about it too. The momentum just changed then. The Mets were probably like, 'Okay, we're tied! We've got life again!' Just like we had life again against the Angels. The Mets got to live for at least another inning."

I then move on to the next strange occurrence in that frame: "A lot of people don't know about what happened next," I say. "With Knight now on second following the wild pitch and taking a *huge* lead, you had a pickoff play on, but Stanley delivered home instead. Because of the pickoff play, you were shaded toward second, which forced Buckner to move toward you to help fill the hole at the second base position, right?"

"Yeah, once Ray Knight got to second," Marty recalls, "he was leading off really far from the bag, and the crowd was going nuts. I know the third base coach [Buddy Harrelson] saw it. So I gave a couple of pickoff calls to Gedman. He gave the 'five signal,' which means there's a pickoff play on, but then it still ended up being a fastball. With that being the case, if you said, 'Okay, I'll take that little ground ball [that Mookie would hit],' I would agree with you ninety-nine times out of a hundred because Bill Buckner's going to field it and flip it to Bobby, and the inning's over. *But who knows?* Maybe we try a pickoff and [Stanley] throws it into centerfield, or something else crazy like that happens, and Knight scores. I'll take the little ground ball as the event that did happen. It's just too bad it did."

"I know you and Buck are close," I say. "It's so unfair the fallout that came from his error."

"Some people think that if Bill Buckner catches that ball, we win the World Series," Barrett says incredulously. "Hey, it's *still* extra innings. It's tough for Bill—just like it's tough for Bobby and Geddy. I'm sure you'd live that every day. You'd replay that a thousand times in your mind, like, 'Did I read it wrong?' Or, 'Should I have charged it a little bit?' Or, 'Should I not have?' It's just constant. But I don't think any of that matters because he'd always catch that ball. And he looked like he got over there in plenty of time. He was perfectly squared up with the ball. I've heard him say in interviews that his glove just closed up instead of opening. Why that happened, I don't know. But Billy Buckner did so much for our team that year—especially in September. When Toronto was starting to get close to us and then we just turned on the afterburners, my recollection is that Buckner probably hit like .340 that month with a bunch of home runs."

"And then of course Buckner was playing with a serious Achilles heel injury that was affecting his range of movement," I say. "To that point there was an opportunity in the eighth inning where Mac could have pinch-hit Buckner for Donnie Baylor with the left-handed Jesse Orosco in the game and the bases loaded. With Buckner out of the game Dave Stapleton would have been inserted as his replacement at first base. Would you have made that move at that time?"

"Yeah, I probably would have," Barrett says. "Although Bill Buckner would hit a bullet off of [Orosco] to center field, I would have made the move to put Baylor in there and have Stapleton go play first. In fact I was at first and said to our first base coach, Walt Hriniak, 'They should pinch hit for Buck.' But Walt said, 'No, no. Buck will get him.' But even then I thought, 'After he hits, go ahead and take him out.'"

"We've talked a lot about momentum shifts today—both in victory and defeat," I say. "Heading into Game Seven, the Mets that I've spoken with say that the World Series was over because of the way the sixth game had ended, while guys like Buckner told me that you guys brushed it off and showed it by jumping out to an early 3–0 lead. How did you feel after Game Six heading into Game Seven?"

"I agree with Buck," Marty is quick to say. "It was just like Game One—just trying to win that game. But the difference was that the winner of this game wins it all, so there was a little more sense of importance in this one. But I don't think there's ever been a game that I've gone into and thought, 'Oh my gosh, we're in for it today!' I've never felt that way. As for the rest of the guys, even right after Game Six, Hurst kind of broke the silence in the clubhouse by saying, 'Gene Mauch must be doing cartwheels right now.' That kind of broke the tension a little bit."

"In a way Game Seven started out much in the same way as Game Six did," I say. "You guys hit Darling really hard and took the early lead. I've always felt that the greatness of this Game Seven is often lost because of all the attention that was paid to Game Six. Despite the Red Sox's losing, you have to admit it was a tremendous ballgame. You guys go up 3–0, the Mets come back to tie it, and then add on to make it 6–3. But then the Red Sox come roaring back to pull to within 6–5 with nobody out and a runner on second. That was a much closer game than the 8–5 final would indicate. I thought it was appropriate that with the superb Series that you had, the Mets had to get you out to end the Series. What were your thoughts after having played so well in that Series to be the one that ultimately made the final out—a strikeout by Jesse Orosco?"

"I'll give you my thoughts on that final at bat," Marty starts out. "I remember looking back at our bench while a smoke bomb was being cleared in center field, wondering if I should swing at the first pitch, like Gary Carter had done when he started the Mets' Game Six rally. I was thinking if [Orosco] had great control, I might as well not let him get ahead of me. Or maybe I should just take a pitch, and he might walk me—a good approach when down three runs. So I decided to take the pitch, and of course it was right down the middle. I kind of twitched my head, wishing that I'd swung at that. I definitely would have put it in play.

"Now the fans are going nuts. I'm still focused, and Orosco throws a couple of balls before getting another strike on me. Now I'm thinking—and this is a *bad* thought really—that the umpire is going to ring me up on anything close, so I've got to really protect the plate. Because I was so locked in, I normally would have taken the pitch that he struck me out on, which was a little up and away. He was probably going to come back after the up and away pitch with a slider. But I swung right through it, threw my right arm down in disgust, and thought to myself, 'This is bullshit.' I just swung at that pitch because I knew [if it's] anything close, the umpire wants to call strike three. I think that's why a lot of guys strike out for the last out of a game. It happens a lot."

"Then you guys had to deal with the Boston media, which was really tough on the Red Sox," I say. "And you had to hear all about how the 'Curse of the Bambino' was living on."

"Yeah, sure; they liked to think there was a curse, but obviously nobody really believed it." Barrett states. "It's just a matter of everything coming together, and then it's over. Just like the 'Curse of the Billy Goat' for the Cubs. If there's a real curse, you'll never win it all, right?"

Barrett's Red Sox career ended in a bit of controversy following the 1990 season. A knee injury midway through the '89 season while he was running out a pinch-hit grounder put him on the disabled list for over two months. However, Barrett alleged that instead of receiving the proper treatment—a surgical reconstruction of his knee—the Red Sox team physician and part-owner of the club, Dr. Arthur Pappas, recommended twenty days of rehabilitation instead. No second opinion allegedly was ever sought by the Red Sox. Barrett charged that the Red Sox intent was to get him back on the field in time for the stretch run of the '89 season—and that his career was shortened by Pappas's negligence. Ultimately Barrett would be vindicated when Pappas was ordered by a U.S. District Court jury to pay him $1.7 million in lost wages in 1995.

"But my relationship with the Red Sox now is fantastic," Barrett tells me. "Everything they do, they do for the players. They have a great alumni group right there in Boston, led by Pam Kenn, who handles everything wonderfully. Back then I didn't handle that 1990 season very well. I got hurt in '89 right after I'd just signed a three-year contract. I tried to come back quick. At that time I didn't know that my ACL had been totally torn. I think I found out in the offseason, but then 1990 came around, and Jody Reed moved over to second and Luis Rivera moved over to short. Rivera did a pretty good job. But since I had come back, I was hitting like .250 and still playing good defense. But Joe Morgan, who was the manager then, let me know that they were going to make a change. We were in first place, and I just thought it was very strange. Nowadays so many managers stick with guys that are hitting .220 or .230 because all of a sudden they get hot at some point. I felt very disappointed, but instead of just digging my nose in and saying, 'Okay, I'll get my chance,' because you always get another chance, I pouted. By the end of the year we made the playoffs, but I didn't play much after that. I had asked them if they would release me because I just didn't think it was a good fit anymore, and they accommodated me. But in hindsight I kind of wish I'd stuck it out. Who knows what would have happened?"

Barrett would play sparingly in his final season with the San Diego Padres before calling it a career.

"Many figured you to become a big league manager," I say. "But you chose to coach your son's little league team instead, while broadcasting games here in Las Vegas with Tim Neverett, who went on to become an announcer with the Pittsburgh Pirates, Red Sox, and now the Dodgers."

"I really enjoyed announcing—especially with Tim," Barrett says. "I love Tim; he's got a great voice. We did some stuff for the Triple-A team here; it was fun. But it was almost like [the grind] of playing baseball. You're just traveling all the time, and my wife wanted me home so we could go out on the weekends during the season—that type of thing. I just felt it was too much on the family."

However, another baseball moment would await Marty: induction into the Red Sox Hall of Fame in 2012.

"What does that honor mean to you?" I ask.

"It means the world to me—it *really* does," Barrett says emotionally. "When they called and told me, I thought, 'Oh my gosh! This is amazing!' That's because the Red Sox have such a rich history—the same as the Yankees do. No disrespect to other teams, but I just think the Yankees and the Red Sox have the richest [history], and to be part of that whole group in the Hall of Fame and to be remembered like that is really neat. I was just one of those guys that wasn't particularly great at anything. But I was *good* at almost everything— ran the bases good, put the ball in play good, those types of things. And the fans in Boston have always been great to me—still are to this day. They *still* recognize me, which is amazing! This summer I went back to Boston, and when I checked into a Hampton Inn, the guy behind the counter goes, 'Marty Barrett! Are you kidding me? Can I get my picture with you?!' It was so cool."

At five feet ten inches and 175 pounds in a lineup of big men, Barrett may have been small in stature for the '86 Red Sox, but he was a giant when they needed him the most.

12.

Lyon-ized

....

I knew if the Red Sox won the World Series, it would make any
other championship in [Boston] look like a third-grade birthday
party. . . . Most of me wanted them to win, but there was a part of
me that didn't.

—STEVE LYONS

By all measures Steve Lyons has the appearance
and demeanor of a man who is living "the dream."
Looking much younger than his years, with Viking-
like long blond hair, pearly white teeth, and a slim and toned
physique thanks to regular Pilates classes, the bachelor Red
Sox analyst, with a two-day-old beard, barefoot, and wearing a
golf shirt and shorts, is at peace with himself in his spacious
two-story Hermosa Beach townhouse, a block away from the
beach. Although originally from Oregon and then playing several years in both Boston and Chicago, Lyons is now the epit-
ome of Southern California cool, lounging in his upstairs living
room near an open balcony door on a pristine, sunny, and
75-degree late January afternoon.

Despite having grown up and currently living on the West
Coast, Steve's heart has always been back East because from
the time he was a child, all he ever wanted to do was play ball
for the Boston Red Sox.

"You're originally from Eugene, Oregon," I say to Steve. "But
your dad, a terrific athlete in his day, grew up in Hudson, Mas-

sachusetts. So you were probably a Red Sox fan because of him, right?"

"A *huge* Red Sox fan," Lyons exclaims. "Back then we only had Saturday baseball on TV—Tony Kubek and Joe Garagiola on the *Game of the Week*. If the Red Sox weren't on, we'd go outside, and my dad would pitch to me and play catch. But if the Red Sox were playing, then we'd sit and watch the game. My dad was a huge Red Sox fan too. His influence on my baseball life in general was overwhelming and why being a Red Sox fan became second nature to me, in the same way kids growing up in New England are Sox fans too—there is no choice; it's the way it is."

"So you must go back to the '67 'Impossible Dream' team," I note. "Back in the earlier days of Yaz and Tony Conigliaro."

"I was seven years old," Lyons recounts. "After Tony C got beaned, I remember an account of it in *Sports Illustrated*. It's funny that I remember that story now. He was saying there was so much blood in his nose and around his eye that, depending on the way he was lying down, he could have literally died by choking on blood because there was no way for him to breathe. He got through that, though, and came back to have a couple of good years, which was pretty amazing. I see his brother [Billy] all the time."

"So you probably have a much better recollection of the pennant-winning '75 team," I say.

"Oh yeah; that's when you start getting into the Rice, Evans, Fisk, and Freddie Lynn period," Lyons says with a grin. "Then, ten years later, I showed up. So you still had the taste of those guys around even though some of them were gone. And later I got to play with Fisk in Chicago. The ghosts of those teams, at the end of the day, underachieved because they were supposed to win but never were able to figure out how to do it."

"Like you said, you came up in 1985, a decade after the club's last division title," I note. "This was your childhood team, a dream so few players realize. You could have ended up with twenty-five other clubs, but you were fortunate enough to end up in Boston. Can you talk about what kind of thrill that must have been for you?"

Lyons leans back in his chair to ponder the question: "You know, it's kind of funny," he starts out philosophically. "Some fathers will say they live vicariously through their sons in a situation like that. But I think I was kind of living through my father in that instance. I was certainly happy to get there. When I got drafted by the Red Sox, that was a big deal for my dad, but I never thought I was going to make it to the big leagues. Even when I was in Triple-A, that was the first time I kind of thought, 'Wow, if someone got hurt, they might actually have to call me up. That would be weird.'"

"You're being very modest," I interject. "I remember when you played center field as a rookie. You had skill; you were an excellent defensive center fielder with a little bit of pop in your bat. Is that really how you felt?"

"If you look at my numbers over my lifetime, [you'll see] I struck out more than I should have for a guy with very little power," Steve says humbly. "I never hit for a high average either. Before [coming to] the big leagues, I was always in the top five in RBIS, runs scored, stolen bases, and even sometimes home runs but would hit like .240. People were like, 'Why don't you get a few more hits somehow?' But the ones I did get caused some damage—[by] driving in runs or whatever. So I always considered that if you were on the other team, you would try not to let [me] hurt you too bad. I wasn't the scariest guy out there—didn't have the numbers of a guy that should be headed straight to the big leagues. But I knew that there wasn't anybody that would outwork me or play harder. I saw guys that were better than me—lots of guys. I was never intimidated by that. I knew I just really had to bust my ass if I was going to do anything. Thankfully things fell into place."

It was also Steve's over-aggressiveness and passion for the game that bestowed upon him one of the best nicknames in baseball history: Psycho.

Lyons laughs when I bring this up: "Early in my career I wasn't noted as—I hesitate to say this—'the smartest player,' as my aggressiveness would sometimes lead me into errors. Everyone always told me, 'Make aggressive mistakes, but don't be stupid.' I think I had some pretty well-known plays that were borderline stupid—and I like to think that I was a guy who really knew the game. I understood how to play it, tried to play it the right way, and always played it hard. But sometimes that over-aggressiveness led to some questionable plays.

"I did have a temper, as well, that I let get away from me more times than I'm proud to say. I marvel at the players today. You rarely see arguments between them and umpires anymore. You rarely see a player get upset and throw his helmet or break something in the dugout. It happens, but when I played, it happened a lot. I guess there were more 'red asses' when I played. I did it a lot but was never proud of that. My father used to call me at times and say stuff like, 'Look, you're not a very good player, but even if you were and you hit .300, you're still gonna make four hundred outs. Are you going to throw your helmet down and be pissed off about every one of them? It looks bad. You're gonna make a lot of outs, so getting upset like that doesn't make sense.' But I could just never get past it, I guess. Anyway that's how I became 'Psycho.'"

Lyons would break into the big leagues out of spring training in 1985—a decision rendered by new manager John McNamara. It brought to mind an encounter between the two of them in an empty Fenway Park well prior to a game that year, and it has stuck in my mind ever since.

"I remember being on the field prior to batting practice as a young reporter," I begin. "You were walking in from the outfield, and McNamara was walking out. Mac kind of snarled at you and said, 'Why don't you get a haircut?' Nothing else—and he kept on walking. It really left an impression on me because here is this young kid busting his ass, making diving plays, and giving his all, and all his manager could think of to say, in a crusty way, was for him to get a haircut. Was that the real Johnny Mac, or did someone just piss in his Wheaties that morning?"

"He was two different guys really," Lyons says. "I think during that time period I was probably a little too much of a pretty boy. I mean, I wanted to be the dirtiest guy on the field at the end of the day, but before the game started, I wanted to look good. My dad always taught me to look like a ballplayer because you might fool somebody on the days when you didn't play like one."

"That's a great line," I tell him.

"So I always tried to look my best—really put together," Steve continues. "Right about then 'hockey hair' was in style. I literally used to get my hair permed, and then it would be long and curly in the back—like a mullet. A lot of guys had mullets back then. Mine was a little longer than most, and [Mac] didn't think I really fit in. Plus nobody wears long hair in Boston—then, now, and always. Everyone looks like they just got out of jail. It's the 'convict do.'" We share a laugh over his colorful description.

"Anyway, Mac was a veterans' manager," Lyons continues. "In '85 there were only two rookies on the team—me and Marc Sullivan. So Mac would send messages to the team through the guys that couldn't really defend themselves—like me. I was kind of like his whipping boy. He was tough. He would yell at me in front of everybody when if by chance I didn't hustle out a ground ball, which was rare, because I usually did. But when one of the veterans, like Jim Rice, did the same thing, he never said a word to them about it. He would send messages through the guys that weren't going to bark back at him. But he would at times, in private, find ways to tell me that he liked what I was doing and would tell me to keep playing hard."

"Psycho" would get plenty of playing time in '85, mostly because star center fielder Tony Armas spent a good portion of the season on the disabled list. But the versatile Lyons also found playing time at third base, shortstop, right field, and left field. He would hit a respectable .264 in over four hundred plate appearances, but with only five home runs and thirty RBIS, he would revert back to being a valuable utility player once Armas returned.

"To say I didn't get a fair shake I don't think would be correct," Lyons says. "I think what happened was that I got tabbed as a utility guy, and they were never going to give me a chance to be more than that. That didn't stop me from continuing to try to be more than that though."

Lyons would play a similar role the following year—unable to become a regular despite signs of brilliance, particularly in the outfield.

"That '86 team was so powerful," Steve recalls. "It was the strongest team I ever played on. We expected to win every night and would get upset if we didn't. Traditionally because you play 162 games, it's not like you get mad every time you lose. You're going to lose a lot. But we would be in disbelief, like, 'How did they beat us?' Or, 'We're going to make them pay and beat the shit out of those guys tomorrow!' That was just the kind of attitude we had; the guys on the team were just like monsters. I was just kind of a guy that fit in."

That would all change on June 29, when Lyons learned that he would be leaving the Red Sox, the only team he had ever wanted to play for, in a trade for living legend Tom Seaver.

"If you're going to get traded," I offer, "it's no small consolation to at least be able to one day tell your grandchildren you were dealt straight up for the guy who, for many years, had the highest vote total of anyone ever elected to the Baseball Hall of Fame. But then again you're being traded from a first-place team that you grew up rooting for. How did this make you feel?"

"A big conflict," Lyons says with a sigh. "Actually pretty disheartening. When I got traded, we were eight games out in front. There was no question we were going to be in first place [at season's end]. The only question was how far we would go [in the postseason]. I got a call that morning from Mac telling me I'd been traded to the Chicago White Sox. I didn't even know who I was traded for initially until I figured it out later.

At the end of the day it doesn't really matter. And I think if you ask Tom Seaver, he'll never tell anybody who he was traded for; it's a little bit more of a feather in my cap than it is in his. But at the same time, with all due respect to Tom Seaver and his greatness—which I was certainly well aware of—he ended up 5-7, hurt his knee, and didn't pitch for them in the playoffs. Then he was done. So it was clearly a Tom Seaver [who was] at the end of his career being traded for a guy that maybe had some up side. As it turned out, I didn't really do anything for the White Sox, so it was kind of a wash. The Red Sox weren't kicking themselves because they got Seaver in his last season. I mean, it wasn't exactly like they'd traded Jeff Bagwell for Larry Anderson!"

The day after the trade, as fate would have it, Armas went down with an injury. Had it happened a matter of hours earlier, Lyons most likely never would have been traded and almost certainly would have been on the roster through the World Series. Instead he missed the party, so to speak.

"After Armas got hurt, did you ever think about what could have been had you not been traded?" I ask.

Lyons is taken aback that he had never really given this scenario any thought. He gives a look of bewilderment over how that could be: "I never really thought of it in terms that you're bringing up to me now, as far as, 'Wow, I might have been the center fielder for a team that had a chance to win the World Series,'" he says. "What I did think a lot about was that for a guy that [the Red Sox] didn't want, they had a tough time replacing [me]. They had a lot of guys out in center field before they ended up with Dave Henderson. [Corner outfielder] Kevin Romine played center after the trade. Then they even tried [infielder] Eddie Romero out there. They must have been like, 'Holy shit, we traded away Steve Lyons; now we don't have a center fielder. What happened?' So [the trade] may have been a misstep on their part. I hate to be spiteful, but I'm proud of the fact that they had a tough time finding a way to replace me instantly after I got traded. But they eventually did, and they should have won the World Series that year. They were the best team in baseball, and it was a fluke play [the 'Buckner play'] that beat them [in Game Six]. Then there's that old adage that you're never going to come back to win Game Seven after that."

"I'm curious," I say. "Did you watch that World Series? If you did, how did you feel in Game Six, when they were one strike away, and then in Game Seven, when they blew a 3–0 lead?"

Lyons seems conflicted by the question but then gives a most honest response: "I put on a good face, as I was living in Boston in a house I had bought," he says. "I was sad and I was mad. I was upset that I wasn't a part of it. I would say there was probably a part of me that was not 100 percent disappointed that that ball went through Buckner's legs. I knew if the Red Sox won the World Series, it would make any other championship in the city look like a third-grade birthday party. I knew the city would explode, and I'd have to sit there and watch it, be on the outside looking in, and feeling sorry [for myself]. I know how that sounds; it sounds immature and spiteful, but that's how I felt. Most of me wanted them to win, but there was a part of me that didn't."

So it was on to Chicago, where Lyons would play for the next four and a half seasons. But his most memorable moment there wouldn't be a game-winning hit or a great catch but rather his mark in YouTube lore for a brain freeze he committed in 1990 in Detroit after beating out an infield bunt single with a dive into first base. While standing on first and attempting to shake the dirt out of his pants, he dropped them, to the amusement of thousands of fans in attendance and countless more on television.

"I told my teenage son I'd be meeting you today; he's a huge baseball fan," I say. "But when I told him you played with the Red Sox, he didn't know that. Then I told him you were once a national baseball analyst for Fox; he didn't know that either. But then when I told him you were the guy who dropped his pants at first base, he shouted, 'Yes! I know him! That's so cool!' So, Steve, you are famous for that; you're in every baseball bloopers movie there is. I've got to ask: was it an honest mistake on your part, or was it done for laughs?"

Lyons, with a big grin, reveals what happened: "Looking back, I go to myself, 'What were you thinking?' But it was an honest mistake. I'm actually flabbergasted when people think that I would have somehow done it on purpose, even while maybe knowing I was a practical joker and someone that tried to keep things loose. I have a good sense of humor and had a good time playing, but between the lines I was dead serious. More than anything, I was afraid—afraid of messing up. I was the biggest hot dog in the world before the game started—like I'd be catching balls behind my back—but I would never think of not catching a fly ball with two hands during a game.

"But getting back to that incident, I just literally forgot I was standing there, and while the two [Detroit Tigers players] argued with the umpire over the call, I felt all the dirt run down the inside of my legs. If you think about it, [you realize that] 50 percent of the time when you slide, you're out, so you run back into the dugout, pull your pants down, and get the dirt out. I just forgot I was still on the field. I get asked about it every day! But knowing that is what I'm known for most is not embarrassing at all. I mean, many guys play their entire careers and live in anonymity. I'm not a star, but people remember that. I think if you're a Major League player, you want to put your mark on the game somewhere, even if it's something as crazy as that. Of course I'd much rather be remembered for hitting a Game Seven home run to win a championship, but that's not in the cards unless I can make a big comeback at fifty-seven!"

Lyons would return not once, not twice, but three times to Boston before calling it a career with the Red Sox in 1993. But his biggest venture in baseball was still ahead of him.

Within three years of retirement Lyons would establish himself as one of the most entertaining studio and game color analysts in the business. He quickly moved up the ranks to cover several division and league championship series for Fox. He had become the star in broadcasting that had eluded him as a player. Aside from his analyst work he would host his own interview show and for two seasons was the voice of the iconic *This Week in Baseball*. But ten years into his life's second act in broadcasting his career became as turbulent as the Pacific Ocean waves breaking along the nearby shore. Steve would be fired for what was perceived by the Fox Sports Network as a racially insensitive remark during a broadcast of the 2006 ALCS.

"I always enjoyed listening to you when you were on Fox because of the comedic style you brought to the broadcast booth—much in the same genre as the great Joe Garagiola," I say. "You made baseball fun. But then after years of broadcasting in a way seemingly encouraged by the network—saying stuff to break up the monotony of the game—you made what some would perceive as a mistake that would cost you your job. Do you think the action that was taken against you was extreme?"

"Absolutely," Lyons exclaims. "To tell you the truth, I didn't get fired for that. I got fired for something that I did two years earlier that I would take accountability for as a slipup of ignorance. There was a Dodger game during Yom Kippur. I'm not Jewish, and I knew even less about Jewish heritage back then. Shawn Green, a Jewish player with the Dodgers, played on that Friday night and hit a home run, but he was not playing on Saturday. He had decided to sit out the game to observe the holiday. As broadcasters, we know not to talk about race, religion, and sex. But in this case it was in the forefront. You couldn't *not* mention it. We had to give the reason why he was sitting out, as the Dodgers were in a playoff hunt with maybe ten games to go in the season. So I said something about why he had sat out."

At this point Lyons becomes more emotional than at any point in our discussion, clearly still agitated by the accusations made against him all these years later.

"Now anyone who thought I'd made a mistake after watching that entire game and came away thinking that I was some type of anti-Semite or that I didn't like Shawn Green, I'll kiss their ass! I spent the entire game talking about how great Shawn Green was and what he meant to the [Dodgers] franchise and how, if you had a brother, you would wish that he was Shawn Green! That's the type of guy he was. On top of which, he was a tremendous player. So the eighth inning rolls around, and Thom Brennaman, who is my partner, says, 'Well, hey Dodgers fans, it's a one-run game, but if you're thinking that Shawn Green's gonna pop out of that dugout and pinch-hit—maybe hit a home run—it's not happening. He's not even in the stadium. He's observing a holiday—the sacred day of Yom Kippur for all Jewish people.'

"The funny thing is that people think I shoot from the hip and don't think too much about what I say—and sometimes that happens—but in this instance I'd actually talked to like three Jewish guys that were on our TV crew, and I gave them the exact same line that I was going to use and asked if they thought it was funny. Not one of them said, 'Oh, I wouldn't say that, Steve, because we don't laugh at ourselves too much.' They were like, 'It's kind of funny. Go ahead.' So I went with it, saying on the air, 'Well, Tom, if you think about it, maybe Shawn is actually sitting out today based on his Jewish heritage much more than his Jewish faith. He's not really a practicing member. He didn't marry a Jewish woman. He doesn't belong to a synagogue. And he never has been bar mitzvah-ed. From what I understand, that's the bad thing because you don't get the money.'

"I guess they got some calls. [Former president of Fox Sports and executive producer] David Hill wanted to fire me. I went in and sat in front of [Fox] lawyers and said, 'I wasn't being malicious. I was trying to bring levity to a situation that was serious. I clearly meant no malice.' They suspended me for a week. That next week before the playoffs and then during the playoffs, I knew the writing was on the wall. They made me sign a piece of paper that said if I ever did anything that was a little off color, they could fire me without cause. So David Hill was just waiting for me [to slip]. The sad part about it was that everybody at Fox loved my work. *Everyone.* Even David Hill, who a year before had told me that I was basically the golden boy. He was going to make me rich and famous is what he told me. Then it turned on a dime just like that. The thing I hated most about it was that David Hill didn't know two shits about baseball. He didn't have a clue about what I did. He had to rely on everyone else saying, 'This guy's really good. You should leave him alone.'

"So I get into the playoffs two years later, and I was trying to redo my deal before the [2006 ALCS] started. [Executive producer] Ed Goren, who always treated me like a son, told me to wait until after the playoffs were over. But I said, 'I don't want to wait because I'm not gonna do anything in the playoffs that's gonna make you want to give me more money. I do what I do. You know what it is. You know I'm up and where my numbers are going to be, so let's just get it done.'"

And then came the perceived slight against Hispanics.

"To me, getting fired for that was for *nothing*," Lyons says. "It was a poor attempt at humor. It really wasn't funny at all. The emphasis of my punch line was on wallet thieves, not on . . . Geez, I can't even remember what I got fired for. 'Making a racially insensitive comment toward Hispanics' is how they phrased it. Well, here's my ignorance again. Number one, I wasn't talking to Lou Piniella [the other analyst], specifically. I was talking to him in general, as my [broadcast] partner. I always thought Piniella was Italian! But he is actually of Spanish descent. They thought I was saying, 'If you're a Spanish-speaking person, you would steal a wallet.' I wasn't saying that at all because I thought Lou was Italian, so I would never be making that reference. Number two, what I was doing was making a call back to something that Lou had said four minutes earlier in the game about finding wallets. He said, 'If I went out and found a wallet on Friday night, I wouldn't be out looking for wallets on Saturday night to see if I could find some more.' Immediately I bit my tongue because what I wanted to say right away was something like, 'Lou, if you found a wallet, wouldn't you look at the license and try to give it back to the guy? Are you keeping his wallet?' Then I thought, 'Don't say that. You're gonna make him look bad.' But I knew I wanted to make a call back to it, and then when he said something in Spanish, I said, 'Now I can't understand you, and my wallet's missing.' I was making a call back to the wallet, nothing about Spanish-speaking people. They fired me before the game was over."

"*Before* the game was over?" I ask incredulously.

"Basically," Lyons answers. "When I went to dinner with our producer, along with Chris Myers and Thom Brennaman, I got a phone call from David Hill. Chris and Thom tried talking with [Hill], asking him basically what he was talking about. In fact Lou [earlier] had said it was kind of the funniest thing we'd done all game. I was like, 'It was all right.' At that time I had no idea that I was in trouble. So when [Hill] fired me, I said to him, 'Go back and look at the tape. I never said anything like that.' People have said things to me about it since then, and a lot of them have said things [to the effect] that, 'If you can make what you said a racist comment, then you're a racist looking at it that way.' I'm always like, 'That makes sense to me.' I don't have a racist bone in my body. My grandson's half Black. I could care less if you're red, blue, or green. You treat me like an asshole, then you're just an asshole. If you treat me fine, then you're going to be good with me. It doesn't matter. So that was just an *ugly, ugly, ugly* time in my career—and I couldn't save it."

"The firing just lit up the media in your defense," I say. "Even some critics of your work defended you, basically pointing out the hypocrisy of how the networks wanted their color guys to be, well, colorful!"

"Right, and I was the first of that [type]," Lyons says. "They hired me to be '*that guy.*' They would be like, 'Go out there, be crazy, be fun, be controversial.' Then the one time I slipped up, they fired me. *Are you fucking kidding me?* Like I said, I think a lot of people don't think I am, but I'm smart enough to draw a line—or at least I thought I was. In this instance I got fired for it. You're never sure how someone else is going to react to it. You're right, Erik. I did see some articles. I saw an article that Gerry Callahan wrote that was very supportive. But then another guy called me a 'deviant.' He called me a deviant! I'm like, 'What? You don't even know who I fucking am, bro!'"

"Do you feel like you were blackballed by the networks after that?" I ask.

"Well, I haven't been able to get national jobs since then," Steve says matter-of-factly. "I don't know if it's blackballed. Maybe I'm not for everyone. But I wouldn't do this job if I didn't think I did an excellent job. I do think I do good work. I pay attention to it. I'm not dabbling in [broadcasting]. It is my career, and I'm serious about it. I think I'm every bit as good as anybody they've put on their networks since I've left and in many, many cases *way better*. I have no problem saying that. [No one's] gonna convince me I'm not better than some of the people that they've had on the air since that time. I mean, it's been more than ten years."

Lyons shakes his head and then, allowing for a pregnant pause, continues his thoughts on the firing and how unheard of it was for the Fox Network to dismiss an on-air talent, while neither Fox Cable [for which Lyons did one hundred pre- and postgame shows] nor the Dodgers organization [for which he did forty-five games] followed suit. Lyons contends that his Fox Network ouster was a personal decision by Hill since the other two organizations did not support his action.

"Here's the funny thing," Steve remarks. "At the time that the Fox Network fired me, I was also working for Fox Cable and the Dodgers. They didn't fire me. So what did I do wrong to get fired by the Fox Network? How do I get fired from the network and not the Dodgers or Fox Cable? Usually if you're fired by the network, anyone else you work for fires you too because they're usually like, 'If the big guys fired him, then we've got to fall in line.' But I didn't even get fired by the same entity on [Fox's] cable side. So what did I really do wrong?"

"At least your tenure with the Dodgers was a good one," I say. "You were there for nine years and seemed to love that job."

"Yeah, it was great!" Lyons says, perking up. "It was great for a lot of reasons. The Dodgers are a good organization with good people to work with for the most part. Plus I lived right there. [With the Red Sox] now I have to move every six months—back and forth between Boston and Los Angeles."

"So what happened at the end of your association with the Dodgers following the 2013 season?" I ask.

"They changed networks to Time Warner, so they got rid of all of the Fox guys," he says. "I guess I had a chance to stay, but the offer that was made to me initially was insulting, and then they brought in their own guy [to replace me]. The funny thing is that the person that took over [the broadcasting division] was the same guy that hired me there originally. So I had a big argument with him about it. I asked him why I wasn't coming back. 'Did I say something wrong? Was I not good enough? Did I not have a good following there? Is there a reason?' All he said was, 'You know, sometimes when a new network comes in, they just want to make changes.' I was like, 'Really? I understand that. That does happen. But you're the guy running the new network, so you're the guy making the change. So tell me what I did wrong?' He couldn't tell me. He was just an ass. So I basically lost my job for no reason at all."

But no matter. The following season Steve returned to Boston and his baseball roots, joining NESN as a studio and occasional game analyst of Red Sox games. So for all the drama in Lyons's life, he's come out on top. He's back working in Beantown, much of the time at the side of his old outfield partner, Jim Rice—right where he's wanted to be all along.

13.

Almost Legend

....

If losing the ['86] World Series was to be my lot in life and not win a World Series, I almost wonder at times if I'd rather lose a World Series with that group of guys than win one with some others. That's because I love those guys.

—BRUCE HURST

Bruce Hurst, one of the greatest southpaws in Red Sox history and a pitcher who tried to single-handedly defeat the Mets in the 1986 World Series, wanted nothing less than to be interviewed for this book. It was nothing personal, but it had been three years since his last interview—at a Red Sox fan festival—and he had promised himself it would be his final one, *forever*. But then an old teammate of his, in disbelief that Hurst wouldn't agree to an interview with me, gave me his number and said to give it a shot. Later that day, when I called and Bruce picked up the phone, to my great delight he sounded as if he was expecting my call. It was clear that he recognized the incoming number and was in good spirits because of it—as though an old friend were giving him a ring. But there was just one problem: he thought I was someone else. In some freakish technological mishap the caller identification mistakenly listed me as "Pam Kenn," the venerable and beloved Red Sox alumni director, whom Bruce has known and liked for many years.

Surely once Hurst figured out that it was a writer and not a friend on the line, he would try to rush me off the phone. But Bruce did just the opposite; he was still very cordial, even if he had no interest in meeting me for an interview. Anyone who knows him wouldn't have been a bit surprised by his kind demeanor. Bruce is a man of the Mormon faith who doesn't smoke, drink alcohol, swear, or ingest caffeine. He's a kind soul. But he wanted no part of reliving his baseball past or, specifically, the disappointment of losing the 1986 World Series. However, after exactly twenty-three minutes of back-and-forth conversation and my numerous attempts to convince him otherwise, he finally acquiesced after I revealed that he was the last remaining player from that '86 pennant-winning team with whom I needed to meet for the book.

"Well, okay, I don't want to be *that guy*," he finally said, not wanting to be the cause of an incomplete picture of the team. After promising him that I would keep the interview short and on point, he exhaled and said, "Erik, if you fly all the way out to Phoenix to see me, I'll give you as much time as you need."

A few weeks later, shortly after I'd landed at Phoenix Sky Harbor Airport on a sunny, late winter afternoon, my cell phone rang, and it was Bruce. For an instant I thought that perhaps he had had a change of heart, that our interview rehashing his days in Boston would be too difficult for him to endure. But the reason for the call was to simply change the venue to my hotel, as the flu was going around his house, and he didn't want me exposed to it. Relieved, I rented a car and drove straight to my hotel. Sitting in the lobby, there to greet me, in a powder blue buttoned-down Ralph Lauren shirt and with his hair combed neatly to the side, was Bruce—still an imposing figure at six feet three inches. He couldn't have been more gracious, and we walked toward the back of the nearly empty hotel restaurant for our chat.

Based on his initial reluctance to talk, my expectations for the interview weren't high. Given all the colorful, outspoken characters from that '86 team, I thought my interview with

Bruce would surely be one of the tamer ones, although in my mind I knew I would be grateful for *any* revelation I could use in the book. As it turned out, I couldn't have been more wrong. My interview with Bruce Hurst would quickly turn into one of the most poignant, emotional, and reflective meetings I've *ever* had with a ballplayer. Bruce had an awful lot to say, even if he really didn't want to say it.

Hurst's road to baseball stardom was unconventional. A Mormon from an LDS community in St. George, Utah, his parents divorced when he was only five, and his mother supported her five children with the money she earned from a bankrupt family variety store the judge awarded her in the settlement.

"In a small town that's big news," Hurst says of the divorce. "Then add to it happening in a Mormon community, and it's a little uncomfortable. That was always hanging over me. But everybody loved my mother, loved our little variety store, and really loved the fight that she had in her. But it was always a stigma that I felt more and more as I got older. I was never a fighter, but I always felt like I had to fight to get what I thought I wanted. That environment helped build a foundation for me on which I could learn to compete on a bigger scale."

Despite Bruce's natural talent and toughness, it would be a bumpy journey to the big leagues, even after he was signed as the heralded number one draft choice of the Red Sox in 1976. He blew out his elbow after nearly leading the A Ball league in innings pitched in '77 and then blew out his shoulder in '78 while pitching in Double-A ball. That's when he began to hear the unfair labels of being "soft" and "lacking toughness."

"When you're injured, at least back then, you're a pariah," Hurst explains. "I had guys telling me, 'You're the biggest waste of a first-round pick we've ever had.'"

"That's pretty terrible," I say.

"No, it's *not* terrible," Hurst shoots back. "That's part of the business. That's part of my having to learn how to defend myself—and I did. Would I have loved to have stayed healthy and had those missed innings to develop and learn? Yeah. But the lessons I learned were valuable to me—painful at times and uncomfortable, but that's not the worst thing in the world that can happen to a guy."

"How about the regular vulgarities spoken around the Minor League clubhouse?" I ask. "Did that bother you?"

"That's where the miss is," Hurst exclaims. "They go, 'Okay, Mormon kid . . . ,' like I couldn't handle it because I don't swear. The language didn't offend me. I grew up in an environment where there was salty language. I didn't have 'virgin ears.' The only thing that was different was when the name of the Lord was used [with bad language]. I was a shade uncomfortable, but I never thought like, 'Oh, I've got to go home now' or, 'I don't want to play baseball anymore.' I would never tell anyone they can't live their life the way they want. I just wanted the same thing from others: not to be judged. [My being a Mormon] was used against me as sort of a character assassination of what I wasn't able to do—that I wasn't tough enough. There was once an article written in the *Boston Globe* saying, '[Hurst's] not tough enough. He's too Mormon.' I was like, 'Are you kidding me?' [Boston Celtics star] Danny Ainge is the same religion as I am, and that guy was in a fight all the time! It was *wonderful!* I wasn't hard-wired that way per se, but it didn't mean that I couldn't compete."

Still Hurst was uncertain about his baseball prospects for other reasons: "My doubts came from being hurt all the time and then thinking, 'Well, what am I going to do with my life here? Do I want to serve a mission? Could I go to college and play basketball? How can I get my education paid for?' Those were the questions going through my mind."

Bruce would end up doing none of those things. Instead he played in a junior college basketball tournament in Phoenix that winter and received some life-changing advice from his coach one morning over breakfast.

"Seeing my shoulder the way it was, [the coach] said, 'Bruce, the best investment you'll ever make in your life is in yourself.

So I encourage you to see Dr. Frank Jobe.' Jobe would make his mark among the most prominent orthopedic surgeons because of all the publicity he got after performing the first 'Tommy John surgery.' So I made the phone call, and the Red Sox gave me permission to see him. Dr. Jobe gave me a cortisone shot, which obviously hit the spot because it hurt so bad for days. I was actually physically ill from the pain. I was miserable, cranky, and irritable; nobody wanted to be around me. But it worked, and I went to spring training in '79, throwing the ball well [for Double-A Bristol]. I went to our Minor League director, Mr. [Edward] Kenney, an absolutely wonderful man who smoked about a foot-long stogie like Branch Rickey— the quintessential baseball man right out of central casting— and said, 'Mr. Kenney, I don't know if this makes sense, but I would like to go back down to Winter Haven [A Ball] to start the season in the warm weather.' He said it was a good idea, so I went down to Winter Haven and came back up to Bristol in the summertime and ended up winning a total of seventeen games that year."

The next season, with some rather unconventional help from Minor League pitching coach and roving instructor Johnny Podres, Bruce got called up to the Majors.

"Pod saw me pitch," Bruce says, "and was quoted in a paper saying things like, 'Hurst is out chasing women. He's drinking now. Now he's ready to pitch in the big leagues.' That kind of thing [which of course wasn't true]. [Podres didn't say] that I had a good changeup or zone strikes or that my curve ball was a plus or whatever—but that I was drinking now and chasing girls; [it was] just kind of like, 'Go get 'em, big fella!' In order to justify my getting into the big leagues, he had to dispel all of the negative things that had been written about me. It's too bad he had to do it that way, but at the same time I'm glad he defended me."

But once up in the Major Leagues, Hurst struggled mightily: "I got to the big leagues and I was awful," he says. "I mean *awful*! In '80 I only got to stay up a month."

And he wasn't exactly getting moral support from the team—not even from "Captain Carl" (Yastrzemski): "I grew up with a poster of Yaz over my bed," Bruce says earnestly. "One day he looked at me and goes, 'You're the *worst* pitcher I've seen in twenty years—bar none. You're the worst!' But I didn't back down. I told him, 'The Red Sox should have traded you and kept Reggie Smith!'"

"You really said that?" I ask. "You were just a rookie."

"Oh yeah, I told him!" Hurst says, smiling. "Oh yeah, I had fire in my belly. I wasn't your typical drink-gallons-of-beer-and-get-into-a-bar-fight guy, but I had some fire."

Soon after, during a particularly bad outing in Baltimore for Hurst that culminated with a mental mistake on his part, a steaming mad Don Zimmer—then the Red Sox manager—came out to the mound to replace him.

"He called me every name in the book," Bruce recalls. "He cussed me out and didn't even stay on the mound to wait for the reliever. I'm walking toward the dugout, and he's following me in. He's like five steps behind me, cussing me out, calling me every name. I was a shade embarrassed, ran up to the clubhouse, and I was like, 'I'm done! This is my big league experience?' I showered and then, with tears in my eyes, walked toward my locker, and [*Boston Globe* columnist] Peter Gammons is standing right there. I put my head down because this was the *last* guy I wanted to see. Number one, this was a writer, but two, it was Peter of all people, so I just took off without saying a word, and he wrote this article about my performance and me running down Thirty-Third Street in Baltimore afterward."

A couple of days later Zimmer was fired. Enter Ralph Houk, with a chance for Hurst to wipe the slate clean—or at least so he thought.

"I go to spring training in '81, and after pitching just *three* innings," Hurst says incredulously, "I get called into Ralph's office; he goes, 'We're sending you down to Pawtucket [Triple-A]. See you later, pal.' I'd just gotten married! So I get to Triple-A, and I'm not pitching very good. After a game in Charleston,

West Virginia, I thought, 'I can't do this anymore. I'm going home. I don't want to play. I'm fighting to get back to the big leagues. Is this what I want in my life?' So I quit. I went home but never unpacked my suitcase. I called a personal friend, and he gave me the good advice to go back. One of the hardest days I ever had was walking back. Most of the guys had taken my stuff and given it away, so I had to beg for my glove and my hat and my shoes. The worst was having to look them in the eye; that was hard. Quitting was a really irrational decision. A friend used to tell me to never make long-term decisions on short-term emotions, which is what I'd done there."

"So how did you get back to the big leagues from there?" I ask.

"We had a pitching coach at Pawtucket named Mike Roark. I went to him and said, 'Mike, I'm yours. What do we do?' He had me filmed in spring training with an eight-millimeter camera, with which you could slow down the video. He said to me one day, 'Come here; I want you to watch yourself pitch.' It was the first time I ever had seen myself pitch, and I just went, 'That's awful!' As a result I never wound up again. Never. What I saw was so bad. He talked to me about things that I'd never heard before. I ended up winning twelve games [with a 2.87 ERA] and got called up to the Red Sox in September—winning both games I pitched. After the second win Yaz said in the paper—never to my face—that 'Bruce Hurst is a big league pitcher and belongs here.' It meant the world to me."

Hurst, while durable, was a remarkably average pitcher over the next four seasons, winning a total of thirty-eight games (including back-to-back 12-12 marks in '83 and '84) with an ERA of nearly 4.50 over that span. He credits Houk with keeping him in the game.

"I owe my career to him," Bruce says with emotion. "He was maybe the smartest, most insightful, patient, and understanding manager around. At one point during my first full season in the Majors I was struggling a bit, and I went to Houk—the only time I'd ever gone into the manager's office—and said, 'Ralph, don't give up on me. I'm trying.' He said, 'Kid, I don't care if you get another out the rest of the year. You're in there every five days. Now get the hell out of my office!' It was beautiful."

"The staff the Red Sox had in the early eighties had three pretty good lefties pitching at right-handed-hitting-friendly Fenway Park: John Tudor, Bobby Ojeda, and you," I say. "Tudor would get traded and go on to become a big winner with the St. Louis Cardinals, and Ojeda was dealt to the Mets and was the ace of their staff in '86. But you remained in Boston."

"Yes, there were three of us, and I have no idea why I was the one that they chose to keep," Hurst says. "It could have easily been any number of scenarios between the three of us."

"It's interesting that all three of your careers really took off around the same time," I note. "What happened in your case? In other words, how did you elevate your game?"

Hurst grins and says, "I can tell you the day. In 1984 at spring training a bunch of guys, including Jack Morris and Dan Petry of the Tigers, started throwing a split-fingered fastball, and it was really becoming a thing. Roger Craig was their pitching coach and taught them how to throw it. One day during BP, Craig was walking across the outfield, and I said, 'Roger, how do you hold that split-finger?' He looked at me like, 'Why are you asking me this? I'm on the opposing team.' But then he grabbed a ball, and while continuing to walk, he showed me. He said, 'Put your finger like this. Put your thumb on the side. You've got to do this.' So I started messing around with it. By the next spring training, in '85, I'm halfway there with the pitch. I can't commit to it yet, and I'm still trying to throw the changeup better. Anyway, we're up in Boston to start the season, and I'm pitching the second game against the Yankees. I'm over at Danny Ainge's house the night before the game, and he says to me, 'You show me nothing if you don't throw [the split-finger] the first pitch of your season.' I go, 'No way.' But he insists, saying, 'You've got to do it.' So I did. But I was still fighting back and forth with it when finally I thought, 'I've got to forget about the changeup. I'm not feeling it. But this split-fingered pitch I can throw.' I ended up pitching a pretty good game against a great Yankee lineup."

Hurst now had his dominant pitch. But another occurrence, which came a couple of months later in a game against the Milwaukee Brewers, elevated his game even more and further distanced the perceived stigma that he lacked toughness on the mound.

"Milwaukee had a great lineup then," Hurst notes. "They had guys like Paul Molitor, Robin Yount, Cecil Cooper, Ben Oglivie, and Ted Simmons that made up the True Blue Brew Crew; they were awesome. I remember facing Molitor after giving up a couple of runs. Geddy called for a changeup away, so I threw my little split out there, and Molitor dove across the plate for it—just fearless—but he missed it, fouling it straight back. Then he gives one of those, 'Oh, I had that bitch' expressions. I looked at him like, 'You don't have anything on me. I don't put any fear in you—not even one bit!' So Geddy puts down a changeup, but I shook him off. He goes curveball, but I shake my head no. He goes fastball away; again I shake him off. I could see his face, and he's [thinking] the only thing left is up and in. I go, 'Yep.' I threw a crossing fastball that went right under Molitor's chin and flipped him as big as Dallas. I took three or four steps in toward the plate and got the ball back from Geddy, who had this huge grin on his face. There's a time in life when 'batting practice is over.' At that moment I said, '*No more!*' If I have to knock you on your you-know-what or if I have to hit you, I hit you, but you're not gonna be diving across the plate having no fear of me anymore. That was my moment! From that time on I was a more effective big league pitcher. All of a sudden I had my little split-finger and had a little more *swag* in today's terms."

By 1986 Hurst was the complete package and ready to roll. He was 13-8 during the regular season, finished strong with a 5-0 September, and watched his ERA drop a run and a half from the previous season to 2.99. If not for a pulled groin, he likely would have won twenty games.

"What was it like for you, after six seasons in the big leagues, to enjoy both stardom and a glorious ride to the division title for the first time?" I ask.

"A couple of things," Hurst begins. "One, I never viewed myself as a star."

"I knew you would say that," I say, chuckling, having observed his modest nature.

"But it's true," Bruce says earnestly. "I never did view myself that way. We had so many guys that really were stars on that team—particularly Clem [Roger Clemens]. Clem changed the dynamic with his pitching. Boston always had enough hitting, but they didn't have strong pitching. Second, I'll give you a story. I had a house in Wellesley at that time. The town didn't have garbage pickup, so you had to have private contractors come and pick up your rubbish. One day our guy, a nice fella, asked me what I thought about the Red Sox. I looked at him and said, 'Oh, I think they're pretty good.' So he goes, 'They don't have the pitching.' I mean, the veins were popping out of my neck!' My wife's grabbing my hand, like 'It's okay, it's okay.' I just said, 'You don't think so, huh?' He had no clue who I was—didn't know I pitched for the Red Sox. He was just on his route, and I could appreciate that, but that was the way it always was. Of course Clem changed all that for us."

In the ALCS the California Angels had their own galaxy of stars like Wally Joyner, Bobby Grich, Reggie Jackson, Brian Downing, and Doug DeCinces, who defeated Clemens convincingly in the opening game, 8–1.

"You were on a roll with your perfect September—the Red Sox's hottest pitcher," I say. "But after the Angels took out your ace—at Fenway—do you recall the importance of Game Two against a team that obviously was riding high after beating Clemens the way it did?"

Hurst leans back in his chair and points toward me with an index finger for emphasis: "Back at the end of the season," he begins, "we had a game against Toronto that I pitched, and if we won it, we would clinch a tie for the division title. I remember going to bed the night before thinking it was the biggest game of my career. It would be the first time I'd ever pitched in that sort of playoff environment. We were competing, playing well, and I was throwing the ball well that September, but nothing had been more significant than this clinching-type of game. At the very least if we won, we'd be in a playoff game. I remember telling my wife Holly the night before that it'd be interesting to see how I responded to that kind of environment. I didn't know if I'd go out there and be a shrinking violet and get my lunch handed to me or if I'd go to battle. Well, I threw a shutout and struck out Jesse Barfield to end the game, and I jumped in the air and did this little shimmy. My wife was crying-laughing, and Geddy had this big smile on his face as we hugged and high-fived each other. It probably wasn't the most important game of the year by any stretch of the imagination, but it did have playoff implications to a degree. Anyway, that game gave me the confidence that I could pitch in this environment, do well, and even relish it. I now looked forward to it and couldn't wait for the next big one.

"But back to Game Two [of the ALCS]. After we lost the first, I didn't want to let Clem down. I had that kind of feeling for him. I also didn't want to let the team or the fans down, and I didn't want the Angels to go out of town with a two-game lead. We just gutted it out and battled every at bat. It wasn't just me; it was the whole team. One of the little mantras that Tom Seaver taught Clemens and me would be to do everything we had to do to throw a shutout inning—to keep the momentum on our side."

Hurst would accomplish just that and more, going the distance in a 9–2 Red Sox victory to even the series.

Boston would again turn to its autumn stopper in the historic Game Five of the ALCS, which the Red Sox entered down three games to one and facing elimination in Anaheim. Hurst pitched well, though he left after the sixth inning down 3–2 and had to sit on the bench and hope his club could rally back after being down 5–2 in the ninth.

"The Red Sox had some insane comebacks throughout the season, but at any point near the end of Game Five—and I wouldn't judge you either way—was there a point where you may have thought, 'You know what, boys, we've had a great run here, but it's just not going to happen'?" I ask.

Bruce doesn't hesitate: "I *never* felt that—never. We were down to our last strike, and it didn't look good for the 'Mudville 9' that day, but you know what? I just never felt that. What *was* amazing to me was how [Angels starter] Mike Witt was taken out in the ninth. He was bulletproof and impenetrable. He would just *destroy* us! The only person he couldn't get out was Geddy. Geddy covered him like he knew what was coming, hitting some absolute rockets off of him. So because of Geddy, Mauch took out Witt for whatever reason. When he did that, it just felt like, 'Oh boy, it's a different game now!' And that's not taking anything away from their bullpen or Gary Lucas or anything like that, but Witt was so good—I mean, *so good*! And then, all of a sudden, the first pitch by Lucas is at Geddy's head [hit by pitch], and it's like what we talked about with momentum: it started to come back to our side of the field."

The next batter, Dave Henderson, would of course hit the memorable go-ahead home run off of reliever Donnie Moore before the Red Sox put it away for good in the eleventh to cut the Angels' lead in the series to 3–2.

"You talk about the importance of momentum," I say. "What about the psyche of the Sox after that thrilling victory? You win that game; you go back to Fenway; you have a new lease on life. Was there any question in your mind that you wouldn't win those last two games to win the pennant?"

"*None*," says Hurst. "Not with Oil Can and Clemens. In Game Six Oil Can was electric. Fenway was electric. And we put the Angels on their heels. You have to remember that in Game Five at Anaheim the [police] horses were on the field, Gene Mauch and Reggie were hugging in the dugout, cops were everywhere, and the stadium was loud. You couldn't hear yourself think. Honest to goodness, it was the loudest place I've ever been because the outfield was closed in. Over sixty-four thousand fans."

"It was basically a football stadium," I interject.

"Yeah, so the echo back in on the field was deafening," Bruce concurs. "But when Don Baylor hit our first home run of the inning and then when Hendu hit his, it was *so quiet*. All we could hear was each other and our section in the stands—that was it! Everything else was just mute. It was like we'd just ripped the heart out from underneath them. It was crazy! I'm not taking anything away from the Angels—they were a good team—but the momentum came to our side. Now we were going to Fenway, and that's a tough place to win one out of two games for any visiting team."

The Red Sox made quick work of the Angels in both games, winning both games back in Boston in routs to capture the pennant and move on to another thrilling series against the Mets in the World Series.

When we take into account at least two factors—first and foremost the Mets total dominance over the National League with 108 regular season wins and, second, a balanced lineup unlike any in the game in 1986—we see that Bruce Hurst's performance over New York in the World Series was rivaled by few pitchers before him. The Mormon from Utah, for so long unfairly labeled with the 'timid' rap, embraced the national stage like few others in his three starts.

"How did you feel and what do you remember about going to the World Series for the first time?" I ask.

"I got off the bus at Shea Stadium before Game One," Hurst begins, "and I had butterflies, but I wasn't scared at all. I must say the playoffs were one thing, but the World Series in New York is quite another. The media were everywhere. You couldn't bend over without knocking five of them over. And the fans were really charged up. I remember thinking, 'Man, the scrutiny isn't just red hot; this is white hot!' But I did my warm-ups and kept my routine as much the same as I could. The fans were all over me, and it was *loud*! But once I was on the mound and after the infielders threw the ball around, I got the ball back from Boggsy and was like, 'Here we go. This is just a ballpark; it's just game time. Nothing else matters.' I just felt comfortable, would just look in on Geddy's glove, and off we would go."

"Like tunnel vision?" I ask.

"Right. The only thing I could control was hitting Geddy's glove," Hurst confirms. "I was going to stay on task, so it didn't matter what was going on around me; the glove was supreme. I would look in at Geddy's glove really close and found a couple of dark spots in it to focus on. And Richie gave absolutely magnificent targets. His glove looked like it was a peach basket. So when I would pick up my leg to throw, I would look for the dark spots. Then it was just like playing catch with Geddy, and it took the butterflies and everything away. Nothing else mattered. And then after an out, as soon as I got the ball back, I looked around at my infielders. There's Marty at second, one of the best guys I've ever been around in my life. And then there's the 'baby rooster,' Spike [Owen], at shortstop. There's Boggsy, one of the greats of the game. And I had Buck over there at first, a guy who had a monster year for us and had been around the block a few times. And I've got my boy, Geddy, behind the plate; make a little eye contact with him, and it was like, 'Let's go brother!' Those are the things you can do in chaotic situations to gain a semblance of normalcy and be able to concentrate on the matters at hand."

Hurst would pitch brilliantly in the first game, just barely outdueling an equally impressive Ron Darling, en route to a 1–0 victory. Bruce would surrender just four hits and strike out eight over eight innings. It was such a terrific pitching match-up that the only run of the game was scored when a ground ball hit by Gedman went through second baseman Tim Teufel's legs to score Rice in the top of the seventh inning.

Hurst would get his second start of the Series in Game Five, with the two clubs knotted in a 2–2 tie. It was the pivotal game in the Series to that point; the winner would go up 3–2 and would be just a victory away from winning the World Series. With the final two games potentially at Shea Stadium, it was even more critical to take this one at Fenway.

"It was chaos," Hurst recalls, letting out a sigh. "While the preparation was the same, we had family and friends staying at our house, and we were scrambling to get them tickets. It was way harder on my wife, bless her soul. She had to manage all that and try to keep things normal for me, but she did it. It also helped to have a good friend like Danny Ainge at that time. He came over one day during the home stand and said, 'Come on, let's go.' I said, 'I can't; I've got all these people around.' But he insisted, saying, 'I don't care.' So he took me out to see a movie; we got some popcorn and drinks and just sat there for a couple of hours. It meant a lot to me. It quieted the world around me a bit and made it where I could get back to doing what we do."

Hurst rose to the occasion once again in the fifth game, shutting out the Mets over the first seven innings before going the distance in a 4–2 victory. So dominant was Hurst in the two games he pitched that when the Red Sox were one out away from winning the sixth game, Bruce had prematurely been voted World Series MVP by the media.

"How would you have felt had the Red Sox gotten just one more strike in Game Six and you were named MVP of the Series?" I ask.

"I would have been humbled and flattered," Hurst says with a grin. "It would have meant a lot. I honestly have wondered at times if we had won and if I'd been named MVP if I ever would've left Boston. It would've been harder to leave and for them to let me leave, but the circumstances played out differently. But the most important thing it would have meant is that we'd won, and that would have been *everything*. It would have meant so much to that club and that town, and it would have exorcized all those demons that were surrounding the team at the time. It would have been so much fun."

At this point Bruce's eyes begin to tear up, and clearly swept up in memories, he takes a moment to compose himself. "Can you imagine what that would've been like to jump up and down in that clubhouse?" Hurst continues softly. "What that would have meant to Mrs. Yawkey and to Haywood Sullivan and to our club? I don't know if I can articulate it the right way, but because I care so much for these guys, if losing the World Series was to be my lot in life and not win a World Series, I almost wonder at times if I'd rather lose a World Series with that group of guys than win one with some others. That's because I love those guys. Immense men. They've all had their issues. We all have our ups and downs and things that've worked out and things that haven't. I don't mean to get emotional here, but that's what they mean to me."

"That's quite a statement, saying that you wonder if you would rather have lost with that special group of guys than . . ."

Hurst cuts me off: "I want to be with those guys . . . ," he says before his voice trails off. "You know, we don't see each other hardly at all. But I'm happy for some of them that went on to win a World Series. Hendu got to win one. Boggsy got one and went on that horse ride around Yankee Stadium. Clem got to win a couple. But for me this group of guys and what we did make me think that sometimes the greatest achievements in life aren't what you accomplish; it's what you overcome. We, as a group, had overcome a lot. We just didn't overcome everything to win it all."

"The Game Six loss set up an epic seventh game," I begin. "Because of a rainout on that Sunday, the game was pushed to Monday night. With the extra day's rest John McNamara would give you the nod over the scheduled starter, Oil Can Boyd. Mac was playing the hot hand. Now this is a Game Seven of the World Series—the pinnacle of the sport. This had to be vastly different for you than a Game One or a Game Five start, right?"

"The circumstances certainly were, but the preparation was not," Hurst answers quickly. "At least not for me. Seaver was *immense* for me during that game because he would talk with me between innings—really in my ear—giving me advice. He'd remind me of things like, 'Get the first out every inning,' 'Get the heavy hitters out,' and, 'Keep throwing strikes.' He kept reminding me of those three things."

Bruce perfectly executed the three goals Seaver kept hammering into his head, retiring the leadoff hitter in every inning through the sixth, when, with a 3–0 Boston lead, things started to unravel after the first out.

"I got the first guy that inning," Hurst recalls, "and that was part of the keys to winning Seaver would discuss with me. After I then gave up a single [to Lee Mazzilli], I was still invested and believed in all the ways to get two outs with one pitch. But after that first out, for the rest of that inning, it just seemed like I could never get on top of things. And then there was the moment of indecision to Keith Hernandez."

With the bases loaded and still just one out Hurst would give up a two-run single to the Mets' first baseman.

"Throughout my entire career," Bruce laments, "whenever I second-guessed one of my pitches, I always got hurt. I can hardly ever remember a time when I second-guessed a pitch and the guy popped it up. So on a pitch to Hernandez I had a changeup in my mind as the best option. Geddy called for a fastball away, and I rationalized that it was probably the smart pitch. But it wasn't the pitch that I was committed to, and I threw a high fastball away that he drove to left-center for a single."

"It was up at eye level, wasn't it?" I ask.

"High, yeah," Bruce responds. "High because it was an uncommitted pitch I threw. In today's world I would've called time out, but I didn't like mound visits then. But that might have been one of those times in my life where I should've called Richie out and said, 'Let's talk about this one.'"

"Keith was such a clutch hitter," I say.

"Oh, he was a great player," Hurst exclaims. "As a pitcher, you know the guys that come up there locked and loaded and ready to play and the others that are like, 'Oh please, don't let me be the goat.' Hernandez wasn't that guy. No, he was up there saying, 'I'm gonna get you!' But those guys were fun to face. That competitiveness—you sensed it. I just had enough doubt and didn't throw a very committed pitch, and that cost us. That is one of those things that *haunts* you. Every losing team has a haunt, and that's mine."

"So the sixth inning ends in a 3–3 tie. Because you were about to hit to lead off the top of the seventh, did you go to Mac about staying in the game, or did he go to you?" I ask.

"Mac said, 'How do you feel?'" Bruce replies. "I said, 'Mac, I'm probably not gonna get a hit here because I suck at hitting, but I think I can get the next part of their order out.' But he said he was going to pinch-hit for me. Those are the National League decisions that are hard for a manager to make. After being taken out, I went down to sit with Seaver, and he said, 'You're tired.' I didn't want to hear that, but maybe I was. Maybe I wasn't being honest with myself. I just felt like I could get the next guys out [in the seventh inning]."

Now removed from the game, Hurst would not be one of the rare pitchers to win three World Series games. But much worse: the Mets would light up the Boston bullpen for three runs in the seventh and two more in the eighth en route to an 8–5 win and a world championship. The second-guessers would have a field day.

Hurst would cement his status as one of the top lefty hurlers in baseball with his best season in 1988, when he tallied an 18-6 mark with a 3.66 ERA. Ironically it was both during and after that stellar season that the Red Sox didn't meet Bruce's request for language in a contract that would have protected him in the event of a lockout or a strike, and then they made things worse by saying his demand was even "immoral." Insulted by the offensive remarks, Hurst would become a free agent and sign with the San Diego Padres.

"[Red Sox general manager] Lou Gorman then made some remarks [to the effect] that Bruce Hurst would be easy to replace and that the Sox would have somebody before long,"

Hurst says with a smirk. "Basically that really left me with a bad feeling."

Those negative sentiments remained for fifteen years until Bruce received a phone call from Gorman, then the coordinator of the Red Sox Hall of Fame, informing him that he had been selected for the 2004 induction class, along with former teammates Wade Boggs and Dennis Eckersley.

"Lou Gorman called, and we had this poignant conversation," Hurst says. "We had a really honest conversation about the past, and he had some really nice things to say to me. We had never spoken since I left, so his call caught me off guard. Afterward I said to my wife, 'You'll never believe this phone call.' After telling her, she goes, 'You're kidding me!' It took me back to one of my last games in 1994 at Fenway Park when I was with the Texas Rangers. The fans were standing and chanting 'MVP!, MVP!' as I took the mound. It was awesome—hardest warm-up pitches I have ever thrown in my life. I don't know how I didn't hit the screen with them. Man, I had tears in my eyes. I even got the win. It meant so much. After the season I called the Red Sox and said, 'All I want to do is come to spring training. If I can make the team, great; if not, I just wanted one more go round in that uniform. But [general manager] Dan Duquette wouldn't let me. All I wanted to do was go back and retire on a note like that, so when I got that call from Lou, that I was going into the Red Sox Hall of Fame, it felt like, 'Okay, I'll hang my last hat.' It mattered to me."

"Your induction was well deserved," I say. "Your career totals with the Red Sox put you in the same conversation as other Boston left-handers like Babe Ruth and Lefty Grove."

"Don't forget Mel Parnell," interrupts Hurst. "You've got to put him in there too! He was the standard my whole time there. Vinnie Orlando, our clubhouse manager, talked about two guys. First, Lefty Grove. He used to tell me, 'You're pretty good, but you're no Lefty Grove!' Second, there was Mel, another lefty that he talked about a lot because he was a modern-era guy."

"So what did it mean for you to get inducted with a couple of Baseball Hall of Famers with whom you were teammates?" I ask.

"I signed with Wade as we were in the same draft in 1976," Hurst begins. "The funny thing about Eck was that in my first baseball card, I had this cheesy, ugly mustache; it was me trying to be like him! The first day of my first spring training I wanted to play catch with Eck. I wanted to see what the mustache looked like. Eck was not only the most honest pitcher, but also the most honest person I've known. He never ever ducked an interview; good day, bad day, he never dodged a question. He always took responsibility; he was amazing. That's not the case for the majority of players, myself included. And what an unbelievable competitor. He competed. He battled. He painted. He did everything. He was *not* gonna lose! He had this will, and I just remember thinking, 'I've got to learn that.'

"Then, with all the things he had to go through in his career, he and I developed a friendship and a little bit of trust. We played basketball during the winters together with a bunch of guys. He meant a lot to me, so to go into [the Red Sox Hall of Fame] with him was great.

"And then to go in with Boggsy, another guy in the 'big Hall of Fame.' I'm just a shmuck compared to those two. But I've known Wade since we were just eighteen. Some things he did were tough on our team. The whole Margo [Adams] thing was a mess."

"The publicity it received sort of split the team, didn't it?" I ask of the four-year extramarital affair that Adams discussed (among other things) in a *Penthouse Magazine* article in 1989, exposing what she claimed were the sexual practices of Boggs and, worse, other unnamed Red Sox players.

"Yeah, it hurt marriages," Bruce confides. "It wasn't easy. All the guys were pissed. *Super* pissed and rightfully so. It was stupid, but Wade was still a great player. He was still my teammate, and I've known all the things he had to overcome. He wasn't a fair-haired boy when he came up. He worked his way up to the big leagues and earned it. My hat's off to him for that."

"So you were back in the Red Sox family," I say enthusiastically. "Here's a story about your mother I love. Until 2004, the year the Sox won their first Fall Classic since 1918, you held the title as the last Red Sox pitcher to win a World Series game. The year before, your mother, just prior to passing away, said that upon reaching Heaven, her first order of business would be to find Babe Ruth and have a word with him about the 'Curse of the Bambino.' What more can you say about that great promise she made to you?"

Hurst starts laughing, and then before answering the question, he gives an anecdote about the 1986 World Series: "My mother, Beth, was this small town girl—wonderful lady—and she flew with my brother-in-law and my sister from Las Vegas to New York for the Series. She gets off the plane at LaGuardia Airport wearing a Red Sox jacket I had given her, and they go outside to catch a cab. Bless her heart, she gets into the taxi, and the driver asks, 'You a Red Sox fan?' She said she was, and he asks why. She goes, 'Well, my son's pitching the first game.' 'Who's your son?' he asks. 'Bruce Hurst,' she answers. The guy goes, 'Bruce Hurst is your son? The Mets are gonna kill him!' My brother-in-law said she just stuck her chin out—so proud and tough—and said, 'We'll see.'

"My mom enjoyed reading, had this wonderful sense of baseball history, and loved stories like *Eight Men Out*. She never liked the idea of the 'Curse of the Bambino,' so she said to me, 'We'll fix that. I'm going to straighten the Babe out!' I can see her pointing that finger of hers because I got that finger pointed at me more than once. I can see her pointing it right at the Babe, saying, 'Let's get this straightened out right now!'"

"After the Red Sox won the World Series the very next season, I heard you celebrated with friends and family as if you were celebrating your own championship," I say.

Again Bruce gets emotional, swallowing hard with misty eyes: "I thought about so many people. I thought about Mrs. Yawkey and Haywood Sullivan. I thought about 'the Voice,' Sherm Feller, our public address announcer. I thought about Johnny

Pesky, Eddie Popowski, and all my Minor League coaches like Frank Malzone, Felix Maldonado, and everyone else that spent a lifetime in the Red Sox organization. It also wasn't lost on any of us players what our fans went through. It was generational. There wasn't a fair-weather fan in Boston. Those do not exist. They are not allowed in that city. You're a fan through thick and thin. When it's thin, they let you know. When it's thick, they let you know too. I thought about what this must have meant to those fans. And I thought about how it must have meant everything to every ten-year-old boy that sent me a letter after we lost the '86 World Series, [boys] that are now grown men. It mattered. I'm sorry I'm so emotional about this."

Wiping tears from his eyes, Hurst says in a whisper, "I didn't expect it."

The interview that Hurst had wanted no part of is now well past three hours old. When I casually bring this up to Bruce to lighten the mood after what has been an impassioned and moving discussion, he doesn't relent.

"I still don't want to talk," Hurst says. "You opened up a lot today—that's why all the emotion. You're peeling back something I've lost. Does that make sense? How do I put this without sounding really whiny—even more whiny than I've probably sounded all day? When I went to Foxwoods for my last interview, I came away feeling like I didn't want to go back. I'm so sick and tired of looking backward, of living my life in reverse. I just felt like such a clown. It was an odd feeling. So there was that, coupled with a bad experience I had working in the Dodgers organization [as Latin American field coordinator in 2015], and I basically told myself, 'I'm done with this.' I need to look forward in my life. I need to do other things. I do not want to only be known for what I did thirty years ago. There are parts of me that really wish I'd never even played—other than the relationships that I have with those men, those people. That matters to me, but the game itself and what it does afterward, if you're not careful . . ."

Bruce paused to reflect further: "There are parts of me that wish I'd gone to college, got an education, gone into a vocation, and worked hard to make a life for myself. Then I would have had a lot more of a future than I would a past. Does that make sense?"

"Bruce, this is the same conversation I have had with so many ex-baseball players," I say sympathetically. "When their careers end, it's very, very difficult."

"It was like a death," Hurst remarks. "I had to mourn. I can't tell you the rides that I've taken by myself just trying to put in place really who I am, not what I was. I don't want to be identified as just a pitcher that had stats comparable to Lefty Grove. I want more than that. I want to be known for more than that to my family, my children, my grandchildren, my nieces, my nephews, my cousins, and my hometown. But that's all I was. And once that ended, finding that footing has been a challenge."

"You say you want to move forward in your life. Does Bruce Hurst ever return to Fenway Park?" I ask.

"I haven't been back since the hundredth anniversary of Fenway Park, when they invited all the living players back," he says. "The only person that could probably take me back right now is my youngest daughter, who was born after I played and would love to go to Fenway Park with me. She's twenty-one now."

"So would you go back for her?" I ask. "You know, the '86 Red Sox who do return are treated like rock stars, sit in luxury boxes, and are introduced to the fans up on the big screen, and the place erupts."

"I would," Hurst says. "I promised her a trip, but I don't want to go back. But if I did, I want to go as incognito as I possibly can. I would rather just buy tickets and have a seat in the stands and watch a game with [my daughter]. I don't want to be Bruce Hurst, 'the ex-pitcher.' I'm done. At least for now. It stung. It hurt."

And with that, a now drained Bruce Hurst and I go outside for some air after what is likely the last interview he'll ever give.

14.

Grace under Fire

··

You're a hero one day and you're a goat the next. That's just the way
the game is.

—CALVIN SCHIRALDI

It's a quiet autumn late afternoon in the suburbs of
Austin, Texas, when my taxi driver pulls up to a spacious yet unpretentious reddish brown and cream
brick house. Numerous bushes and a few potted plants line
the front, while tall trees now cast a shadow over most of the
property. After I ring the doorbell, a yellow Labrador barks and
wags its tail excitedly as the former hard-throwing relief pitcher
for the Red Sox, Calvin Schiraldi, and his lovely wife of thirty-
four years, Debbie, greet me at the door.

"Don't mind Ruger," Calvin says of the dog while grinning.
"He's a dumb ass, but he's a *good* dumb ass."

Schiraldi had just come back from a friend's ranch, still clad
in a brown T-shirt, fatigue pants, and snake boots used to fend
off the rattlesnakes, coral snakes, and black indigos in that part
of Texas. A "T" ring, which signifies that he lettered at the University of Texas for two years and graduated from the school, is
proudly worn on his right hand. He's a large man, still every bit
the six feet five inches he was in the big leagues but is now far
more brawny, and with a full, mostly gray beard, he is downright rugged looking. It's a far cry from the clean-shaven boy-
ishness that he exuded in the eighties.

Initially I didn't carry much hope that I would get to meet with Calvin. Through mutual acquaintances I had heard that Schiraldi generally didn't grant interview requests about his Red Sox days. And who could blame him? Like his old teammates Buckner and Stanley, he has had to live with enduring scorn from a demanding fan base for not closing out Game Six of the '86 World Series. He has widely been regarded—unfairly, I would add [more about this below]—as one of the scapegoats, as someone who buckled under the pressure of the moment.

But I had an ace in the hole. I had become buddies with one of Calvin's longtime friends and former Minor League teammates in the Mets' organization, Ed Hearn, whom I interviewed in my book on the '86 Mets, *Kings of Queens.*

"He's a good fella, low key, and he looks for *the good* in stories," is how Hearn described me and my writing acumen to Schiraldi via a text message. "He's very interested in your story, not just with the Red Sox, but also with what you've done at St. Michael's [Catholic Academy]."

With that endorsement from Hearn, Schiraldi agreed to a meeting at his home. Before the interview even began, there was a trust factor that my questions would be fair—unlike many of the ones that I found in the voluminous newspaper clippings that I went through in preparation for this meeting.

Calvin's smile and demeanor were warm, his brown eyes twinkling—like a gentle giant, so to speak. He has a deep baritone voice and measured cadence to his speech. For all he's been through, which included a battle with alcoholism, he immediately came across to me as someone who is now comfortable in his own skin. He leans back on his sofa, legs crossed with his snake boots on, and a dip of tobacco tucked under his bottom lip, when Ruger climbs up and puts his head on Calvin's lap. Debbie offers me a more comfortable chair as she brings me a glass of water. The couple has had a trying few days as their daughter, Samantha, and her family had to evacuate their home in Santa Rosa, California, and head south because of recent fires in that state. Their son, Lukas, a former Minor

League pitcher with great promise, is now done with baseball and is attending engineering school at Texas Tech.

"Did you encourage Lukas to play ball?" I ask.

"No, I didn't," Schiraldi says. "I didn't want to be one of those dads that did that, so I just said, 'Whenever you want to go play catch, let me know, and we'll go outside.' He was fifteen when he decided he wanted to try baseball."

Lukas would quickly follow in his father's footsteps, becoming a standout high school pitcher, an All-American college hurler, and, finally, a Minor Leaguer in both the Seattle Mariners' and Miami Marlins' organizations for the last six years.

"And Samantha—did she play ball as well?" I ask.

"She did not," Calvin says with a grin. "She was a cheerleader at St. Michael's Catholic Academy. Both of my kids went there."

Practically from the time Schiraldi was finished with baseball as a professional, his name has been synonymous with St. Michael's. It's what happens when you have over three hundred wins as the coach of the baseball team.

"After all these years as coach of the Crusaders, do you do it for the love of the game or some other reason?" I ask.

"I do it because I love the game," Calvin says without hesitation. "And I think I'm pretty good at it. I became a part of the St. Michael's community, and my kids grew up there. From the time Sam was six and Lucas was three, they would come to the games. And then they attended school there. So it's kind of been a big part of my life for the last twenty-five years."

"What are some of the things that you learned from your own baseball career that you teach your players?" I ask.

"'Do as I say, not as I do,'" Calvin says with a sly grin before getting serious. "But really, by just relying on a lot of my experiences in baseball, I can see situations coming that I know are going to happen, and I try to avoid them. That's why I think I'm pretty good at coaching high school kids. I can tell them what's going to happen, and they go, 'How do you know that?' Well, I just do because I've been there and done that at all levels. So they have a comfort zone with me that I think benefits us. We're a small, private school and play public school teams that are bigger and better than we are—and we beat three of them last year. Plus we lost a close game to San Antonio Reagan, a team that went on to the state tournament. But that's the only way to get better. The players have confidence in me, and I try to put them in situations where they can succeed."

"Have any of your players gone on to the Major Leagues?" I ask.

Calvin's eyes light up: "I had one get to the big leagues with the Red Sox—Kyle Martin," he exclaims. "He got called up two years ago, and it was really cool. I was in California visiting my daughter, and I got a phone call from him saying, 'Coach, I just got called up!' I said, 'That's awesome!' And he goes, 'I'm going to be in Anaheim tomorrow.' With my daughter living in Huntington Beach at the time, I told Kyle I needed tickets [to his game]. So I actually got to go to his second game, a relief appearance. He gave up a home run to the first batter he faced—Martin Maldonado—but then set down the next three straight. It was really cool to watch."

The pride Calvin takes in Kyle's early development is evident. Schiraldi loves being a coach.

Calvin's first exposure to serious baseball was at the University of Texas, where he played with future Red Sox teammates Roger Clemens and Spike Owen. So dominating was Schiraldi as a college pitcher that Alan Simpson, the editor of *Baseball America*, famously said that he thought Calvin was a slightly better prospect than Clemens. In 1983 it wasn't such a stretch, as Schiraldi won the MVP award of the College World Series and was named *Baseball America*'s College Pitcher of the Year. Despite the accolades, Schiraldi doesn't choose to reflect on personal achievements.

"The kinship the three of us had was pretty good," Schiraldi recalls fondly. "In '82, my sophomore year, we were 57-4 and went to the [College] World Series. We had won something like thirty-three straight games and were pretty damn good. It didn't work out at the World Series, but Roger came in and was the big man on campus. I've never seen anything like what he did in the playoffs, where he pitched thirty-five consecutive scoreless innings—an NCAA record back then. That was just *ridiculous.* So there was always that bond with the three of us from that season. But after Spike left after '82, it was Roger and me and a great group of others. I think we had ten or eleven Major Leaguers on that '83 team that won the [College] World Series. When I got traded from the Mets to the Red Sox, knowing somebody there like Roger was a blessing in the sense that I wasn't completely lost. I was still just twenty-three, and the fact that he'd been there and knew the guys made the transition a lot easier for me. And then when Spike came over, that was just icing on the cake and was fun."

"After all these years do you still get together with those guys?" I ask.

"I do," he says. "Spike lives out in Spanish Oaks, and I just spoke with him last week. Roger comes into town and we still get together."

"I have already interviewed them both," I point out to Calvin. "Spike looks great and is the same enthusiastic guy that he always was. And I spoke to Roger for hours; he was fantastic."

"People really get [Roger] wrong," Schiraldi is quick to interject. "And that pisses me off. He's as giving as anybody can be, and people just don't understand that. They see a persona [on the mound], and that's how they think the person is."

"I think they see his tenacity and intensity on the baseball field, Calvin, and they think, 'Wow, he really brushes guys back.' But Roger told me that intimidation is winning—that you've got to pitch inside. People have asked me since the interview, 'So what's Roger like?' I always tell them, 'He is the nicest guy in the world.'"

Schiraldi nods in agreement before driving home his point: "Yeah, he certainly is. I wish people understood that, but I don't change people's minds."

With all the negativity that surrounded Schiraldi's failure to close out the Mets in Game Six of the World Series, it's easy to overlook how dominant a reliever he was in the final two months of the season and through Game One of the Fall Classic. The best part of the story is that he emerged out of nowhere.

Calvin struggled in limited action with the Mets in 1985 before being dealt to the Red Sox, along with three other prospects, for Bobby Ojeda. His spring training performance in '86 was dreadful, as he posted an ERA of just under 15.00 after developing bicep tendonitis in his right arm. It is not surprising that he was sent to Pawtucket to try to work through his issues while the club converted him from starter to reliever. The results were impressive: twelve saves in thirty-one games and a 2.86 ERA. So when reliever Sammy Stewart went on the disabled list in late July, Schiraldi was called up—and he never looked back. With nine saves, four wins, and a 1.41 ERA in the final two months of the season, he quickly became the toast of the town.

"You were blowing hitters away," I recall. "Bill Fischer said, in early September of '86, that he 'didn't know where the team would be without you.' Bob Duca of the *Cape Cod Times* described it this way: 'It's like little leaguers pitted against Nolan Ryan.' There were injuries in the Boston bullpen. There was inconsistency. But then you burst onto the scene as the fireball closer that the Red Sox needed—a *savior* of sorts. It would have been a *much* closer race without you. When looking back, do you understand the positive impact you had on the Red Sox winning the division title?"

"I felt I was doing my job," the ever-humble Schiraldi replies calmly. "I was doing fairly well, but that was my job. It was the first year I had ever relieved, so I didn't really know what the hell was going on. I was just throwing what I knew. But as far as knowing the impact—no. I was just doing what I thought I was supposed to do, just trying to make a living."

Schiraldi's new role as a closer is another part of the equation that often gets lost on those critical of his performance in the World Series. Being thrown into that role would be daunting for any starter at any juncture, much less on baseball's biggest stage.

"How did you take to being converted into a reliever?" I ask.

"I liked being a starter—and completing games," he says. "In high school and at the University of Texas I finished most of the games I started. Then, in the Minor Leagues, I had success as a starter. That's what I knew, so I was not a big fan of relieving. But it turned out okay [in '86]."

"Even though you were on a roll as a closer then, is it safe to say you wanted to become a starter again?" I ask.

"No, because when I went down to Pawtucket and had success [relieving], I kind of got used to it and therefore could see myself doing that," Schiraldi confesses. "I still wanted to start—and still had a starter's mentality—but I could see myself now as a reliever. I liked getting into more games. Of course there are more chances to screw it up, but you're now mentally *into* more games. I mean, as a starter, you don't have to be into the games you don't pitch. Being a reliever made 162 games a year a lot better. And I think that helped me later on with my coaching. I was always watching what managers and coaches were doing and how they handled different situations. As a starter, I could be BS-ing with 'Joe Blow' over here and not paying attention to what's going on in the game. Being a reliever grew on me."

Calvin's first real sign of trouble in '86 didn't occur until Game Four of the ALCS against the California Angels. Even that was hardly what you would call a meltdown. With Boston down two games to one he was called on in the bottom of the ninth in relief of Roger Clemens, with the Red Sox leading, 3–1, but with the Angels threatening with men on first and second and just one out. Gary Pettis would greet him by lofting a fly ball to left field; Rice misjudged it by coming in a few steps on the ball before watching it drift over his head for a double to cut the lead to 3–2 and put runners in scoring position. After an intentional walk loaded the bases, Schiraldi struck out the always tough Bobby Grich and was now just one out away from knotting the series at two games apiece. But after jumping ahead with two quick strikes on Brian Downing, he would end up hitting him with an inside curveball to tie the game. Still he composed himself enough to get Reggie Jackson to ground out to second to end the Angels' bases-loaded threat.

After retiring the Angels in order in the tenth, Calvin would surrender a game-winning single to Grich in the eleventh to give California the victory and a commanding 3–1 edge in the series. A deeply dejected Schiraldi walked slowly off the field into the dugout, took a seat on the bench, and agonizingly covered his head with a towel to hide the tears from the television cameras.

"Game Four of the ALCS didn't go well for me," Schiraldi says solemnly. "I went back to the hotel and read the Bible because that's what I did. I just read it continuously, from chapter to chapter from the beginning. I got to Romans 5:3, which says, 'Not only so, but be thankful for our tribulations, knowing that our tribulation produces perseverance; and perseverance, character; and character, hope, and hope is what we have in the Lord.' That's what I read that night."

Schiraldi then exhales before continuing, still clearly in awe over what happened next: "Thirty minutes later I get a phone call," he recounts. "That's *not* supposed to happen because I had a lock on my phone at the hotel. It was a phone call from a fireman in San Francisco who watched the game. He just wanted to call to say that he and all his buddies at the station were praying for me. And that was it. I was like, 'Okay, He [the Lord] is trying to tell me something here.' The next day comes, the last inning of Game Five, and I'm facing the same hitter [as the night before]—Brian Downing—and again get two strikes on him. But instead of throwing him a curveball, this time I throw him a fastball, and he pops it up to first for the final out. So, I thought [of the Lord], 'Okay, You're telling me something. You're trying to talk to me here. So it's my job to listen.'"

Schiraldi was back and would close out Game Seven at Fenway for the pennant-clincher and then Game One of the World Series in New York against the Mets.

"Can you comment on what those major successes under the brightest of lights in the postseason meant to you as a young pitcher?" I ask.

"You don't really remember those," Schiraldi says with a shrug. "That's because it's a result-based game. The *final* results weren't what they were supposed to be. That's what gets publicized; that's what gets remembered more by the public, by me, and by pretty much everybody. Not the regular successes because those go day to day. You're a hero one day, and you're a goat the next. That's just the way the game is. The end results didn't come out the way that I had wanted them to. But like I've learned over the years, tell God your plan, and he'll decide on that too. He's often got other plans for you, so that's the way you have to look at it—or at least that's the way I have to look at it. What I wanted wasn't His plan, so now I have to try to figure out what it is."

Admittedly Schiraldi has leaned heavily on his faith. As he talks about God's plan for him, he claims to have *always* been a devout Christian—through good times and bad. In his family room are symbols of his beliefs: a cross on his mantle, a picture frame with spiritual references, and a book written by former NFL head coach Tony Dungy titled *Uncommon Life*, which reflects on living a Christian lifestyle.

Calvin notices me taking note of them all. "They're little remembrances, little reminders of what's important," Schiraldi says with a smile.

After the Red Sox overcame the Angels in seven games, no one on the club knew the upcoming World Series opponent, the Mets, better than Schiraldi. For three years he had played in three different levels in their Minor League system, as well as having two stints on their big league roster. He knew how deeply talented they were from the top down.

"Even in '84 you could see how good they were going to be a mile away," Calvin tells me. "You knew they were going to be special. Even in '83, on the Jackson team, we had Herm Winningham, Kevin Mitchell, and Roger McDowell. On our Lynchburg team we had Dwight Gooden, Lenny Dykstra, Mark Carreon, Wes Gardner, Randy Milligan, and myself. That Lynchburg team won more games than anybody in baseball in '83. The Mets were loaded; you knew they would be really good, really soon. It's just like what happened with the [modern-day] Astros; it's the same dang thing. On the big league club the guy I really respected was Keith Hernandez. Keith just had a professional way of going about his business, and he took younger guys under his wing in spring training, that type of thing. You listened to him even more than you listened to the manager. By the way, I think Keith would have been a *great* manager."

Schiraldi counted several of the Mets players as some of his closest friends at the time, particularly Mitchell and Ed Hearn. In fact, so tight was Schiraldi with Hearn that the Mets' backup catcher was dating Calvin's sister, Rhonda, at the time of the World Series.

"Did you ever ask your sister for whom she was rooting in that Series?" I ask.

"I don't think so," Calvin says. "But I think it's one of those things where no matter who won, she would have been fine with it."

As for Mitchell, he and Schiraldi would face one another in the most pivotal point of the '86 World Series—with the Mets trailing, 5–3, with two outs and a man on in the bottom of the tenth inning of Game Six.

"I was on the phone with our mutual friend Kevin Mitchell last week and told him that we were going to get together," I tell Schiraldi. "Right away he brought up the time you both were in the Minors and talked about how you would pitch against him should you ever face him in a game. He said you told him you would get him out on a slider."

"Yeah, he couldn't hit one back then—not in Double-A, not in Triple-A," Calvin confirms.

"So when you faced him in Game Six, were you thinking at all about that conversation you two had?" I ask.

"No, that never even entered my mind," Schiraldi says with a slight grin. "Not until I was reminded of it after everything was over. And then I went, 'Oh yeah, that did happen.' I definitely remember talking to him about it because it was in Syracuse, New York, and we were facing Toronto's [Minor League team]. I said, 'You can't hit a bleepin' slider. I'd get your ass out with a slider.' It's just one of those things where I thought, 'I know I can get him out with a slider, but I just can't hang it.' So yes, I do remember saying that to Mitchell, but I just wasn't thinking about it during that particular game. That was not running through my head."

Recalling that long-ago conversation with Schiraldi, Mitchell, looking for a slider all the way, served a single into center field to put runners on first and second.

"Mitchell's hit was the second of three in a row in that inning after you got the first two outs—none of them hit particularly hard," I note. "Ray Knight got that third hit after you got ahead of him 0-2. You were one strike away from ending the World Series. What was going through your mind, needing just one more strike to win a World Series?"

"I remember what I forgot, which was to *never* give up an 0-2 base hit," Calvin says, clearly still annoyed that he'd let that happen. "I think instead of *pitching*, I just threw because that was my pet peeve all the time: never give up a hit on 0-2. I don't care if it hit the frickin' back screen, you can't give up an 0-2 hit. With the Red Sox we would get fined in Kangaroo Court for 0-2 hits."

"From Baylor, right?" I ask.

"Yes, Don would [fine] you $25 for a single, $50 for a double, and $75 for a triple, and if you gave up an 0-2 home run, it was $250. A grand slam was $500. This was done so you wouldn't do it. And I didn't remember that at the time. I don't know where my brain was, but it wasn't there."

"It sounds like you just wanted to end the game," I remark.

"Yeah, win the game—then let's party!" exclaims Calvin. "But it didn't happen."

"At that point McNamara took you out of the game and brought in Stanley. Of the sixteen pitches you made in the tenth inning—your third inning of work, by the way—twelve were strikes, and like I said earlier, none were hit particularly hard. Clearly you made some good pitches. In retrospect does that lessen any of the sting—that is, the fact that you pitched well but that the Mets' hitters just fought off some pretty damned good pitches?"

Calvin doesn't hesitate: "No, not in our game," he says. "Not in the World Series. It's a results-based thing, so that means zero."

The misfortunes for the Red Sox would continue in their quest for that final out. The Stanley wild pitch and the Buckner error allowed the Mets to knot the World Series at three games apiece.

Schiraldi would get another chance in Game Seven— unbeknown to the two of us at the time of our interview that it was *exactly* thirty-three years earlier to the day. He was summoned back to the mound by McNamara to start the bottom of the seventh inning of a 3–3 tie. But a leadoff home run by Ray Knight and then a Rafael Santana RBI single later in the inning ended Schiraldi's night, with the Red Sox trailing 5–3. Two innings later the Mets extinguished the Red Sox's hopes for their first championship in sixty-eight years, winning the game, 8–5.

"Again, you can count on one hand the number of tough outings you had in '86," I say. "But because two of them were in the final two games of a World Series, they were magnified. Or like you've said, they're what people tend to remember. How did that, if at all, affect the rest of your career?"

"I don't think that affected my career," Schiraldi says thoughtfully. "I think the thing that affected my career the most was going from starter to reliever and then from reliever to starter and back again to reliever. From the time I started in the Major

Leagues, I don't think there was a year back to back that I held the same [role]. At least not after '86 and '87 with the Red Sox as a reliever."

"Is that extremely difficult for a pitcher?" I ask.

"Yes, it's not easy," Calvin confirms. "That's because before the season starts I'm preparing to be a reliever, and then, all of a sudden, they say you're going to be a starter. And then they would do the reverse—from starter to back to the bullpen. I think that had the most effect on how the rest of my career went."

"With the sixty-eight-year world championship drought Boston fans would have gone out of their minds had the Red Sox won in '86," I surmise. "Do you ever give any thought to how your life and the lives of your teammates would have been different had you ended the so-called curse that year?"

"No, I don't like dwelling on the past," Schiraldi says. "And I don't like dwelling on what could have been. I deal with the *now*. Would I change what happened? No. And the reason is because what happened then, as well as [what happened in] the rest of my career, made me who I am. Granted, I've not always been a great person, but I think I'm a good human being. I have had my problems with alcohol and stuff. I'm a recovering alcoholic, but it wasn't baseball that caused that. I mean, I was drinking before college. But alcoholism and just the whole life thing, it's one day at a time—not dwelling on what could be or what has been. I live in the present—or try to live in the present."

"It's easy to forget that Red Sox fans still celebrated after the World Series loss," I recall. "It's easy to forget, given the negativity that followed in the ensuing years, but the City of Boston threw you guys a massive parade and rally at Government Center."

Schiraldi gives a big grin when recalling that bright, shiny day in Boston: "That was *phenomenal!*" he exclaims. "I remember being on a tractor-trailer thing and that there were like five hundred thousand people there. It was an awesome way to end the season, even though we weren't MLB champions. We were *still* American League champions. So that was just really cool."

Calvin's relatively short tenure in Boston would end following the '87 season, when he was traded to the Chicago Cubs as part of a deal that brought future Hall of Fame closer Lee Smith to the Red Sox. After additional stops in San Diego and Texas, he would call it a career following the 1991 season. But despite playing for five big league clubs in eight seasons, he will forever be indelibly linked with the '86 Red Sox and how he took Boston by storm in the second half that season yet couldn't quite finish off the Mets in the World Series.

But on this evening in Austin none of that mattered much anymore. Schiraldi is clearly a man at peace with his world.

15.

Two for the Ages

I'd like to be remembered as that guy who, in a two-week span, stole the show. . . . For two or three weeks I just did things that superstars were supposed to do.

—DAVE HENDERSON

You talk about a leader. We had Evans and Rice and Buckner, but it was Don [Baylor] who started to sow the seeds of winning for us.

—RICH GEDMAN

Perhaps never before in baseball history have two teammates been so indelibly linked to one historic game yet were so different. The first of the duo, Don "Groove" Baylor, was already a bona fide star. A former MVP, Baylor was an imposing and stoic figure who had proudly accepted the role of leader, big brother, and enforcer for Boston after the Sox acquired him from the Yankees prior to the '86 season.

"We were no longer going to be messed with," Marty Barrett told me. "If a pitcher threw at one of our hitters, there was going to be retaliation, and Donnie Baylor was going to be right down in the middle of the fight. He always had his game face on and was a great offensive force. I think it was really good for Jim Rice to have Baylor on the team because he was the same type of guy."

A fixture in the middle of their lineup, Baylor led the Red Sox with thirty-one home runs and had the dubious achievement of getting hit by a career-high thirty-five pitches in '86, an uncanny "art form" he mastered during his career that exemplified his toughness.

"I remember when he walked into our clubhouse in Winter Haven, Florida, the first day of spring training," Bruce Hurst recalled. "I looked across the room, and the first thought I had was, 'This guy's huge! What do I do now? He scared the crap out of me for the last five years, and now I've got to be nice to him? I've tried to have anything but fear and trepidation with this guy and stand my ground—and now he's my teammate?' But he came over, shook my hand, and said, 'It's nice to be here. I'm looking forward to playing with you this year.' I then thought, 'Man, this is a good guy.'"

Even some of the veterans immediately saw the intangibles that Groove brought to the club: "We knew what we had in Baylor in spring training," Dwight Evans said. "Not only was there his talent, but his leadership by example. I thought, '[This team] is looking really good now.'" "When we brought over Don Baylor," Wade Boggs added, "he was the veteran solidifying presence that our club needed, and he fit in perfectly for us."

The second of the duo was the relatively anonymous Dave Henderson, the affable, fun-loving, gap-toothed outfielder with the thousand-watt smile acquired in a mid-August '86 trade with the Mariners along with shortstop Spike Owen. Hendu, as he was called by everyone, was to be used strictly as a backup to center fielder Tony Armas. He would hit a paltry .196 with but a single home run in his limited playing time down the stretch. Unlike Baylor, who made an immediate impact, Hendu's initial contributions to the club were muted, and his abilities went largely unnoticed.

"We didn't really take the Mariners seriously back then," Bruce Hurst told me. "They had all this young talent, but they were really under the radar. So when we got Hendu from them, we had no idea what a phenomenal athlete he was—as athletic as anybody I ever played with or against." "We already had Armas, who was an excellent center fielder," Dwight Evans added. "So when we got Dave, we didn't know where he would fit in."

But on a brilliant, sun-splashed afternoon in Southern California on October 12, 1986, all that would change. Baylor and Henderson would become synonymous in Red Sox lore.

The scene was Anaheim Stadium, Game Five of the 1986 ALCS, with the Angels leading the series three games to one. The Red Sox were trailing 5–2 with one out and one on in the ninth and facing elimination when Baylor stepped to the plate. Angels ace Mike Witt was pitching a gem when Baylor, using his tremendous strength, reached for a pitch on the outside part of the plate and pulled it over the left-center-field fence—just out of the reach of a leaping Gary Pettis—to make it a 5–4 game.

Then three batters later, with a man on and now two outs, Hendu, who had entered the game in the bottom of the fifth for an ailing Armas (who had badly injured an ankle after crashing into the outfield wall the previous inning), came to the plate against Angels closer Donnie Moore.

"Dave was hurt too," Hurst recalled, referring to the torn cartilage Hendu had in his right knee. "He had a bad leg—a *really* bad leg. It was hurt way more than anybody knew."

The fans, nearly sixty-five thousand, rose to their feet—many of them ready to storm the field in jubilation—and roared in anticipation of the Angels' first trip to the World Series in their twenty-five-year history; it was now just one out away.

"With the stadium cops standing on the top step of our first base dugout, ready to keep the fans off the field, we're looking at Henderson between their legs from four steps down," Dwight Evans recalled incredulously.

The hard-throwing Moore would start by firing two fastballs right by Hendu, who didn't look comfortable at all. "He was hitting off one leg," Hurst recalled. "If you remember the first two swings he took, he was a day late and a dollar short. He wasn't even close." "Hendu looked like an old man swinging at those pitches," was how Buckner described it.

The Angels were ready to celebrate—a scene that is etched in Boggs's mind. "When I looked over [at their dugout] and there were two outs," he said, "I saw Reggie [Jackson] hugging [Angels manager] Gene Mauch and then taking his glasses off and putting them into his shirt. They thought it was done."

And that's when an incredible turn of events occurred. Down to his last strike, Henderson would lunge out in front of a Donnie Moore forkball and plant it into the left-field stands for a two-run homer to give the Red Sox a 6–5 lead.

"It was like, '*Boom!*'" Boggs exclaimed. "Brian Downing goes back [for Henderson's fly ball] and then hits the wall as the home run goes out. I see all of the Angels in their dugout; all of their mouths just dropped. They did *not* want to go back to Boston. That was putting the paddles on them and jump-starting things again for us."

"When you're in the dugout and don't have control over what's going on, you're just wishing and hoping something would change—and it did," Clemens added. "It was pretty incredible."

Some, like Dwight Evans, gave it added significance: "Henderson's home run, to me, was the greatest I *ever* saw," said Evans, who had witnessed teammate Carlton Fisk's iconic 1975 World Series walk-off in Game Six. "It was also the most important and the most dramatic home run I ever saw. Just off the charts."

Just as memorable was the twirl and leap Hendu jubilantly took—bad knee and all—as he watched the ball sail out of the park—easily the most famous reaction to a home run since, well, the aforementioned Fisk home run.

"That was just Hendu's boyish exuberance that came out and manifested into this beautiful leap—an Olympic-type thing," Hurst noted. "But when he landed, he wobbled a little bit because he was hurt."

Clemens recalled the same thing: "If you'd watched him jump, when he turned [in the air], you'd've seen him come down and his knee buckled—his foot cross-eyed with that bad knee. But Hendu sucked it up for us and ended up playing a great World Series."

But the heroics weren't finished yet for Hendu and Bay-lor in *this* game. After the Angels tied it up in the bottom of the ninth to move the game into extra innings, Baylor led off the top of the eleventh by getting hit by a pitch. Later in the inning Hendu drove him home with a sacrifice fly to cen-ter to give the Red Sox what would prove to be the winning run in their miraculous 7–6 victory. The Angels would never recover from that devastating defeat, and the Red Sox steam-rolled over them in the final two games at Fenway to advance to the World Series.

"The [ALCS] was *over* after that game," Barrett told me emphat-ically. "With what happened in that game, we were flying high going back to Boston; it was just so awesome. We just went into Fenway, and the last two games weren't even close."

A lot has been written and said about how 1986 was a heart-breaking continuation of the so-called Curse of the Bambino. Thus it's easy to forget the stunningly remarkable victory in Game Five of the ALCS that catapulted the Red Sox into the World Series. It was nothing short of one of the last century's greatest and most dramatic occurrences in all of sports.

Before the heroics of Baylor and Henderson in the ALCS vaulted them into iconic status among the Fenway faithful, there was a great deal going on with them, both professionally and per-sonally, that received little public fanfare.

Baylor acted as judge of the Red Sox "Kangaroo Court" throughout the '86 season. While it served to lighten up the clubhouse atmosphere, it more importantly served to remind the players how to conduct themselves more professionally.

"Donnie really was a gentle giant," Barrett told me. "I used to love to see him laugh because he was so stoic all the time. He had this demeanor about him that was so interesting. He ran the Kangaroo Court the first year we ever had one. He would give out little fines for not doing things correctly during a game or not following the unwritten rules of baseball. If you broke one of them, the Kangaroo Court would hold a meeting."

Hurst recounted that Baylor took his job as judge seriously: "During that season Mike Witt and I had the same agent—Nick Lampros," Hurst said. "I didn't know Mike real well, but because we had this in common, we had a marginal relationship. But because we were on opposite teams, one of Baylor's Kangaroo Court rules was that I couldn't talk to him on the field. If I did, it would cost me fifty bucks."

Baylor brought some levity to his Kangaroo Court. For example, he fined Clemens five dollars after he struck out twenty Mariners in one game. The reason? He'd allowed the relatively light-hitting Spike Owen, still a Mariner at the time, to single off of him.

From the very start of his career Baylor had a quiet confidence about himself. In 1970, while at the Orioles' Triple-A affiliate in Rochester, he led the Minor Leagues in doubles, triples, runs scored, and games played. Hurst loves telling the story of how this breakout season earned Baylor his nickname, Groove: "In Baltimore they had an outfield of Frank Robinson, Paul Blair, and Don Buford," Bruce told me. "Now Baylor's like the Minor League Player of the Year, so he comes into spring training and is asked, 'How are you going to crack this outfield?' He goes, 'Once I get in the groove.' So Robinson started calling him Groove, and it stuck."

Of most importance to Hurst was the effort Baylor made in getting to know his teammates and the leadership role he played aside from being the judge of the Kangaroo Court: "We found out we liked the same music, and he would take me to a music warehouse he knew about in Cleveland on every trip there," Hurst recounted. "We talked about music and Groove and I developed a friendship that was a lot of fun. He also was always pulling for his teammates, getting guys together for dinner on the road, and keeping us centered on baseball. He was a really good man. After I got traded, I remember I had to face him when he was in Oakland, and I was like, 'I don't want to get him out. Can you just let somebody else hit?' I didn't just like Groove; I *loved* him."

Henderson had a baby boy to worry about; few people knew about the situation at the time. His older son, Chase, was born just four months before Hendu's dramatic ALCS home run with a neurogenetic disorder called Angelman Syndrome, which in this case caused seizures and motor delay to the infant. He ultimately became handicapped.

"When I think about the 1986 season," Hendu told the *Boston Herald*'s Steve Buckley a decade later, "I think of all the time I spent that summer at the UMass Medical Center in Worcester. So when people ask me if that home run [in the ALCS] was the biggest thrill in my life, well, no it isn't. The biggest thrill of my life is any day when my son is healthy. And right now he is healthy. And I'm thrilled."

Evans, whose two sons had their own serious medical challenges, was like a kindred spirit to Hendu: "He was always smiling and happy and had that little gap in his teeth," Evans recalled. "This despite his child having that serious condition that put him in a wheelchair. After [Henderson] and his wife divorced, he took the child. That shows you what kind of guy he was. I don't know what the issues were, but he took the kid and took care of him in Seattle. A great guy with a smile that was contagious. I can see that smile right now."

Boggs felt the same way about him: "I loved Hendu," he told me. "You could be having your worst day and walk into the clubhouse and just see his smile, which was so infectious, and he would literally pick you up and say everything's going to be better. He made you believe that we just needed to go out and focus and win that day. He was a tremendous team leader, and I was very honored to call him a close friend."

Everyone quickly found out something else about Henderson after he was acquired: his freakishly impressive jumping ability. It was the stuff of legend. All the Red Sox I spoke with about Hendu brought this up with their own stories.

"He could jump higher than *anyone* I ever saw," Buckner exclaimed. "He once jumped over the trainer's table. I couldn't believe my eyes. He reminded me of these little goats that live on these rocky mountains I saw on the show *Planet Earth*. They're like Spider-Man, jumping straight down a hundred feet and not slipping. Hendu was like that!"

"Hendu was just chiseled—not an ounce of fat," Evans recalled. "Two hundred twenty pounds of muscle, and he never lifted a weight. He would jump from the dugout floor standing sideways—his right shoulder toward first base—up onto the playing field. His leaping ability and athleticism was off the charts."

And there was this from Rich Gedman: "If we had a grocery cart, he'd stand next to it and say, 'I can jump over this standing straight up.' You would look at him going, 'No way.' And then he'd go ahead and do it. He was just so big, strong, and confident. But his greatest attribute was still his smile."

Incredibly Henderson would continue to do in the World Series against the Mets what he'd shockingly done to the Angels, and he'd come ever so close to carrying the Red Sox to their first championship in sixty-eight years. By clubbing two of the Red Sox five home runs, batting .400, and, most memorably, hitting a lead-off homer in the top of the tenth inning of the infamous Game Six, he appeared to put Boston on the brink of finishing off the Mets.

So how does a relatively obscure player like Hendu go from pedestrian ballplayer to a star on the rise, capable of dominating serious October baseball and leaving some of the Mets to wonder, "Who is this guy?"

Spike Owen, who knew Hendu longer than anyone on the team—going back to their years together in Seattle—wasn't shocked one bit by his newfound success: "He was one of the best teammates I ever had," the shortstop told me. "He loved to play the game but didn't get the coverage in Seattle that he got in Boston and then later in his heyday with Oakland. So his performance didn't surprise me at all. With Hendu you never knew when something big was gonna happen. He always came ready to play, and if he got an opportunity, he would thrive.

The ['86 postseason] was his time. I was up next and waiting for him at home plate after his home run in Game Six in New York. A shot of that is on one of my favorite baseball cards."

Hurst had another theory: "He was a younger player with other young players in Seattle," the southpaw said. "As a player with the talent he had, to come to Boston and now be surrounded by guys like Rice, Baylor, Clemens, Evans, Armas, Boggsy, and Buckner, he could just be himself. He didn't have to be 'the franchise' or necessarily 'the man' like he had with the Mariners. But he certainly did become 'the man,' a big part of what we accomplished, and he *loved* 'the big moment.' I mean, his at bat against Donnie Moore might have been the greatest at bat I ever saw. And then the World Series he had was amazing. I know they were going to name me the MVP of that World Series [had the Red Sox won], but he or Marty could easily have been MVP as well."

All Gedman could do was admire the intestinal fortitude of the man: "Some people have to grind, but Hendu didn't," the catcher explained to me. "It's a gift when you can smile in the face of danger, if you will. He wouldn't allow the game to beat him up. That's a tremendous thing for any baseball player who can do that. You don't see many of them that can."

Because the World Series invoked the designated hitter (DH) rule for only the three games at Fenway, Baylor's playing time was understandably limited. However, he was disappointed when McNamara passed him over in a couple of key pinch-hitting spots in New York. Still he was able to contribute the game-winning RBI in Game Five and provide invaluable leadership from the bench throughout the Series.

If not for the unlikeliest of finishes in Game Six and yet another comeback by the Mets in Game Seven, both Baylor and Henderson would have forever been sacred cows in Boston. With his exploits in the World Series you could make the argument that Henderson's postseason would have gone down as the greatest in Major League history. But it wasn't to be, and the departure of both Groove and Hendu, almost unfathomably, would fall on the exact same day less than a year later, when, on September 1, 1987, Baylor was dealt to the Minnesota Twins and Henderson to the San Francisco Giants. Two players so richly engrained in Red Sox history were like shooting stars, both in Boston for less than two seasons. Henderson, despite all the adulation and fame, only saw action in 111 games in a Red Sox uniform (rookie Ellis Burks would become the primary center fielder in '87). Both he and Baylor would ultimately win their elusive World Series championships elsewhere—Baylor with the '87 Twins and Hendu with the '89 A's—and they would reunite as teammates on the pennant-winning '88 A's in Don's last big league season. It is not surprising that Baylor would utilize his leadership skills in becoming a big league manager for the expansion Colorado Rockies and then later with the Chicago Cubs—with varying degrees of success. Hendu would blossom into a star with the A's and become one of the most beloved players in club history, though he retired early to be home in Seattle with his two sons before embarking on a broadcasting career with the Mariners.

Sadly Hendu and Baylor would ultimately share something else: they would be the first of the '86 Red Sox players to pass away. Considering the physical specimen that Henderson was during his playing career, the news of his premature death in 2015 from a massive heart attack—suffered two months after his having undergone a successful kidney transplant—was nothing short of shocking. And the idea that he was the *first* of the '86 Red Sox to die is almost incomprehensible. He was just fifty-seven years old.

"It hit me hard when he passed away," Boggs confided to me. "But he came in at the right time. He was the person we needed and sort of took us on his shoulders in the California series and said, 'You know what? Let's go! Just jump on, and we're going to do this!' He always made you laugh, whether he was doing his little 'dancey' catch in the outfield or his flippy throws back in. Oh, I can just see him right now."

Barrett and Clemens echoed much of Boggs's sentiments. "Hendu, man, he just kept everyone loose," Marty recounted. "I'll just always remember that gap tooth of his and how he didn't have a worry in the world—always laughing. I remember he was the worst batting practice hitter you've ever seen, but in the game he'd be awesome. That was a smoking good trade we made to get him. For a guy who just came over, he acted like he'd been with us for twenty years."

"Hendu was cut from the same mold as Kirby Puckett," Clemens said. "I don't think I ever saw him upset or without a smile on his face. He was always upbeat and was never scared of any challenge that was facing him."

And then there was this sentimental view from his long-time teammate Owen, who believes he was a better player for having observed the way Hendu conducted himself: "If he had a really bad night, you would never know. It showed me that, okay, this is the way it works here; this is a tough game, the competition is hard, and you're not going to shine all the time. And when you don't shine, so what? You just come back and get them the next day. Hendu never realized what he meant to me as far as my watching him and the way he did things. He taught me to have fun while playing and be able to just move from day to day. I learned a lot and respect him for that."

But the modest outfielder with the magnificent smile downplayed his impact on the Red Sox, once telling a throng of reporters at a Boston Baseball Writers' dinner in 1996, "I'd like to be remembered as that guy who, in a two-week span, stole the show. It's not like I was a great ballplayer in Boston. But for two or three weeks I just did things that superstars were supposed to do."

Don Baylor's passing in 2017 followed a fourteen-year battle with multiple myeloma, a cancer of the blood plasma cells. He was sixty-eight. The news of his death was tragic, though less of a surprise than Henderson's.

"You talk about a leader," Gedman said. "We had Evans and Rice and Buckner, but it was Don who started to sow the seeds of winning for us. He'd be like, 'Win a series, and they can't catch us. Win another series, and they can't catch us.' And that's exactly what we did all the way to winning the [division title]."

In 1986 Boston it may have been the summer of Clemens and his winning the rare combination of both the Cy Young Award and the MVP. And it may have been Jim Rice's last great season of his storied career. And it may have been Boggs's most courageous year, winning yet another batting title in the face of personal tragedy. But for high drama the '86 postseason will forever belong to a duo that left the Red Sox, and this earth, too quickly—Groove and Hendu.

Epilogue

One of the greatest challenges when writing a book about a team that had such a profound effect on baseball like the '86 Red Sox is to capture as many significant angles as possible. And I have often found that some of the most intriguing stories don't necessarily come from the brightest stars on a club but often from those to whom nothing came easily or from those who made their most notable impact behind the scenes. By limiting my literary portraits in this book to the regular position players, starting pitching staff, primary relievers, and a couple of players with fascinating human interest stories, the rest of the team members—including the manager—from the 1986 Red Sox World Series roster weren't given their own chapters. But this does not diminish the contributions each of them made to the '86 Red Sox. The reality is that just to make it to the Major Leagues, much less to be the rare individual to appear in a World Series, is a Herculean achievement that makes for wonderful story lines of great skill and determination. Thus to round out the full picture of this storied team, the following sections describe the critical roles each of them played on the '86 Red Sox and what became of them after that fateful season.

Tony Armas was a prolific power hitter, hitting more home runs from 1980 through 1985 than any other American League player. In 1984 he was the Red Sox co-MVP and placed seventh in the league MVP voting. But by 1986, although he was still the regular center fielder for Boston, recurring leg injuries put a dent into his playing time—including in the ALCS—opening the door for the heroics of his replacement, Dave Henderson.

A humble man who enjoyed his Bud Lights and Winston cigarettes in the clubhouse after games, Armas's popular catch phrase after making a great catch, according to Joe Castiglione, was, "If you don't hit, you gotta do something. You *must* do something."

Tony signed a free agent contract with the Angels in 1987, and he finished out his career with them two years later. His son, Tony Jr., pitched for three Major League teams over ten seasons through 2008.

Armas currently lives in Venezuela, where he is the batting coach for the Leones del Caracas in the Venezuelan Professional Baseball League. He earned induction into both the Venezuelan Baseball Hall of Fame and Museum and the Caribbean Baseball Hall of Fame.

Steve "Shag" Crawford was a big, strong versatile pitcher on whom the Red Sox relied for seven seasons. In '86 he had the distinction of going winless during the regular season but getting credit for the win in the epic Game Five of the ALCS and then in Game Two of the World Series.

Still a regular at Red Sox fantasy camps, Crawford resides in Salina, Oklahoma, just outside of Commerce.

Mike "the Gator" Greenwell was a worthy successor to the storied triumvirate of Red Sox left fielders—Ted Williams, Carl Yastrzemski, and Jim Rice—playing his entire twelve-season career in the shadow of the Green Monster. A part-time player in '86, he came into his own the following year by finishing fourth in the Rookie of the Year voting. By 1988 he was one of the best players in the game, setting career highs with 22 home runs, 119 RBIS, and a .325 batting average and finishing second in the MVP race to Jose Canseco. With revelations that came out later about Canseco's admitted steroid use that season, Greenwell publicly wondered if the award should go to him. "I do have a problem with losing the MVP to an admitted steroids user," Greenwell told the *Fort Myers News-Press* in 2005. "Where's my MVP? He's an admitted steroid user. I was clean. If they're going to start putting asterisks by things, let's put one by the MVP."

Greenwell currently resides in Alva, Florida, where he owns a ranch where he grows fruits and vegetables. He once owned a Cape Coral amusement park named Mike Greenwell's Bat-a-Ball and Family Fun Park, which he recently sold and which is now called Gator Mike's.

Mike has a wife, Tracy, and two sons—Bo, a Minor Leaguer for eight years, and Garrett, who played college ball.

John McNamara was named AL Manager of the Year for guiding the Red Sox to the '86 pennant. But McNamara would last only another season and a half in Boston after a disappointing 1987 campaign and slow first-half start the following season. He would go on to pilot the Cleveland Indians before his final managerial stop in an interim role with the California Angels in 1996.

Shortly after the '96 season ended, extreme tragedy struck McNamara's family when his son-in-law shot and killed John's two young grandchildren before turning the gun on himself in a murder-suicide.

McNamara passed away on July 28, 2020, from natural causes.

Al Nipper was used primarily as a back-of-the-rotation starter for the '86 Red Sox, pitching a total of five seasons in Boston. He appeared twice in the World Series, first as the starting pitcher in Game Four and then in a relief role in Game Seven.

Nipper would be traded, along with Calvin Schiraldi, in a blockbuster deal that brought future Hall of Fame closer Lee Smith to Boston following the 1987 season. Nipper's last big league appearance would be with the Cleveland Indians in 1990.

Following his playing career Nipper worked as a Major and Minor League pitching coach and scout for several teams, including the Red Sox. He currently resides in the St. Louis suburb of Chesterfield, Missouri.

Ed Romero was a seasoned veteran when the Red Sox acquired him following the 1985 season from the Milwaukee Brewers. Splitting time at shortstop with Rey Quinones for much of the '86 regular season, he served as Spike Owen's backup at the position following the late-season trade with Seattle that brought Owen to Boston. Romero would appear in three World Series games that fall.

Following his playing career Ed would serve as third base and bench coach for the Houston Astros after managerial stints for several Minor League clubs in the Padres' and Brewers' organizations. Most recently he was the manager of the Tri-City Valley Cats of the New York–Penn League. His son, Eddie, is currently the executive vice president and assistant general manager for the Red Sox.

Joe Sambito was the left-handed specialist the Red Sox bullpen desperately needed in '86. Following an All-Star beginning to his career with the Astros, ligament damage in his pitching elbow necessitated Tommy John surgery. After a lengthy rehabilitation and long road back to the big leagues, a determined Sambito made the Red Sox roster out of spring training prior to the '86 season—ironically after being released by the Mets (his favorite boyhood team and Boston's World Series foe) late the previous season. He would save twelve games for the Red Sox in '86—his first saves in more than three seasons.

"I was playing Triple-A for the Mets when they released me," Joe told me. "I thought it was the end of the road. I went home to St. Petersburg, Florida, and by October I was regularly throwing off the mound at the Cardinals' Minor League facility. Their farm director, Lee Thomas, approached me one day and asked if I was willing to go to Venezuela to pitch for six weeks.

The Triple-A field manager in Venezuela was Jim Fregosi. I agreed to go, and I pitched well enough to attract some attention. One of the interested teams was the Red Sox. They had a need for a left-handed reliever as there was only one on the roster. I went from 'dead in the water' to spring training with the Red Sox to a World Series in the fall. It was my only World Series, and my two years in Boston were incredible. It was a case of preparation and opportunity coming together for me."

Sambito would retire from baseball in mid-1988. But just two months later he was busy in the Florida Instructional League, recruiting players for Hendricks Sports Management, the sports agency that had represented him as a player. The following year Joe became the first ex–Major Leaguer to be certified by the Major League Baseball Players' Association as a player agent, a role in which he would thrive for twenty-nine years.

Joe currently resides in Irvine, California, with his second wife, Jennifer. He has three children—Sophia, Giovanni, and Marisa—and a stepson, Michael.

Dave Stapleton played his entire seven-year career with the Red Sox, serving as the starting first baseman for two seasons until Boston acquired Bill Buckner in 1984. The versatile Stapleton covered six different positions during his time with the Red Sox but is best remembered as the ailing Buckner's late-inning defensive replacement throughout the '86 season. And it was because of that that McNamara's decision to leave Stapleton in the dugout during the tenth inning of Game Six of the World Series stirred so much controversy soon after Buckner's error on Mookie Wilson's groundball allowed the winning run to score in the Mets' come-from-behind victory.

As it turned out, with Stapleton's release by the Mariners the following spring, that '86 World Series would mark the end of his Major League career.

Stapleton currently lives in Daphne, Alabama.

ACKNOWLEDGMENTS

I owe a special debt of gratitude to my dear friend Tim Neverett, the former Red Sox and current Dodgers broadcaster. It was Tim who encouraged me to pursue "the other side of the story" following the success of my book *Kings of Queens: Life Beyond Baseball with the '86 Mets.*

I also want to thank my literary agent, Robert Wilson, a master at his craft who is a true co-pilot on my various projects.

Any author deeply values support and encouragement. Above anybody else, the person that exemplifies this for me is my dear friend Jeanne Glazer, who has been nothing short of a godsend. For Jeanne's love of baseball and the arts, and her enthusiasm for my book projects, I give my eternal gratitude.

My utmost appreciation goes to the University of Nebraska Press and most notably to senior acquisitions editor Rob Taylor and associate acquisitions editor Courtney Ochsner for believing in and understanding the relevance of this Red Sox team in the annals of baseball history. It was a privilege working with them and the rest of the team, which included senior project editor Sara Springsteen, copyeditor Bojana Ristich, publicist Anna Weir, publicity manager Rosemary Sekora, and the manager of editorial, design, and production Ann Baker.

This book could not have happened without the assistance of the venerable Red Sox vice president of community, alumni, and player relations Pam Kenn, the manager of alumni and player relations Sheri Rosenberg, Red Sox team historian Gordon Edes, and Pawtucket Red Sox vice president of communications and community relations Bill Wanless, all of whom put me in touch with many of the '86 Red Sox players.

Special recognition should also go to the staff at the National Baseball Hall of Fame and Museum, with a nod of appreciation to Bruce Markusen, manager of digital and outreach learning, and Matt Rothenberg, manager of the Giamatti Research Center. Their opening up of the vast resources of the Hall of Fame to me was invaluable.

And last, various publications and websites aided me in my research of the men that made up the '86 Red Sox team. Much of that information came from the "bible" of baseball record-keeping, the website BaseballResearch.com. Other sources included the *Boston Globe*, the *Boston Herald*, the *Providence Journal-Bulletin*, the *Patriot Ledger*, Boston.com, the *Sporting News*, *Grantland*, *USA Today*, the *National Sports Daily*, the *New York Post*, the *New York Daily News*, the *New York Times*, the *Washington Post*, *Newsday*, the *Los Angeles Times*, *Rocky Mountain News*, *Sport Magazine*, the *Mercury News*, Associated Press, *Curbed Austin*, the *Daily Texan*, *Sports Collectors Digest*, *Diamond Days*, the *Hartford Courant*, the *Albany Times*, NESN.com, the *New Hampshire Union Leader*, the *Enterprise*, the *Detroit Free Press*, the *Kansas City Star*, the *Huffington Post*, the *Chicago Tribune*, ESPN.com, the *New Yorker*, the *Deseret News*, MLB.com, and *Sports Illustrated*.